THE NEW FOLGER LIBRARY SHAKESPEARE

Designed to make Shakespeare's great plays available to all readers, the New Folger Library edition of Shakespeare's plays provides accurate texts in modern spelling and punctuation, as well as scene-by-scene action summaries, full explanatory notes, many pictures clarifying Shakespeare's language, and notes recording all significant departures from the early printed versions. Each play is prefaced by a brief introduction, by a guide to reading Shakespeare's language, and by accounts of his life and theater. Each play is followed by an annotated list of further readings and by a "Modern Perspective" written by an expert on that particular play.

Barbara A. Mowat is Director of Academic Programs at the Folger Shakespeare Library, Executive Editor of *Shakespeare Quarterly*, Chair of the Folger Institute, and author of *The Dramaturgy of Shakespeare's Romances* and of essays on Shakespeare's plays and on the editing of the plays.

Paul Werstine is Professor of English at the Graduate School and at King's University College at the University of Western Ontario. He is general editor of the New Variorum Shakespeare and author of many papers and articles on the printing and editing of Shakespeare's plays.

The Folger Shakespeare Library

The Folger Shakespeare Library in Washington, D.C., a privately funded research library dedicated to Shakespeare and the civilization of early modern Europe, was founded in 1932 by Henry Clay and Emily Jordan Folger. In addition to its role as the world's preeminent Shakespeare collection and its emergence as a leading center for Renaissance studies, the Folger Library offers a wide array of cultural and educational programs and services for the general public.

EDITORS

BARBARA A. MOWAT
Director of Academic Programs
Folger Shakespeare Library

PAUL WERSTINE
Professor of English
King's University College at the University of
Western Ontario, Canada

FOLGER SHAKESPEARE LIBRARY

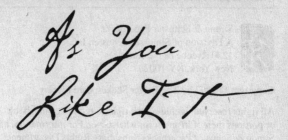

As You Like It

By
WILLIAM SHAKESPEARE

EDITED BY BARBARA A. MOWAT
AND PAUL WERSTINE

SIMON & SCHUSTER PAPERBACKS
NEW YORK LONDON TORONTO SYDNEY

Simon & Schuster Paperbacks
A Division of Simon & Schuster, Inc.
1230 Avenue of the Americas
New York, NY 10020

Copyright © 1997 by The Folger Shakespeare Library

All rights reserved, including the right to reproduce this book
or portions thereof in any form whatsoever. For information, address
Simon & Schuster Paperbacks Subsidiary Rights Department,
1230 Avenue of the Americas, New York, NY 10020.

Washington Square Press New Folger Edition April 1997
This Simon & Schuster paperback edition June 2009

SIMON & SCHUSTER PAPERBACKS and colophon are
registered trademarks of Simon & Schuster, Inc.

For information regarding special discounts for bulk purchases,
please contact Simon & Schuster Special Sales at
1-866-506-1949 or business@simonandschuster.com.

The Simon & Schuster Speakers Bureau can bring authors to your
live event. For more information or to book an event, contact the
Simon & Schuster Speakers Bureau at 1-866-248-3049 or visit our
website at www.simonspeakers.com.

Manufactured in the United States of America

20 19 18 17 16 15 14 13

ISBN 978-0-7434-8486-2

From the Director of the Library

For over four decades, the Folger Library General Reader's Shakespeare provided accurate and accessible texts of the plays and poems to students, teachers, and millions of other interested readers. Today, in an age often impatient with the past, the passion for Shakespeare continues to grow. No author speaks more powerfully to the human condition, in all its variety, than this actor/playwright from a minor sixteenth-century English village.

Over the years vast changes have occurred in the way Shakespeare's works are edited, performed, studied, and taught. The New Folger Library Shakespeare replaces the earlier versions, bringing to bear the best and most current thinking concerning both the texts and their interpretation. Here is an edition which makes the plays and poems fully understandable for modern readers using uncompromising scholarship. Professors Barbara Mowat and Paul Werstine are uniquely qualified to produce this New Folger Shakespeare for a new generation of readers. The Library is grateful for the learning, clarity, and imagination they have brought to this ambitious project.

Werner Gundersheimer,
Director of the Folger Shakespeare Library
from 1984 to 2002

Contents

Contents

Editors' Preface

In recent years, ways of dealing with Shakespeare's texts and with the interpretation of his plays have been undergoing significant change. This edition, while retaining many of the features that have always made the Folger Shakespeare so attractive to the general reader, at the same time reflects these current ways of thinking about Shakespeare. For example, modern readers, actors, and teachers have become interested in the differences between, on the one hand, the early forms in which Shakespeare's plays were first published and, on the other hand, the forms in which editors through the centuries have presented them. In response to this interest, we have based our edition on what we consider the best early printed version of a particular play (explaining our rationale in a section called "An Introduction to This Text") and have marked our changes in the text—unobtrusively, we hope, but in such a way that the curious reader can be aware that a change has been made and can consult the "Textual Notes" to discover what appeared in the early printed version.

Current ways of looking at the plays are reflected in our brief prefaces, in many of the commentary notes, in the annotated lists of "Further Reading," and especially in each play's "Modern Perspective," an essay written by an outstanding scholar who brings to the reader his or her fresh assessment of the play in the light of today's interests and concerns.

As in the Folger Library General Reader's Shakespeare, which this edition replaces, we include explanatory notes designed to help make Shakespeare's language clearer to a modern reader, and we place the notes on the page facing the text that they explain. We also follow the earlier edition in including illustrations—of objects, of clothing, of mythological figures—from books and manuscripts in the Folger Library collection. We provide fresh accounts of the life of Shakespeare, of the publishing of his plays, and of the theaters in which his plays were performed, as well as an introduction to the text itself. We also include a section called "Reading Shakespeare's Language," in which we try to help readers learn to "break the code" of Elizabethan poetic language.

For each section of each volume, we are indebted to a host of generous experts and fellow scholars. The "Reading Shakespeare's Language" sections, for example, could not have been written had not Arthur King, of Brigham Young University, and Randall Robinson, author of *Unlocking Shakespeare's Language*, led the way in untangling Shakespearean language puzzles and shared their insights and methodologies generously with us. "Shakespeare's Life" profited by the careful reading given it by the late S. Schoenbaum, "Shakespeare's Theater" was read and strengthened by Andrew Gurr and John Astington, and "The Publication of Shakespeare's Plays" is indebted to the comments of Peter W. M. Blayney. Among the texts we consulted in editing *As You Like It*, we found Richard Knowles' New Variorum edition of the play invaluable for its meticulous compilation of commentary and scholarship on the play. We, as editors, take sole responsibility for any errors in our editions.

We are grateful to the authors of the "Modern Perspectives"; to Leeds Barroll and David Bevington for their generous encouragement; to the Huntington and Newberry Libraries for fellowship support; to King's College for the grants it has provided to Paul Werstine; to the Social Sciences and Humanities Research Council of Canada, which provided him with a Research Time Stipend for 1990–91; to R. J. Shroyer of the University of

Western Ontario for essential computer support; to Joan Ozark Holmer for sharing her expertise on sixteenth-century dueling manuals; and to the Folger Institute's Center for Shakespeare Studies for its fortuitous sponsorship of a workshop on "Shakespeare's Texts for Students and Teachers" (funded by the National Endowment for the Humanities and led by Richard Knowles of the University of Wisconsin), a workshop from which we learned an enormous amount about what is wanted by college and high-school teachers of Shakespeare today; and especially to Steve Llano, our production editor at Pocket Books, whose expertise and attention to detail are essential to this project.

Our biggest debt is to the Folger Shakespeare Library—to Werner Gundersheimer, Director of the Library, who made possible our edition; to Deborah Curren-Aquino, who provides extensive editorial and production support; to Jean Miller, the Library's Art Curator, who combs the Library holdings for illustrations, and to Julie Ainsworth, Head of the Photography Department, who carefully photographs them; to Peggy O'Brien, former Director of Education at the Folger and now Director of Education Programs at the Corporation for Public Broadcasting, and her assistant at the Folger, Molly Haws, who gave us expert advice about the needs being expressed by Shakespeare teachers and students (and to Martha Christian and other "master teachers" who used our texts in manuscript in their classrooms); to Jessica Hymowitz and Wazir Shpoon for their expert computer support; to the staff of the Academic Programs Division, especially Amy Adler, Mary Tonkinson, Kathleen Lynch, Linda Johnson, Carol Brobeck, Toni Krieger, and Rebecca Willson; and, finally, to the staff of the Library Reading Room, whose patience and support are invaluable.

Barbara A. Mowat and Paul Werstine

"All the men and women merely players." (2.7.147)
From [William Alabaster,] *Roxana tragaedia . . .* (1632).

Shakespeare's *As You Like It*

Readers and audiences of *As You Like It* have for centuries greeted the play with delight. In large part, it seems to belong to the culture of those who read and go to see plays—a culture of leisure in which people have time for conversation. The play speaks to lovers of witty verbal exchange because, whatever else the play's characters may be, they are brilliant conversationalists. The Princesses Rosalind and Celia shine in this respect early in the play, as does Touchstone, the professional Fool or jester, whose function it is to entertain these princesses and others at court. When these three go into exile in the exotic Forest of Arden, where most of the play is set, they find new conversational partners to engage. In the forest, Touchstone immediately becomes an object of fascination for one of the exiled courtiers, Jaques, who finds in the Fool a model of world-weary cynicism. Jaques' conversation becomes celebration and quotation of Touchstone: " 'Tis but an hour ago since it was nine, / And after one hour more 'twill be eleven. / And so from hour to hour we ripe and ripe, / And then from hour to hour we rot and rot." Yet this disillusioned pair have to share the forest and the conversational stage with a good number of clever idealists, especially the young lovers Rosalind and Orlando, who can sometimes be more than a match for them.

Acknowledging the brilliance of the dialogue, recent critics and scholars have been attending to the play's shimmering verbal exchanges from perspectives that ground the dialogue in some of the more serious issues of late sixteenth-century England. One of these issues is the practice of primogeniture, the "courtesy of nations," as the play euphemistically refers to it, according to which property passes directly from the father to his eldest son, leaving younger sons either dependent on their older brother or destitute and desperate. Looked at from the perspective of primogeniture, *As You Like It* suddenly becomes remarkable for its depiction of intense conflict between pairs of brothers. At the play's highest social level, Duke Frederick, younger and therefore dependent brother to Duke Senior, has overthrown his older brother and forced him to live homeless in the Forest of Arden. The rivalry between Orlando and his elder brother Oliver is no less bitter, as Oliver seeks a solution to Orlando's demand for a share of their father's patrimony by plotting his brother's death early in the play. Orlando escapes his brother only to come close to death by starvation in his homelessness. Orlando is driven, in turn, to threaten with death the exiled duke and his followers when he encounters them in possession of the food he needs in order to survive. Thus, *As You Like It* exposes the cost in human suffering that primogeniture entails and shows how primogeniture, in its preservation of property, contradictorily provokes crimes against property.

A second new perspective on the play attends to the issue of crossdressing, a prominent feature in the plot and an equally prominent feature of the theatrical culture in which the play was first performed. Most of Orlando's courtship of Rosalind takes place while Rosalind is disguised as a man, calling herself "Ganymede." Rosalind-as-Ganymede persuades Orlando to pretend that Ganymede is his beloved "Rosalind." In her male disguise, Rosalind takes over prerogatives within the fiction of the play that, in its time, were exclusively male, such as the prerogative of choosing her own mate and directing his courtship of her, prerogatives that would conventionally belong to her father. Rosalind even takes over the play's epilogue, its formal farewell to the audience, commenting on how unusual it is for the female lead to do so. But, of course, as "she" reveals in her epilogue, "she," the actor playing Rosalind on the sixteenth-century English stage, is male, as were all the actors who played female roles on the stage of Shakespeare's time. The complications of gender in this play, where a boy plays a girl playing a boy pretending to be a girl, are today seen as more than an amusing tour de force. Adding weight to the fun of the play's love games are questions now being asked about the nature of the attraction between/among genders and about female power in a patriarchal world and on a transvestite stage.

It is reassuring to see that our new awareness of the serious social issues of inheritance, poverty, and gender relations in *As You Like It* does not dilute the joy of reading, performing, or attending a performance of the play. The dialogue remains brilliant and the characters intriguing, and the Forest of Arden remains a place we "willingly could waste [our] time in."

After you have read the play, we invite you to turn to the essay printed after it, *"As You Like It: A Modern Perspective,"* written by Professor Emeritus Susan Snyder of Swarthmore College.

Reading Shakespeare's Language: *As You Like It*

For many people today, reading Shakespeare's language can be a problem—but it is a problem that can be solved. Those who have studied Latin (or even French or

German or Spanish) and those who are used to reading poetry will have little difficulty understanding the language of Shakespeare's poetic drama. Others, though, need to develop the skills of untangling unusual sentence structures and of recognizing and understanding poetic compressions, omissions, and wordplay. And even those skilled in reading unusual sentence structures may have occasional trouble with Shakespeare's words. Four hundred years of "static" intervene between his speaking and our hearing. Most of his immense vocabulary is still in use, but a few of his words are not, and, worse, some of his words now have meanings quite different from those they had in the sixteenth century. In the theater, most of these difficulties are solved for us by actors who study the language and articulate it for us so that the essential meaning is heard—or, when combined with stage action, is at least *felt*. When reading on one's own, one must do what each actor does: go over the lines (often with a dictionary close at hand) until the puzzles are solved and the lines yield up their poetry and the characters speak in words and phrases that are, suddenly, rewarding and wonderfully memorable.

Shakespeare's Words

As you begin to read the opening scenes of a play by Shakespeare, you may notice occasional unfamiliar words. Some are unfamiliar simply because we no longer use them. In the opening scenes of *As You Like It*, for example, you will find the words *misconsters* (misconstrues, misunderstands), *unkept* (uncared for), *illfavored* (ugly), *misprized* (scorned, despised), and *quintain* (a wooden post used for jousting practice or in rural games). Words of this kind are explained in notes to the text and will become familiar the more of Shakespeare's plays you read.

More numerous and more problematic are the words in Shakespeare's plays that we still use but that we use with a different meaning. In the opening scenes of *As You Like It*, for example, the word *profit* has the meaning of "proficiency," *avoid* is used where we would say "get rid of," *envious* means "malicious," and *stubborn* is used where we would say "ruthless, fierce." Such words will be explained in the notes to the text, but they, too, will become familiar as you continue to read Shakespeare's language.

Some words are strange not because of the "static" introduced by changes in language over the past centuries but because these are words that Shakespeare is using to build dramatic worlds that have their own space, time, history, and background mythology. Shakespeare opens *As You Like It* on the estate of Oliver, heir of Sir Rowland de Boys. The language which constructs that world centers on inheritance, money, and what we would now call class structure. It is a world where horses are "taught their manage" and are "fair with their feeding," where a "gentleman of birth" demands that he be "bred" properly and allowed his "exercises," and where "the courtesy of nations" (i.e., the law of primogeniture) makes the eldest son "nearer to his [father's] reverence." When the action moves to the Forest of Arden in 2.1, the language constructs a world "exempt from public haunt," which views the "envious court" as a place of "painted pomp" and prides itself on confronting nothing more perilous than "the churlish chiding of the winter's wind." In this forest world of "antique roots" and brooks that brawl along the wood, courtiers dressed "like foresters" "moralize" natural spectacles and "gore" with "forkèd heads [i.e., arrowheads]" the "round haunches" of deer ("poor dappled fools," "native burghers of this desert city"). These and other language worlds together create the complex terrain that Orlando, Rosalind, Touchstone, Duke Senior, and their companions and relatives inhabit.

As You Like It is constructed with yet one more set of unusual words. This play depends heavily on allusions. The life of Duke Senior and his men is in part constructed through allusions to Robin Hood and his merry men and to descriptions of the golden age in Hesiod and Ovid. Orlando alludes to the biblical prodigal son narrative to tell his own story. The wrestling match is given a mythological context through allusion to Hercules' match with Antaeus. Rosalind and Celia describe their friendship through allusion to Juno's swans. Biblical, mythological, and learned allusions abound in this play, introducing us to (or reminding us of) words and images that significantly enlarge the play's scope.

Shakespeare's Sentences

In an English sentence, meaning is quite dependent on the place given each word. "The dog bit the boy" and "The boy bit the dog" mean very different things, even though the individual words are the same. Because English places such importance on the positions of words in sentences, on the way words are arranged, unusual arrangements can puzzle a reader. Shakespeare frequently shifts his sentences away from "normal" English arrangements—often to create the rhythm he seeks, sometimes to use a line's poetic rhythm to emphasize a particular word, sometimes to give a character his or her own speech pattern or to allow the character to speak in a special way. When we attend a good performance of the play, the actors will have worked out the sentence structures and will articulate the sentences so that the meaning is clear. In reading for yourself, do as the actor does. That is, when you become puzzled by a character's speech, check to see if words are being presented in an unusual sequence.

Look first for the placement of subject and verb. Shakespeare often places the verb before the subject (i.e., instead of "He goes" we find "Goes he") or places the subject between the auxiliary and the main verbs (i.e., instead of "He will go," we find "Will he go"). In *As You Like It*, we find such a construction in Charles the wrestler's "Marry, *do I*, sir," as well as in Oliver's "Now *will I stir* this gamester." Touchstone's "yet *was* not *the knight* forsworn" is another example of inverted subject and verb.

Such inversions rarely cause much confusion. More problematic is Shakespeare's frequent placing of the object before the subject and verb (i.e., instead of "I hit him," we might find "Him I hit"). Orlando's "My brother Jaques he keeps at school" is an example of such an inversion (the normal order would be "He keeps my brother Jaques at school"), as is his "the something that nature gave me his countenance seems to take from me." Other examples are Celia's "The like do you" (i.e., you do the same thing) and Rosalind's "Let me the knowledge of my fault bear with me," where the normal order would be "Let me bear with me the knowledge of my fault."

Inversions are not the only unusual sentence structures in Shakespeare's language. Often in his sentences words that would normally appear together are separated from each other. (Again, this is often done to create a particular rhythm or to stress a particular word.) Take, for example, the First Lord's lines describing the place where "a poor sequestered stag / That from the hunter's aim had ta'en a hurt / Did come to languish"; here the clause "That from the hunter's aim had ta'en a hurt" separates the subject ("stag") from its verb ("Did come"). Or take his description of the deer itself: "And thus the hairy fool, / Much markèd of the melancholy Jaques, / Stood on th' extremest verge of the swift brook," where the normal construction "And thus the hairy fool stood on th' extremest verge of the swift brook" is interrupted by parenthetical material. In order to create for yourself sentences that seem more like the English of everyday speech, you may wish to rearrange the words, putting together the word clusters ("stag did come to languish," "fool stood on th' extremest verge"). You will usually find that the sentence will gain in clarity but will lose its rhythm or shift its emphasis.

Locating and rearranging words that "belong together" is especially necessary in passages that separate basic sentence elements by long delaying or expanding interruptions. When Rosalind tells Duke Frederick that she is innocent of treachery ("I never did offend your Highness"), she uses a construction that delays the main sentence elements until subordinate material is presented:

> If with myself I hold intelligence
> Or have acquaintance with mine own desires,
> If that I do not dream or be not frantic—
> As I do trust I am not—then, dear uncle,
> *Never* so much as in a thought unborn
> *Did I offend your Highness.*

In these lines, note that the main sentence elements ("Never did I offend your Highness") are themselves interrupted with additional material, as is the clause *"If that I do not dream or be not frantic, then . . . ,"* in which the "if-then" structure is significantly qualified by the interpolated "As I do trust I am not." In some of Shakespeare's plays (*Hamlet*, for instance), long, interrupted sentences and sentences in which the basic elements are significantly delayed are used frequently, sometimes to catch the audience up in the narrative and sometimes as a characterizing device. They appear only occasionally in *As You Like It*, where sentences tend to be structurally straightforward.

Finally, in many of Shakespeare's plays, sentences are sometimes complicated not because of unusual structures or interruptions but because Shakespeare omits words and parts of words that English sentences normally require. (In conversation, we, too, often omit words. We say, "Heard from him yet?" and our hearer supplies the missing "Have you.") Frequent reading of Shakespeare—and of other poets—trains us to supply such missing words. In some plays (*Twelfth Night*, for example), omissions are rare and seem to be used to affect the tone of the speech or for the sake of speech rhythm. In others (especially plays written very late in his career), Shakespeare uses omissions both of verbs and of nouns to great dramatic effect. *As You Like It* is a play with relatively few omissions, many of them like Rosalind's "is there any else longs to see this broken music" (where "one" is omitted after "any" and "who" is omitted after "else") and like Orlando's "Thus must I from the smoke into the smother" (where "go" is omitted after "I"). Occasionally, however, one finds interesting omissions, such as in Celia's "I was too young that time to value her" (where "at" is omitted before "that time," the omission creating a regular iambic pentameter line and giving a secondary meaning to Celia's memory of "that time"). Equally interesting is Charles the wrestler's description of Celia's love for Rosalind—"her cousin so loves her, being ever from their cradles bred together, that she would have followed her exile or have died to stay behind her." Here the compression is rather severe. The full phrases would read, "have followed her [into] exile or have died [if she had been forced] to stay behind her." What's more, the compressed phrasing is also part of an interrupted structure that separates the elements of "so loves her that" with the memorable "being ever from their cradles bred together."

Shakespearean Wordplay

Shakespeare plays with language so often and so variously that entire books are written on the topic. Here we will mention only two kinds of wordplay, puns and metaphors. A pun is a play on words that sound the same but that have different meanings (or on a single word that has more than one meaning). In *As You Like It*, for example, when Amiens sings that the winter wind is not "so unkind as man's ingratitude," the word "unkind" means both (1) unnatural and (2) inconsiderate. Touchstone's comment that "the truest poetry is the most feigning" plays with "feigning" as (1) imaginative and (2) deceitful, while Jaques' comment that Touchstone is a "material fool" puns on "material" as (1) full of good sense and (2) earthy or coarse. When Corin asks Touchstone "how like you this shepherd's life?" Touchstone replies "as there is no more plenty in it, it goes much against my stomach," playing on "stomach" as (1) inclination and (2) belly. When Rosalind describes the remarkably sudden love of Celia and Oliver, who, she says, "have . . . made a pair of stairs to marriage, which they will climb incontinent, or else be incontinent before marriage," she plays with "incontinent" as (1) at once and (2) unchaste, sexually unrestrained. And Celia's request "I pray you bear with me" elicits from Touchstone the response "I had rather bear with you than bear you. Yet I should bear no cross if I did bear you, for I think you have no money in your purse," a response that plays not only with multiple meanings of "bear" but, more interestingly, puns on "cross" as the name of an Elizabethan coin stamped with a cross and on the familiar biblical verse "whosoever doth not bear his cross and come after me cannot be my disciple."

Many of the puns in *As You Like It* occur in elaborate combinations. For example, in the following dialogue about a poem found hanging on a tree, Celia and Rosalind pun on "feet" (as divisions of a verse), "bear" (as "allow" and "carry"), "lame" (as "crippled" and "metrically defective"), and "without" ("in the absence of" and "outside of"):

CELIA Didst thou hear these verses?
ROSALIND O yes, I heard them all, and more too,
     for some of them had in them more feet than
     the verses would bear.
CELIA That's no matter. The feet might bear the
     verses.
ROSALIND Ay, but the feet were lame and could
     not bear themselves without the verse, and
     therefore stood lamely in the verse.

Another interweaving of puns supports Celia's charge that "the oath of a lover is no stronger than the word of a tapster. They are both the confirmer of false reckonings." The truth of Celia's second sentence here depends on complicated puns on the words "confirmer" ([1] establisher, ratifier, and [2] encourager) and "reckonings" ([1] bills and [2] expectations). As a "confirmer of false reckonings," the tapster, she claims, is an establisher or ratifier of inaccurate tavern bills; the lover is an encourager of false expectations.

To take one final example: Touchstone's comment to Audrey, "I am here with thee and thy goats, as the most capricious poet, honest Ovid, was among the Goths," is an elaborate and learned joke that compares Touchstone in the forest to the Roman love poet Ovid exiled among the Getae, often confused in Shakespeare's day with the Goths (pronounced, at that time, "gotes"). It has been suggested that there is not only a pun on goats/Goths, but also that "capricious" may here mean "lascivious, goat-like," from wordplay on the Latin *caper*—i.e., goat. Because puns occur often and in complex combinations in *As You Like It*, the language in this play must be listened to carefully if one wishes to catch all its meanings.

A metaphor is a play on words in which one object or idea is expressed as if it were something else, something with which it shares common features. When Rosalind describes herself as "one out of suits with fortune," she is using metaphorical language, speaking as if she were a servant no longer allowed to wear Fortune's livery. Orlando, unable to speak to Rosalind, explains his sudden muteness with a metaphor, asking himself, "What passion hangs these weights upon my tongue?" The old servant Adam uses metaphor to convey his sense that Orlando's very strengths have placed him in a dangerous situation: "Your virtues, gentle master, / Are sanctified and holy traitors to you." In turn, Orlando uses a gardening metaphor to say that, if Adam shares his savings with him, the money will probably be wasted: "poor old man, thou prun'st a rotten tree / That cannot so much as a blossom yield / In lieu of [i.e., in exchange for] all thy pains and husbandry [i.e., thrift]."

Often in *As You Like It* metaphors are rather straightforward. Human life is "a wide and universal theater" presenting "woeful pageants." Time is a horse that "travels in divers paces with divers persons." The pains of love are "wounds invisible that love's keen arrows make"; to be in love is to be a "prisoner" in a "cage of rushes," or to be "fathom deep" in an ocean that "cannot be sounded" [i.e., whose depth cannot be measured] because it "hath an unknown bottom, like the Bay of Portugal."

Sometimes, however, the play's metaphoric language is richly complex or highly allusive. Take, for example, Oliver's "Begin you to grow upon me? I will physic your rankness." This statement of Oliver's malign intent upon Orlando draws simultaneously from the worlds of gardening and of sixteenth-century medicine, so that Orlando is, for Oliver, both an overgrown plant in need of cutting down and an illness that must be cured through bloodletting. In quite a different kind of complex metaphor, Silvius declares his adoration for Phoebe by translating his "poverty of grace" into physical poverty:

> So holy and so perfect is my love,
> And I in such a poverty of grace,
> That I shall think it a most plenteous crop
> To glean the broken ears after the man
> That the main harvest reaps. Loose now and then
> A scattered smile, and that I'll live upon.

Silvius's extended metaphor, in which he is a poor man living off scattered ears of grain left behind by the reapers, draws on two biblical passages, one in which the Israelites are told by the Lord that, when reaping the harvest, they are to leave some grain unharvested for the poor and the stranger, and one in which Ruth asks to "glean and gather after the reapers among the sheaves." In this allusive metaphorical context, Phoebe's smiles, loosed like broken ears of grain, become Silvius's sustenance.

In most of Shakespeare's plays, metaphors tend to be used when the idea being conveyed is hard to express, and the speaker is thus given language that helps to carry the idea or the feeling to his or her listener—and to the audience. In *Romeo and Juliet*, for example, Romeo's metaphors of Juliet-as-saint and Juliet-as-light employ images from the poetic tradition that seem designed to portray a lover struggling to express the overpowering feelings that come with being in love. In *As You Like It*, metaphors occasionally have this kind of power. More often, though, they are simply one of many ways that characters converse, one kind of language-thread in the intricate weave of words that creates this play.

Implied Stage Action

Finally, in reading Shakespeare's plays we should always remember that what we are reading is a performance script. The dialogue is written to be spoken by actors who, at the same time, are moving, gesturing, picking up objects, weeping, shaking their fists. Some stage action is described in what are called "stage directions"; some is suggested within the dialogue itself. We must learn to be alert to such signals as we stage the play in our imagination. When, in *As You Like It*, Orlando says to Oliver, "Wert thou not my brother, I would not take this hand from thy throat till this other had pulled out thy tongue," it is clear that Orlando has seized Oliver by the throat. Again, when, in the course of the wrestling bout, Duke Frederick says "No more, no more," Orlando replies "Yes, I beseech your Grace. I am not yet well breathed," and the conversation continues with the news that Charles "cannot speak" and the order to "Bear him away," one knows that Charles has been thrown down.

At several places in *As You Like It*, signals to the reader are not quite so clear. When, for example, Adam offers his life savings to Orlando with the words "Here is the gold. All this I give you," the dialogue does not indicate whether the actor playing Orlando should take the purse. Again, when Orlando and Adam are on their journey to the woods, it is clear that, in his exhaustion, Adam lies down. (He says "Here lie I down and measure out my grave.") However, at the end of the scene, when Orlando says "Come, I will bear thee to some shelter" and the Folio text has them exit, the fact that the word "bear" has several meanings creates ambiguity about the stage action, allowing the director (and the reader, in imagination) either to have Orlando "pick up Adam" (as some editions say) and carry him off or to have Orlando simply support him as they walk off together. Learning to read the language of stage action repays one many times over when one reads the play's final scene, with Touchstone's bravura performance of dueling punctilio, with the unexpected entrance of Hymen "bringing" Rosalind, the yet-more-unexpected entrance of the Second Brother, and the final dance. Here, as in so much of *As You Like It*, implied stage action vitally affects our response to the play.

It is immensely rewarding to work carefully with Shakespeare's language so that the words, the sentences, the wordplay, and the implied stage action all become clear—as readers for the past four centuries have discovered. It may be more pleasurable to attend a good performance of a play—though not everyone has thought so. But the joy of being able to stage one of Shakespeare's plays in one's imagination, to return to passages that continue to yield further meanings (or further questions) the more one reads them—these are pleasures that, for many, rival (or at least augment) those of the performed text, and certainly make it worth considerable effort to "break the code" of Elizabethan poetic drama and let free the remarkable language that makes up a Shakespeare text.

Shakespeare's Life

Surviving documents that give us glimpses into the life of William Shakespeare show us a playwright, poet, and actor who grew up in the market town of Stratford-upon-Avon, spent his professional life in London, and returned to Stratford a wealthy landowner. He was born in April 1564, died in April 1616, and is buried inside the chancel of Holy Trinity Church in Stratford.

We wish we could know more about the life of the world's greatest dramatist. His plays and poems are testaments to his wide reading—especially to his knowledge of Virgil, Ovid, Plutarch, Holinshed's *Chronicles*, and the Bible—and to his mastery of the English language, but we can only speculate about his education. We know that the King's New School in Stratford-upon-Avon was considered excellent. The school was one of the English "grammar schools" established to educate young men, primarily in Latin grammar and literature. As in other schools of the time, students began their studies at the age of four or five in the attached "petty school," and there learned to read and write in English, studying primarily the catechism from the Book of Common Prayer. After two years in the petty

CATECHISMVS

paruus pueris primùm Latinè
qui ediscatur, proponendus
in Scholis.

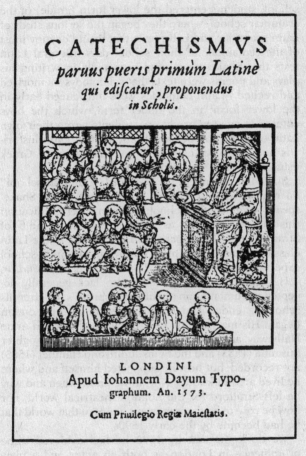

LONDINI
Apud Iohannem Dayum Typo-
graphum. An. 1573.

Cum Priuilegio Regiæ Maiestatis.

Title page of a 1573 Latin and Greek catechism
for children.

school, students entered the lower form (grade) of the grammar school, where they began the serious study of Latin grammar and Latin texts that would occupy most of the remainder of their school days. (Several Latin texts that Shakespeare used repeatedly in writing his plays and poems were texts that schoolboys memorized and recited.) Latin comedies were introduced early in the lower form; in the upper form, which the boys entered at age ten or eleven, students wrote their own Latin orations and declamations, studied Latin historians and rhetoricians, and began the study of Greek using the Greek New Testament.

Since the records of the Stratford "grammar school" do not survive, we cannot prove that William Shakespeare attended the school; however, every indication (his father's position as an alderman and bailiff of Stratford, the playwright's own knowledge of the Latin classics, scenes in the plays that recall grammar-school experiences—for example, *The Merry Wives of Windsor*, 4.1) suggests that he did. We also lack generally accepted documentation about Shakespeare's life after his schooling ended and his professional life in London began. His marriage in 1582 (at age eighteen) to Anne Hathaway and the subsequent births of his daughter Susanna (1583) and the twins Judith and Hamnet (1585) are recorded, but how he supported himself and where he lived are not known. Nor do we know when and why he left Stratford for the London theatrical world, nor how he rose to be the important figure in that world that he had become by the early 1590s.

We do know that by 1592 he had achieved some prominence in London as both an actor and a playwright. In that year was published a book by the playwright Robert Greene attacking an actor who had the audacity to write blank-verse drama and who was "in his own conceit [i.e., opinion] the only Shake-scene in a country." Since Greene's attack includes a parody of a line from one of Shakespeare's early plays, there is little doubt that it is Shakespeare to whom he refers, a "Shake-scene" who had aroused Greene's fury by successfully competing with university-educated dramatists like Greene himself. It was in 1593 that Shakespeare became a published poet. In that year he published his long narrative poem *Venus and Adonis;* in 1594, he followed it with *The Rape of Lucrece.* Both poems were dedicated to the young earl of Southampton (Henry Wriothesley), who may have become Shakespeare's patron.

It seems no coincidence that Shakespeare wrote these narrative poems at a time when the theaters were closed because of the plague, a contagious epidemic disease that devastated the population of London. When the theaters reopened in 1594, Shakespeare apparently resumed his double career of actor and playwright and began his long (and seemingly profitable) service as an acting-company shareholder. Records for December of 1594 show him to be a leading member of the Lord Chamberlain's Men. It was this company of actors, later named the King's Men, for whom he would be a principal actor, dramatist, and shareholder for the rest of his career.

So far as we can tell, that career spanned about twenty years. In the 1590s, he wrote his plays on English history as well as several comedies and at least two tragedies (*Titus Andronicus* and *Romeo and Juliet*). These histories, comedies, and tragedies are the plays credited to him in 1598 in a work, *Palladis Tamia,* that in one chapter compares English writers with "Greek, Latin, and Italian Poets." There the author, Francis Meres, claims that Shakespeare is comparable to the

Latin dramatists Seneca for tragedy and Plautus for comedy, and calls him "the most excellent in both kinds for the stage." He also names him "Mellifluous and honey-tongued Shakespeare": "I say," writes Meres, "that the Muses would speak with Shakespeare's fine filed phrase, if they would speak English." Since Meres also mentions Shakespeare's "sugared sonnets among his private friends," it is assumed that many of Shakespeare's sonnets (not published until 1609) were also written in the 1590s.

In 1599, Shakespeare's company built a theater for themselves across the river from London, naming it the Globe. The plays that are considered by many to be Shakespeare's major tragedies (*Hamlet, Othello, King Lear,* and *Macbeth*) were written while the company was resident in this theater, as were such comedies as *Twelfth Night* and *Measure for Measure.* Many of Shakespeare's plays were performed at court (both for Queen Elizabeth I and, after her death in 1603, for King James I), some were presented at the Inns of Court (the residences of London's legal societies), and some were doubtless performed in other towns, at the universities, and at great houses when the King's Men went on tour; otherwise, his plays from 1599 to 1608 were, so far as we know, performed only at the Globe. Between 1608 and 1612, Shakespeare wrote several plays—among them *The Winter's Tale* and *The Tempest*—presumably for the company's new indoor Blackfriars theater, though the plays seem to have been performed also at the Globe and at court. Surviving documents describe a performance of *The Winter's Tale* in 1611 at the Globe, for example, and performances of *The Tempest* in 1611 and 1613 at the royal palace of Whitehall.

Shakespeare wrote very little after 1612, the year in which he probably wrote *King Henry VIII.* (It was at a performance of *Henry VIII* in 1613 that the Globe caught fire and burned to the ground.) Sometime between 1610 and 1613 he seems to have returned to live in Stratford-upon-Avon, where he owned a large house and considerable property, and where his wife and his two daughters and their husbands lived. (His son Hamnet had died in 1596.) During his professional years in London, Shakespeare had presumably derived income from the acting company's profits as well as from his own career as an actor, from the sale of his play manuscripts to the acting company, and, after 1599, from his shares as an owner of the Globe. It was presumably that income, carefully invested in land and other property, which made him the wealthy man that surviving documents show him to have become. It is also assumed that William Shakespeare's growing wealth and reputation played some part in inclining the crown, in 1596, to grant John Shakespeare, William's father, the coat of arms that he had so long sought. William Shakespeare died in Stratford on April 23, 1616 (according to the epitaph carved under his bust in Holy Trinity Church) and was buried on April 25. Seven years after his death, his collected plays were published as *Mr. William Shakespeares Comedies, Histories, & Tragedies* (the work now known as the First Folio).

The years in which Shakespeare wrote were among the most exciting in English history. Intellectually, the discovery, translation, and printing of Greek and Roman classics were making available a set of works and worldviews that interacted complexly with Christian texts and beliefs. The result was a questioning, a vital intellectual ferment, that provided energy for the period's amazing dramatic and literary output and that fed directly into Shakespeare's plays. The Ghost in *Hamlet*, for example, is wonderfully complicated in part because he is a figure from Roman tragedy—the spirit of the dead returning to seek revenge—who at the same time inhabits a Christian hell (or purgatory); Hamlet's description of humankind reflects at one moment the Neoplatonic wonderment at mankind ("What a piece of work is a man!") and, at the next, the Christian disparagement of human sinners ("And yet, to me, what is this quintessence of dust?").

As intellectual horizons expanded, so also did geographical and cosmological horizons. New worlds—both North and South America—were explored, and in them were found human beings who lived and worshiped in ways radically different from those of Renaissance Europeans and Englishmen. The universe during these years also seemed to shift and expand. Copernicus had earlier theorized that the earth was not the center of the cosmos but revolved as a planet around the sun. Galileo's telescope, created in 1609, allowed scientists to see that Copernicus had been correct; the universe was not organized with the earth at the center, nor was it so nicely circumscribed as people had, until that time, thought. In terms of expanding horizons, the impact of these discoveries on people's beliefs—religious, scientific, and philosophical—cannot be overstated.

London, too, rapidly expanded and changed during the years (from the early 1590s to around 1610) that Shakespeare lived there. London—the center of England's government, its economy, its royal court, its overseas trade—was, during these years, becoming an exciting metropolis, drawing to it thousands of new citizens every year. Troubled by overcrowding, by poverty, by recurring epidemics of the plague, London was also a mecca for the wealthy and the aristocratic, and for those who sought advancement at court, or power in government or finance or trade. One hears in Shakespeare's plays the voices of London—the struggles for power, the fear of venereal disease, the language of buying and selling. One hears as well the voices of Stratford-upon-Avon—references to the nearby Forest of Arden, to sheep herding, to small-town gossip, to village fairs and markets. Part of the richness of Shakespeare's work is the influence felt there of the various worlds in which he lived: the world of metropolitan London, the world of small-town and rural England, the world of the theater, and the worlds of craftsmen and shepherds.

That Shakespeare inhabited such worlds we know from surviving London and Stratford documents, as well as from the evidence of the plays and poems themselves. From such records we can sketch the dramatist's life. We know from his works that he was a voracious reader. We know from legal and business documents that he was a multifaceted theater man who became a wealthy landowner. We know a bit about his family life and a fair amount about his legal and financial dealings. Most scholars today depend upon such evidence as they draw their picture of the world's greatest playwright. Such, however, has not always been the case. Until the late eighteenth century, the William Shakespeare who lived in most biographies was the creation of legend and tradition. This was the Shakespeare who was supposedly caught poaching deer at Charlecote, the estate of Sir Thomas Lucy close by Stratford; this was the Shakespeare who fled from Sir Thomas's vengeance and made his way in London by taking care of horses outside a playhouse; this was the Shakespeare who reportedly could barely read but whose natural gifts were extraordinary, whose father was a butcher who allowed his gifted son sometimes to help in the butcher shop, where William supposedly killed calves "in a high style," making a speech for the

"It was a lover and his lass." (5.3.16–39)
From Thomas Morley, *The first booke of ayres . . .* (1600).

2 Betweene the Akers of the rie,
   With a hay, with a ho and a hay nonie no,
   These prettie Countrie fooles would lie,
   In spring time, the onely prettie ring time,
   When Birds doe sing, hay ding a ding a ding,
   Sweete louers loue the spring.

3 This Carrell they began that houre,
   With a hay, with a ho and a hay nonie no,
   How that a life was but a flower,
   In spring time, the onely prettie ring time,
   When Birds doe sing, hay ding a ding a ding,
   Sweete louers loue the spring.

4 Then prettie louers take the time,
   With a hay, with a ho and a hay nonie no,
   For loue is crowned with the prime,
   In spring time, the onely prettie ring time,
   When Birds doe sing, hay ding a ding a ding,
   Sweete louers loue the spring.

The lute airs of Shakespeare's time were often published so that the lutenist, singers, and viol player could sit around a table and read from one book.

occasion. It was this legendary William Shakespeare whose Falstaff (in *1* and *2 Henry IV*) so pleased Queen Elizabeth that she demanded a play about Falstaff in love, and demanded that it be written in fourteen days (hence the existence of *The Merry Wives of Windsor*). It was this legendary Shakespeare who reached the top of his acting career in the roles of the Ghost in *Hamlet* and old Adam in *As You Like It*—and who died of a fever contracted by drinking too hard at "a merry meeting" with the poets Michael Drayton and Ben Jonson. This legendary Shakespeare is a rambunctious, undisciplined man, as attractively "wild" as his plays were seen by earlier generations to be. Unfortunately, there is no trace of evidence to support these wonderful stories.

Perhaps in response to the disreputable Shakespeare of legend—or perhaps in response to the fragmentary and, for some, all-too-ordinary Shakespeare documented by surviving records—some people since the mid-nineteenth century have argued that William Shakespeare could not have written the plays that bear his name. These persons have put forward some dozen names as more likely authors, among them Queen Elizabeth, Sir Francis Bacon, Edward de Vere (earl of Oxford), and Christopher Marlowe. Such attempts to find what for these people is a more believable author of the plays is a tribute to the regard in which the plays are held. Unfortunately for their claims, the documents that exist that provide evidence for the facts of Shakespeare's life tie him inextricably to the body of plays and poems that bear his name. Unlikely as it seems to those who want the works to have been written by an aristocrat, a university graduate, or an "important" person, the plays and poems seem clearly to have been produced by a man from Stratford-upon-Avon with a very good "grammar-school" education and a life of experience in London and in the world of the London theater. How this particular man produced the works that dominate the cultures of much of the world almost four hundred years after his death is one of life's mysteries—and one that will continue to tease our imaginations as we continue to delight in his plays and poems.

Shakespeare's Theater

The actors of Shakespeare's time are known to have performed plays in a great variety of locations. They played at court (that is, in the great halls of such royal residences as Whitehall, Hampton Court, and Greenwich); they played in halls at the universities of Oxford and Cambridge, and at the Inns of Court (the residences in London of the legal societies); and they also played in the private houses of great lords and civic officials. Sometimes acting companies went on tour from London into the provinces, often (but not only) when outbreaks of bubonic plague in the capital forced the closing of theaters to reduce the possibility of contagion in crowded audiences. In the provinces the actors usually staged their plays in churches (until around 1600) or in guildhalls. While surviving records show only a handful of occasions when actors played at inns while on tour, London inns were important playing places up until the 1590s.

The building of theaters in London had begun only shortly before Shakespeare wrote his first plays in the 1590s. These theaters were of two kinds: outdoor or public playhouses that could accommodate large numbers of playgoers, and indoor or private theaters for much smaller audiences. What is usually regarded as the first London outdoor public playhouse was called simply the Theatre. James Burbage—the father of Richard Burbage, who was perhaps the most famous actor in Shakespeare's company—built it in 1576 in an area north of the city of London called Shoreditch. Among the more famous of the other public playhouses that capitalized on the new fashion were the Curtain and the Fortune (both also built north of the city), the Rose, the Swan, the Globe, and the Hope (all located on the Bankside, a region just across the Thames south of the city of London). All these playhouses had to be built outside the jurisdiction of the city of London because many civic officials were hostile to the performance of drama and repeatedly petitioned the royal council to abolish it.

The theaters erected on the Bankside (a region under the authority of the Church of England, whose head was the monarch) shared the neighborhood with houses of prostitution and with the Paris Garden, where the blood sports of bearbaiting and bullbaiting were carried on. There may have been no clear distinction between playhouses and buildings for such sports, for we know that the Hope was used for both plays and baiting and that Philip Henslowe, owner of the Rose and, later, partner in the ownership of the Fortune, was also a partner in a monopoly on baiting. All these forms of entertainment were easily accessible to Londoners by boat across the Thames or over London Bridge.

Evidently Shakespeare's company prospered on the Bankside. They moved there in 1599. Threatened by difficulties in renewing the lease on the land where their first theater (the Theatre) had been built, Shakespeare's company took advantage of the Christmas holiday in 1598 to dismantle the Theatre and transport its timbers across the Thames to the Bankside, where, in 1599, these timbers were used in the building of the Globe. The weather in late December 1598 is recorded as having been especially harsh. It was so cold that the Thames was "nigh [nearly] frozen," and there was heavy snow. Perhaps the weather aided Shakespeare's company in eluding their landlord, the snow hiding their activity and the freezing of the Thames allowing them to slide the timbers across to the Bankside without paying tolls for repeated trips over London Bridge. Attractive as this narrative is, it remains just as likely that the heavy snow hampered transport of the timbers in wagons through the London streets to the river. It also must be remembered that the Thames was, according to report, only "nigh frozen" and therefore as impassable as it ever was. Whatever the precise circumstances of this fascinating event in English theater history, Shakespeare's company was able to begin playing at their new Globe theater on the Bankside in 1599. After the first Globe burned down in 1613 during the staging of Shakespeare's *Henry VIII* (its thatch roof was set alight by cannon fire called for by the performance), Shakespeare's company immediately rebuilt on the same location. The second Globe seems to have been a grander structure than its predecessor. It remained in use until the beginning of the English Civil War in 1642, when Parliament officially closed the theaters. Soon thereafter it was pulled down.

The public theaters of Shakespeare's time were very different buildings from our theaters today. First of all, they were open-air playhouses. As recent excavations of the Rose and the Globe confirm, some were polygonal or roughly circular in shape; the Fortune, however, was square. The most recent estimates of their size put the diameter of these buildings at 72 feet (the Rose) to 100 feet (the Globe), but we know that they held vast audiences of two or three thousand, who must have been squeezed together quite tightly. Some of these spectators paid extra to sit or stand in the two or three levels of roofed galleries that extended, on the upper levels, all the way around the theater and surrounded an open space. In this space were the stage and, perhaps, the tiring house (what we would call dressing rooms), as well as the so-called yard. In the yard stood the spectators who chose to pay less, the ones whom Hamlet contemptuously called "groundlings." For a roof they had only the sky, and so they were exposed to all kinds of weather. They stood on a floor that was sometimes made of mortar and sometimes of ash mixed with the shells of hazelnuts. The latter provided a porous and therefore dry footing for the crowd, and the shells may have been more comfortable to stand on because they were not as hard as mortar. Availability of shells may not have been a problem if hazelnuts were a favorite food for Shakespeare's audiences to munch on as they watched his plays. Archaeologists who are today unearthing the remains of theaters from this period have discovered quantities of these nutshells on theater sites.

Unlike the yard, the stage itself was covered by a roof. Its ceiling, called "the heavens," is thought to have been elaborately painted to depict the sun, moon, stars, and planets. Just how big the stage was remains hard to determine. We have a single sketch of part of the interior of the Swan. A Dutchman named Johannes de Witt visited this theater around 1596 and sent a sketch of it back to his friend, Arend van Buchel. Because van Buchel found de Witt's letter and sketch of interest, he copied both into a book. It is van Buchel's copy, adapted, it seems, to the shape and size of the page in his book, that survives. In this sketch, the stage appears to be a large rectangular platform that thrusts far out into the yard, perhaps even as far as the center of the circle formed by the surrounding galleries. This drawing, combined with the specifications for the size of the stage in the building contract for the Fortune, has led scholars to conjecture that the stage on which Shakespeare's plays were performed must have measured approximately 43 feet in width and 27 feet in depth, a vast acting area. But the digging up of a large part of the Rose by archaeologists has provided evidence of a quite different stage design. The Rose stage was a platform tapered at the corners and much shallower than what seems to be depicted in the van Buchel sketch. Indeed, its measurements seem to be about 37.5 feet across at its widest point and only 15.5 feet deep. Because the surviving indications of stage size and design differ from each other so much, it is possible that the stages in other theaters, like the Theatre, the Curtain, and the Globe (the outdoor playhouses where we know that Shakespeare's plays were performed), were different from those at both the Swan and the Rose.

After about 1608 Shakespeare's plays were staged not only at the Globe but also at an indoor or private playhouse in Blackfriars. This theater had been constructed in 1596 by James Burbage in an upper hall of a former Dominican priory or monastic house. Although Henry VIII had dissolved all English monasteries in the 1530s (shortly after he had founded the Church of England), the area remained under church, rather than hostile civic, control. The hall that Burbage had purchased and renovated was a large one in which Parliament had once met. In the private theater that he constructed, the stage, lit by candles, was built across the narrow end of the hall, with boxes flanking it. The rest of the hall offered seating room only. Because there was no provision for standing room, the largest audience it could hold was less than a thousand, or about a quarter of what the Globe could accommodate. Admission to Blackfriars was correspondingly more expensive. Instead of a penny to stand in the yard at the Globe, it cost a minimum of sixpence to get into Blackfriars. The best seats at the Globe (in the Lords' Room in the gallery above and behind the stage) cost sixpence; but the boxes flanking the stage at Blackfriars were half a crown, or five times sixpence. Some spectators who were particularly interested in displaying themselves paid even more to sit on stools on the Blackfriars stage.

Whether in the outdoor or indoor playhouses, the stages of Shakespeare's time were different from ours. They were not separated from the audience by the dropping of a curtain between acts and scenes. Therefore the playwrights of the time had to find other ways of signaling to the audience that one scene (to be imagined as occurring in one location at a given time) had ended and the next (to be imagined at perhaps a different location at a later time) had begun. The customary way used by Shakespeare and many of his contemporaries was to have everyone onstage exit at the end of one scene and have one or more different characters enter to begin the next. In a few cases, where characters remain onstage from one scene to another, the dialogue or stage action makes the change of location clear, and the characters are generally to be imagined as having moved from one place to another. For example, in *Romeo and Juliet*, Romeo and his friends remain onstage in Act 1 from scene 4 to scene 5, but they are represented as having moved between scenes from the street that leads to Capulet's house into Capulet's house itself. The new location is signaled in part by the appearance onstage of Capulet's servingmen carrying napkins, something they would not take into the streets. Playwrights had to be quite resourceful in the use of hand properties, like the napkin, or in the use of dialogue to specify where the action was taking place in their plays because, in contrast to most of today's theaters, the playhouses of Shakespeare's time did not use movable scenery to dress the stage and make the setting precise. As another consequence of this difference, however, the playwrights of Shakespeare's time did not have to specify exactly where the action of their plays was set when they did not choose to do so, and much of the action of their plays is tied to no specific place.

Usually Shakespeare's stage is referred to as a "bare stage," to distinguish it from the stages of the last two or three centuries with their elaborate sets. But the stage in Shakespeare's time was not completely bare. Philip Henslowe, owner of the Rose, lists in his inventory of stage properties a rock, three tombs, and two mossy banks. Stage directions in plays of the time also call for such things as thrones (or "states"), banquets (presumably tables with plaster replicas of food on them), and beds and tombs to be pushed onto the stage. Thus the stage often held more than the actors.

The actors did not limit their performing to the stage alone. Occasionally they went beneath the stage, as the Ghost appears to do in the first act of *Hamlet*. From there they could emerge onto the stage through a trapdoor. They could retire behind the hangings across the back of the stage (or the front of the tiring house), as, for example, the actor playing Polonius does when he hides behind the arras. Sometimes the hangings could be drawn back during a performance to "discover" one or more actors behind them. When performance required that an actor appear "above," as when

Juliet is imagined to stand at the window of her chamber in the famous and misnamed "balcony scene," then the actor probably climbed the stairs to the gallery over the back of the stage and temporarily shared it with some of the spectators. The stage was also provided with ropes and winches so that actors could descend from, and reascend to, the "heavens."

Perhaps the greatest difference between dramatic performances in Shakespeare's time and ours was that in Shakespeare's England the roles of women were played by boys. (Some of these boys grew up to take male roles in their maturity.) There were no women in the acting companies, only in the audience. It had not always been so in the history of the English stage. There are records of women on English stages in the thirteenth and fourteenth centuries, two hundred years before Shakespeare's plays were performed. After the accession of James I in 1603, the queen of England and her ladies took part in entertainments at court called masques, and with the reopening of the theaters in 1660 at the restoration of Charles II, women again took their place on the public stage.

The chief competitors for the companies of adult actors such as the one to which Shakespeare belonged and for which he wrote were companies of exclusively boy actors. The competition was most intense in the early 1600s. There were then two principal children's companies: the Children of Paul's (the choirboys from St. Paul's Cathedral, whose private playhouse was near the cathedral); and the Children of the Chapel Royal (the choirboys from the monarch's private chapel, who performed at the Blackfriars theater built by Burbage in 1596, which Shakespeare's company had been stopped from using by local residents who objected to crowds). In *Hamlet* Shakespeare writes of "an aerie [nest] of children, little eyases [hawks], that cry out on the top of question and are most tyrannically clapped for 't. These are now the fashion and . . . berattle the common stages [attack the public theaters]." In the long run, the adult actors prevailed. The Children of Paul's dissolved around 1606. By about 1608 the Children of the Chapel Royal had been forced to stop playing at the Blackfriars theater, which was then taken over by the King's Men, Shakespeare's own troupe.

Acting companies and theaters of Shakespeare's time were organized in different ways. For example, Philip Henslowe owned the Rose and leased it to companies of actors, who paid him from their takings. Henslowe would act as manager of these companies, initially paying playwrights for their plays and buying properties, recovering his outlay from the actors. Shakespeare's company, however, managed itself, with the principal actors, Shakespeare among them, having the status of "sharers" and the right to a share in the takings, as well as the responsibility for a part of the expenses. Five of the sharers themselves, Shakespeare among them, owned the Globe. As actor, as sharer in an acting company and in ownership of theaters, and as playwright, Shakespeare was about as involved in the theatrical industry as one could imagine. Although Shakespeare and his fellows prospered, their status under the law was conditional upon the protection of powerful patrons. "Common players"—those who did not have patrons or masters—were classed in the language of the law with "vagabonds and sturdy beggars." So the actors had to secure for themselves the official rank of servants of patrons. Among the patrons under whose protection Shakespeare's company worked were the lord chamberlain and, after the accession of King James in 1603, the king himself.

We are now perhaps on the verge of learning a great

deal more about the theaters in which Shakespeare and his contemporaries performed—or at least of opening up new questions about them. Already about 70 percent of the Rose has been excavated, as has about 10 percent of the second Globe, the one built in 1614. It is to be hoped that soon more will be available for study. These are exciting times for students of Shakespeare's stage.

The Publication of Shakespeare's Plays

Eighteen of Shakespeare's plays found their way into print during the playwright's lifetime, but there is nothing to suggest that he took any interest in their publication. These eighteen appeared separately in editions called quartos. Their pages were not much larger than the one you are now reading, and these little books were sold unbound for a few pence. The earliest of the quartos that still survive were printed in 1594, the year that both *Titus Andronicus* and a version of the play now called *2 King Henry VI* became available. While almost every one of these early quartos displays on its title page the name of the acting company that performed the play, only about half provide the name of the playwright, Shakespeare. The first quarto edition to bear the name Shakespeare on its title page is *Love's Labor's Lost* of 1598. A few of these quartos were popular with the book-buying public of Shakespeare's lifetime; for example, quarto *Richard II* went through five editions between 1597 and 1615. But most of the quartos were far from best-sellers; *Love's Labor's Lost* (1598), for instance, was not reprinted in quarto until 1631. After

Shakespeare's death, two more of his plays appeared in quarto format: *Othello* in 1622 and *The Two Noble Kinsmen*, coauthored with John Fletcher, in 1634.

In 1623, seven years after Shakespeare's death, *Mr. William Shakespeares Comedies, Histories, & Tragedies* was published. This printing offered readers in a single book thirty-six of the thirty-eight plays now thought to have been written by Shakespeare, including eighteen that had never been printed before. And it offered them in a style that was then reserved for serious literature and scholarship. The plays were arranged in double columns on pages nearly a foot high. This large page size is called "folio," as opposed to the smaller "quarto," and the 1623 volume is usually called the Shakespeare First Folio. It is reputed to have sold for the lordly price of a pound. (One copy at the Folger Library is marked fifteen shillings—that is, three-quarters of a pound.)

In a preface to the First Folio entitled "To the great Variety of Readers," two of Shakespeare's former fellow actors in the King's Men, John Heminge and Henry Condell, wrote that they themselves had collected their dead companion's plays. They suggested that they had seen his own papers: "we have scarce received from him a blot in his papers." The title page of the Folio declared that the plays within it had been printed "according to the True Original Copies." Comparing the Folio to the quartos, Heminge and Condell disparaged the quartos, advising their readers that "before you were abused with divers stolen and surreptitious copies, maimed, and deformed by the frauds and stealths of injurious impostors." Many Shakespeareans of the eighteenth and nineteenth centuries believed Heminge and Condell and regarded the Folio plays as superior to anything in the quartos.

Once we begin to examine the Folio plays in detail, it becomes less easy to take at face value the word of

Heminge and Condell about the superiority of the Folio texts. For example, of the first nine plays in the Folio (one quarter of the entire collection), four were essentially reprinted from earlier quarto printings that Heminge and Condell had disparaged; and four have now been identified as printed from copies written in the hand of a professional scribe of the 1620s named Ralph Crane; the ninth, *The Comedy of Errors*, was apparently also printed from a manuscript, but one whose origin cannot be readily identified. Evidently then, eight of the first nine plays in the First Folio were not printed, in spite of what the Folio title page announces, "according to the True Original Copies," or Shakespeare's own papers, and the source of the ninth is unknown. Since today's editors have been forced to treat Heminge and Condell's pronouncements with skepticism, they must choose whether to base their own editions upon quartos or the Folio on grounds other than Heminge and Condell's story of where the quarto and Folio versions originated.

Editors have often fashioned their own narratives to explain what lies behind the quartos and Folio. They have said that Heminge and Condell meant to criticize only a few of the early quartos, the ones that offer much shorter and sometimes quite different, often garbled, versions of plays. Among the examples of these are the 1600 quarto of *Henry V* (the Folio offers a much fuller version) or the 1603 *Hamlet* quarto (in 1604 a different, much longer form of the play got into print as a quarto). Early in this century editors speculated that these questionable texts were produced when someone in the audience took notes from the plays' dialogue during performances and then employed "hack poets" to fill out the notes. The poor results were then sold to a publisher and presented in print as Shakespeare's plays. More recently this story has given way to another in which the shorter versions are said to be recreations from memory of Shakespeare's plays by actors who wanted to stage them in the provinces but lacked manuscript copies. Most of the quartos offer much better texts than these so-called bad quartos. Indeed, in most of the quartos we find texts that are at least equal to or better than what is printed in the Folio. Many of this century's Shakespeare enthusiasts have persuaded themselves that most of the quartos were set into type directly from Shakespeare's own papers, although there is nothing on which to base this conclusion except the desire for it to be true. Thus speculation continues about how the Shakespeare plays got to be printed. All that we have are the printed texts.

The book collector who was most successful in bringing together copies of the quartos and the First Folio was Henry Clay Folger, founder of the Folger Shakespeare Library in Washington, D.C. While it is estimated that there survive around the world only about 230 copies of the First Folio, Mr. Folger was able to acquire more than seventy-five copies, as well as a large number of fragments, for the library that bears his name. He also amassed a substantial number of quartos. For example, only fourteen copies of the First Quarto of *Love's Labor's Lost* are known to exist, and three are at the Folger Shakespeare Library. As a consequence of Mr. Folger's labors, twentieth-century scholars visiting the Folger Library have been able to learn a great deal about sixteenth- and seventeenth-century printing and, particularly, about the printing of Shakespeare's plays. And Mr. Folger did not stop at the First Folio, but collected many copies of later editions of Shakespeare, beginning with the Second Folio (1632), the Third (1663–64), and the Fourth (1685). Each of these later folios was based on its immediate predecessor and was edited anonymously. The first editor of Shakespeare whose name we know was Nicholas Rowe, whose first edition came out in 1709. Mr. Folger collected this edition and many, many more by Rowe's successors.

An Introduction to This Text

As You Like It was first printed in the 1623 collection of Shakespeare's plays now known as the First Folio. The present edition is based directly upon the First Folio version.* For the convenience of the reader, we have modernized the punctuation and the spelling of the Folio. Sometimes we go so far as to modernize certain old forms of words; for example, when *a* means *he,* we change it to *he;* we change *mo* to *more* and *ye* to *you.* But it is not our practice in editing any of the plays to modernize words that sound distinctly different from modern forms. For example, when the early printed texts read *sith* or *apricocks* or *porpentine,* we have not modernized to *since, apricots, porcupine.* When the forms *an, and,* or *and if* appear instead of the modern form *if,* we have reduced *and* to *an* but have not changed any of these forms to their modern equivalent, *if.* We also modernize and, where necessary, correct passages in foreign languages, unless an error in the early printed text can be reasonably explained as a joke.

Whenever we change the wording of the First Folio or add anything to its stage directions, we mark the change by enclosing it in superior half-brackets (⌐ ⌐). We want our readers to be immediately aware when we have

---

*We have also consulted the computerized text of the First Folio provided by the Text Archive of the Oxford University Computing Centre, to which we are grateful.

intervened. (Only when we correct an obvious typographical error in the First Folio does the change not get marked.) Whenever we change either the First Folio's wording or its punctuation so that the meaning changes, we list the change in the textual notes at the back of the book, even if all we have done is fix an obvious error.

We regularize a number of proper names, as is the usual practice in editions of the play. For example, the Folio sometimes calls Le Beau by the name "Le Beu," sometimes names Rosalind "Rosaline," and sometimes refers to Sir Rowland de Boys as "Sir Roland de Boys." We, however, use only the forms Le Beau, Rosalind, and Sir Rowland de Boys.

This edition differs from many earlier ones in its efforts to aid the reader in imagining the play as a performance rather than as a series of actual events. Thus, stage directions and speech prefixes are written with reference to the stage. For example, when one goes to a production of *As You Like It*, one is always aware, after the actors playing Rosalind and Celia have donned their disguises, that they no longer look like princesses. Instead, the actor playing Rosalind looks like a man from the country called Ganymede, and the actor playing Celia, now named Aliena, looks like Ganymede's sister. Only the two princesses and Touchstone know that Ganymede and Aliena are assumed identities. In an effort to reproduce in our edition the effect that an audience experiences, we have added their "disguise names" to the speech prefixes ROSALIND and CELIA whenever these characters are in dialogue with characters who think they are conversing with Ganymede and/or Aliena rather than with the princesses. With the addition of such directions to the speech prefixes, we hope to give our readers a greater opportunity to stage the play in their own imaginations.

For the same reason, whenever it is reasonably certain, in our view, that a speech is accompanied by a particular action, we provide a stage direction describing the action. (Occasional exceptions to this rule occur when the action is so obvious that to add a stage direction would insult the reader.) Stage directions for the entrance of characters in mid-scene are, with rare exceptions, placed so that they immediately precede the characters' participation in the scene, even though these entrances may appear somewhat earlier in the early printed texts. Whenever we move a stage direction, we record this change in the textual notes. Latin stage directions (e.g., *Exeunt*) are translated into English (e.g., *They exit*).

We expand the often severely abbreviated forms of names used as speech headings in early printed texts into the full names of the characters. We also regularize the speakers' names in speech headings, using only a single designation for each character, even though the early printed texts sometimes use a variety of designations. Variations in the speech headings of the early printed texts are recorded in the textual notes.

In the present edition, as well, we mark with a dash any change of address within a speech, unless a stage direction intervenes. When the *-ed* ending of a word is to be pronounced, we mark it with an accent. Like editors for the past two centuries, we print metrically linked lines in the following way:

SILVIUS
    Phoebe, with all my heart.
PHOEBE   I'll write it straight.

However, when there are a number of short verse lines that can be linked in more than one way, we do not, with rare exceptions, indent any of them.

The Explanatory Notes

The notes that appear on the pages facing the text are designed to provide readers with the help that they may need to enjoy the play. Whenever the meaning of a word in the text is not readily accessible in a good contemporary dictionary, we offer the meaning in a note. Sometimes we provide a note even when the relevant meaning is to be found in the dictionary but the word has acquired since Shakespeare's time other potentially confusing meanings. In our notes, we try to offer modern synonyms for Shakespeare's words. We also try to indicate to the reader the connection between the word in the play and the modern synonym. For example, Shakespeare sometimes uses the word *head* to mean "source," but, for modern readers, there may be no connection evident between these two words. We provide the connection by explaining Shakespeare's usage as follows: "**head:** fountainhead, source." On some occasions, a whole phrase or clause needs explanation. Then, if space allows, we rephrase in our own words the difficult passage, and add at the end synonyms for individual words in the passage. When scholars have been unable to determine the meaning of a word or phrase, we acknowledge the uncertainty.

AS YOU LIKE IT

Characters in the Play

ORLANDO, youngest son of Sir Rowland de Boys
OLIVER, his elder brother
SECOND BROTHER, brother to Orlando and Oliver, named Jaques
ADAM, servant to Oliver and friend to Orlando
DENNIS, servant to Oliver

ROSALIND, daughter to Duke Senior
CELIA, Rosalind's cousin, daughter to Duke Frederick
TOUCHSTONE, a court Fool

DUKE FREDERICK, the usurping duke
CHARLES, wrestler at Duke Frederick's court
LE BEAU, a courtier at Duke Frederick's court
FIRST LORD
SECOND LORD } *attending Duke Frederick*

DUKE SENIOR, the exiled duke, brother to Duke Frederick

JAQUES
AMIENS
FIRST LORD
SECOND LORD } *Lords attending Duke Senior in exile*

FIRST PAGE
SECOND PAGE } *attending Duke Senior in exile*

CORIN, a shepherd
SILVIUS, a young shepherd in love
PHOEBE, a disdainful shepherdess

3

AUDREY, a goat-keeper
WILLIAM, a country youth in love with Audrey
SIR OLIVER MARTEXT, a parish priest

HYMEN, god of marriage

Lords, Attendants, Musicians

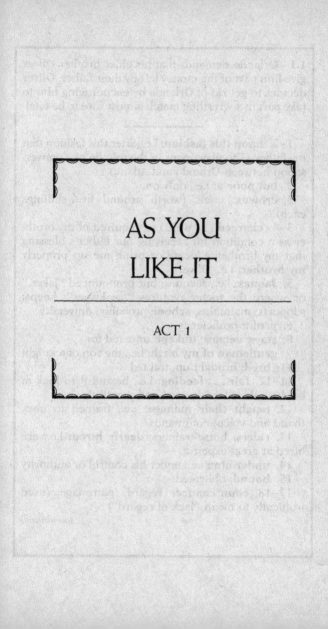

AS YOU LIKE IT

ACT 1

1.1 Orlando demands that his elder brother Oliver give him part of the money left by their father. Oliver decides to get rid of Orlando by encouraging him to take part in a wrestling match almost sure to be fatal.

———————

1–2. **upon this fashion:** i.e., after this fashion that my father (The play opens in the middle of a conversation between Orlando and Adam.)

2. **but poor a:** i.e., only one

3. **crowns:** coins (worth around five shillings each)

3–4. **charged . . . well:** i.e., required of my brother as a condition for receiving our father's blessing that my brother educate or bring me up properly **my brother:** i.e., Oliver

5. **Jaques:** i.e., Jacques, but pronounced "jakes," or where the meter requires, "jay-kwees"; **keeps:** supports, maintains; **school:** probably, university

6. **profit:** proficiency

8. **stays:** detains; **unkept:** uncared for

9. **gentleman of my birth:** i.e., the son of a knight

11. **bred:** brought up, trained

11–12. **fair . . . feeding:** i.e., beautiful to look at because their feed is good and plentiful

12. **taught their manage:** i.e., trained to obey (hand and voice) commands

13. **riders:** horse-trainers; **dearly hired:** i.e., are hired at great expense

14. **under him:** i.e., under his control or authority

15. **bound:** obligated

17–18. **countenance:** regard, patronage (used ironically to mean "lack of regard")

(continued)

6

ACT 1

Scene 1
Enter Orlando and Adam.

ORLANDO As I remember, <u>Adam</u>, it was upon this
fashion bequeathed me by will but poor a <u>thousand
crowns</u>, and, as thou sayst, charged <u>my brother</u> on
<u>his blessing to breed me well.</u> And there begins my
sadness. My brother <u>Jaques</u> he keeps at <u>school</u>, and   5
report speaks <u>goldenly of his profit.</u> For my part, he
keeps me rustically at home, or, to speak more
properly, stays me here at home <u>unkept;</u> for call you
that "keeping" for a <u>gentleman of my birth,</u> that
differs not from the <u>stalling of an ox?</u> <u>His horses</u> are   10
bred <u>bette</u>r, for, besides that they are <u>fair with their
feeding,</u> they are <u>taught their manage</u> and, to <u>that</u>
<u>end,</u> riders dearly hired. But I, his brother, <u>gain
nothing under him but growth,</u> for the which his
<u>animals on his dunghills</u> are as much bound to him   15
as I. Besides this nothing that he so plentifully gives
me, the something that nature gave me his countenance seems to take from me. He lets <u>me feed with
his hinds, bars me the place of a brother, and, as</u>
much as in <u>him lies, mines my gentility</u> with my   20
<u>education.</u> This is it, Adam, that grieves me, and the
<u>spirit</u> of <u>my father,</u> which I think is within me,
begins to mutiny against this <u>servitude.</u> I will no

7

19. **hinds:** servants; **bars me:** i.e., excludes me from

19-20. **as much . . . lies:** i.e., to the extent that he can

20. **mines:** undermines; **gentility:** status as a gentleman by birth

21. **education:** i.e., lack of education

25. **avoid:** get rid of

27. **Go apart:** i.e., step aside

28. **shake me up:** harass me

29. **make you:** i.e., are you doing (In Orlando's reply in line 30, **make** has the usual sense of "create.")

31. **mar:** Proverbial: "to **make** or **mar**"

32. **Marry:** i.e., indeed (originally an oath on the name of the Virgin Mary)

35. **be naught:** (1) keep silent; or (2) go away

37-38. **Shall . . . spent:** In Luke 15.11–32, the **prodigal** son, having foolishly wasted his patrimony **(portion),** is given a job feeding **hogs,** and, in his hunger, envies them the **husks** he feeds them. **prodigal portion . . . spent:** (1) prodigal's portion have I spent (2) portion have I prodigally spent

40. **where:** i.e., in whose presence (Orlando's reply is to the sense of **where** as "in what place.")

41. **orchard:** garden (See page 22.)

43. **him:** i.e., he whom

44-45. **in the gentle . . . know me:** i.e., you should acknowledge that we both were born gentlemen **condition:** attribute, quality

45-47. **The courtesy . . . first-born:** i.e., the custom of primogeniture (according to which the eldest son inherited the whole of his father's estate) acknowledges you as superior to me (See longer note, page 207.)

(continued)

longer endure it, though yet I know no wise remedy
how to avoid it.   25

Enter Oliver.

ADAM   Yonder comes my master, your brother.
ORLANDO   Go apart, Adam, and thou shalt hear how he
will shake me up.   ⌜*Adam steps aside.*⌝
OLIVER   Now, sir, what make you here?
ORLANDO   Nothing. I am not taught to make anything.   30
OLIVER   What mar you then, sir?
ORLANDO   Marry, sir, I am helping you to mar that
which God made, a poor unworthy brother of
yours, with idleness.
OLIVER   Marry, sir, be better employed, and be naught   35
awhile.
ORLANDO   Shall I keep your hogs and eat husks with
them? What prodigal portion have I spent that I
should come to such penury?
OLIVER   Know you where you are, sir?   40
ORLANDO   O sir, very well: here in your orchard.
OLIVER   Know you before whom, sir?
ORLANDO   Ay, better than him I am before knows me. I
know you are my eldest brother, and in the gentle
condition of blood you should so know me. The   45
courtesy of nations allows you my better, in that you
are the first-born, but the same tradition takes not
away my blood, were there twenty brothers betwixt
us. I have as much of my father in me as you, albeit I
confess your coming before me is nearer to his   50
reverence.
OLIVER, ⌜*threatening Orlando*⌝ What, boy!
ORLANDO, ⌜*holding off Oliver by the throat*⌝ Come,
come, elder brother, you are too young in this.
OLIVER   Wilt thou lay hands on me, villain?   55
ORLANDO   I am no villain. I am the youngest son of Sir

48. **blood:** parentage, lineage
50. **coming before me:** i.e., being older than I
54. **young in this:** i.e., inexperienced at fighting
55. **villain:** scoundrel (Orlando's reply, lines 56–58, plays on the word's sense of "low-born peasant.")
61. **on:** i.e., against
62. **patient:** calm
63. **at accord:** reconciled
69. **qualities:** accomplishments
70. **allow:** provide
71. **exercises:** practice for the sake of improvement
72. **allottery:** perhaps, allotment (This is the only recorded appearance of this word.)
73. **fortunes:** condition or standing in life; perhaps some position at court
77. **will:** wishes (with wordplay, perhaps, on the portion left to Orlando in their father's **will**)
81–82. **lost my teeth:** an allusion to the fable in Aesop where a dog, beaten for letting game escape from him, says: "Thou hast loved me catching game, thou hast hated me being slow and toothless."
84–85. **grow upon . . . rankness:** an image from gardening (in which overgrown plants are cut down) and from medicine (in which corrupt blood is released through bloodletting) **grow upon:** take liberties with (with wordplay on **grow**) **physic:** treat with medicine, especially with a purgative **rankness:** rebelliousness (with wordplay on "rank" as "grown too large" and "corrupt")
86. **Holla:** a shout to get someone's attention
87. **your Worship:** a title of honor

Rowland de Boys. He was my father, and he is thrice a villain that says such a father begot villains. Wert thou not my brother, I would not take this hand from thy throat till this other had pulled out thy tongue for saying so. Thou hast railed on thyself. 60

ADAM, ⌜*coming forward*⌝ Sweet masters, be patient. For your father's remembrance, be at accord.

OLIVER, ⌜*to Orlando*⌝ Let me go, I say.

ORLANDO I will not till I please. You shall hear me. My father charged you in his will to give me good education. You have trained me like a peasant, obscuring and hiding from me all gentlemanlike qualities. The spirit of my father grows strong in me, and I will no longer endure it. Therefore allow me such exercises as may become a gentleman, or give me the poor allottery my father left me by testament. With that I will go buy my fortunes. 65 70

⌜*Orlando releases Oliver.*⌝

OLIVER And what wilt thou do—beg when that is spent? Well, sir, get you in. I will not long be troubled with you. You shall have some part of your will. I pray you leave me. 75

ORLANDO I will no further offend you than becomes me for my good.

OLIVER, ⌜*to Adam*⌝ Get you with him, you old dog. 80

ADAM Is "old dog" my reward? Most true, I have lost my teeth in your service. God be with my old master. He would not have spoke such a word.

Orlando ⌜*and*⌝ *Adam exit.*

OLIVER Is it even so? Begin you to grow upon me? I will physic your rankness, and yet give no thousand crowns neither.—Holla, Dennis! 85

Enter Dennis.

DENNIS Calls your Worship?

90. **So please you:** i.e., yes (literally, so may it please you)

94. **morrow:** morning

102. **good leave:** i.e., unqualified permission

106. **the Duke's . . . her cousin:** i.e., Celia

108. **she:** i.e., Celia; **her:** i.e., Rosalind's

109. **to stay:** i.e., if she had been forced to stay; **She:** i.e., Rosalind

110. **of:** i.e., by

113. **Forest of Arden:** In Thomas Lodge's *Rosalynde*, the early novel that Shakespeare here dramatizes, the **Forest of Arden** is in France. There is, however, a Forest of Arden in Shakespeare's native Warwickshire.

114. **a many:** i.e., many; **merry:** happy

115. **Robin Hood:** legendary fourteenth-century knight forced off his land into Sherwood Forest, where he joined with a band of outlaws (known in the legends and ballads as his **merry** men) until, together, they recovered his land (See longer note, page 207.)

117. **fleet the time:** pass the time quickly; **carelessly:** free of care or anxiety

117–18. **golden world:** i.e., the mythological "golden age," always long ago, when humankind, free of the need to work, enjoyed the bounty of the earth in a continual springtime (See longer note, pages 207–8, and illustration, page 186.)

119. **What:** an interjection introducing a question or exclamation

OLIVER Was not Charles, the Duke's wrestler, here to
speak with me?

DENNIS So please you, he is here at the door and   90
importunes access to you.

OLIVER Call him in. ⌜*Dennis exits.*⌝ 'Twill be a good
way, and tomorrow the wrestling is.

Enter Charles.

CHARLES Good morrow to your Worship.

OLIVER Good Monsieur Charles, what's the new news   95
at the new court?

CHARLES There's no news at the court, sir, but the old
news. That is, the old duke is banished by his
younger brother the new duke, and three or four
loving lords have put themselves into voluntary   100
exile with him, whose lands and revenues enrich
the new duke. Therefore he gives them good leave
to wander.

OLIVER Can you tell if Rosalind, the Duke's daughter,
be banished with her father?   105

CHARLES O no, for the Duke's daughter her cousin so
loves her, being ever from their cradles bred together, that ⌜she⌝ would have followed her exile or have
died to stay behind her. She is at the court and no
less beloved of her uncle than his own daughter,   110
and never two ladies loved as they do.

OLIVER Where will the old duke live?

CHARLES They say he is already in the Forest of Arden,
and a many merry men with him; and there they
live like the old Robin Hood of England. They say   115
many young gentlemen flock to him every day and
fleet the time carelessly, as they did in the golden
world.

OLIVER What, you wrestle tomorrow before the new
duke?   120

122. **a matter:** i.e., a certain matter

123–24. **a disposition:** an intention

125. **fall:** wrestling bout

128. **for your love:** i.e., for your sake; **foil:** throw, and thereby defeat

131. **withal:** i.e., with this news

131–32. **stay . . . intendment:** prevent him from carrying out his intention

133. **as:** i.e., that; **run into:** incur

134. **search:** i.e., seeking

138. **underhand:** unobtrusive; not open or obvious

140. **stubbornest:** most ruthless, fierce

141. **envious emulator:** malicious disparager

142. **parts:** abilities; **contriver:** plotter

143. **natural brother:** i.e., brother by blood

144. **had as lief:** i.e., had just as soon

145. **thou . . . to 't:** i.e., you had better beware

146–47. **mightily . . . thee:** i.e., gain a great reputation at your expense

147. **practice:** lay schemes

149. **leave:** stop interfering with; **ta'en:** i.e., taken

153. **brotherly:** i.e., with the reserve appropriate to a brother

CHARLES Marry, do I, sir, and I came to acquaint you
     with a matter. I am given, sir, secretly to under-
     stand that your younger brother Orlando hath a
     disposition to come in disguised against me to try a
     fall. Tomorrow, sir, I wrestle for my credit, and he   125
     that escapes me without some broken limb shall
     acquit him well. Your brother is but young and
     tender, and for your love I would be loath to foil
     him, as I must for my own honor if he come in.
     Therefore, out of my love to you, I came hither to   130
     acquaint you withal, that either you might stay him
     from his intendment, or brook such disgrace well
     as he shall run into, in that it is a thing of his own
     search, and altogether against my will.
OLIVER Charles, I thank thee for thy love to me, which   135
     thou shalt find I will most kindly requite. I had
     myself notice of my brother's purpose herein, and
     have by underhand means labored to dissuade him
     from it; but he is resolute. I'll tell thee, Charles, it is
     the stubbornest young fellow of France, full of   140
     ambition, an envious emulator of every man's good
     parts, a secret and villainous contriver against me
     his natural brother. Therefore use thy discretion. I
     had as lief thou didst break his neck as his finger.
     And thou wert best look to 't, for if thou dost him   145
     any slight disgrace, or if he do not mightily grace
     himself on thee, he will practice against thee by
     poison, entrap thee by some treacherous device,
     and never leave thee till he hath ta'en thy life by
     some indirect means or other. For I assure thee—   150
     and almost with tears I speak it—there is not one so
     young and so villainous this day living. I speak but
     brotherly of him, but should I anatomize him to
     thee as he is, I must blush and weep, and thou must
     look pale and wonder.   155
CHARLES I am heartily glad I came hither to you. If he

158. **go alone:** walk without help; **more:** again

161. **stir:** urge on; **gamester:** (1) athlete; (2) person full of high-spirited fun

164. **learned:** educated; **device:** ingenuity, desire, opinion

165. **sorts:** kinds (of people); **enchantingly:** i.e., as if by enchantment

166–67. **my own people:** i.e., my retinue, followers, servants

168. **misprized:** scorned, despised

169. **kindle:** inflame, rouse

1.2 Orlando wins the wrestling match and, at the same time, wins the heart of Rosalind, daughter of the legitimate duke, now banished by his usurping brother, Duke Frederick. Orlando is equally attracted to Rosalind.

1. **sweet my coz:** i.e., my sweet cousin

3. **would . . . merrier:** i.e., do you wish I were even merrier; or, do you nevertheless wish I were merrier

5. **learn:** teach

8. **that:** i.e., with which

10. **so:** i.e., as long as; **still:** always

12–13. **righteously tempered:** rightly constituted

14. **estate:** prosperity

come tomorrow, I'll give him his payment. If ever
he go alone again, I'll never wrestle for prize more.
And so God keep your Worship.

⌜OLIVER⌝ Farewell, good Charles.   ⌜*Charles*⌝ *exits.*   160
Now will I stir this gamester. I hope I shall see an
end of him, for my soul—yet I know not why—
hates nothing more than he. Yet he's gentle, never
schooled and yet learned, full of noble device, of all
sorts enchantingly beloved, and indeed so much in   165
the heart of the world, and especially of my own
people, who best know him, that I am altogether
misprized. But it shall not be so long; this wrestler
shall clear all. Nothing remains but that I kindle the
boy thither, which now I'll go about.   170
                                        He exits.

Scene 2
Enter Rosalind and Celia.

CELIA I pray thee, Rosalind, sweet my coz, be merry.
ROSALIND Dear Celia, I show more mirth than I am
    mistress of, and would you yet ⌜I⌝ were merrier?
    Unless you could teach me to forget a banished
    father, you must not learn me how to remember   5
    any extraordinary pleasure.
CELIA Herein I see thou lov'st me not with the full
    weight that I love thee. If my uncle, thy banished
    father, had banished thy uncle, the Duke my father,
    so thou hadst been still with me, I could have taught 10
    my love to take thy father for mine. So wouldst thou,
    if the truth of thy love to me were so righteously
    tempered as mine is to thee.
ROSALIND Well, I will forget the condition of my estate
    to rejoice in yours.   15

17. **like:** likely

19. **perforce:** forcibly

24. **sports:** amusements, diversions (Celia's response, line 26, plays on **to make sport,** or treat as a joke.)

26. **prithee:** i.e., pray thee; **withal:** with

27. **in good earnest:** seriously

28. **neither:** i.e., either; **a pure blush:** (1) a simple or mere **blush;** (2) the blush of a **pure** woman

29. **come off:** escape

31–32. **housewife Fortune . . . wheel:** The goddess **Fortune,** who turns the **wheel** on which people's fortunes rise and fall, is here compared to a **housewife** at a spinning-wheel. There is also wordplay on "housewife" and "hussy" (words that were almost interchangeable at the time), since the goddess Fortune is said to grant favors to all, but to be true to none. See note to 4.3.30, and illustration, page 32.

35. **blind:** Fortune is often depicted wearing a blindfold.

36. **mistake:** go wrong, err

37. **fair:** beautiful; **scarce:** seldom, rarely

38. **honest:** chaste

39. **ill-favoredly:** ugly

44. **by fortune:** (1) by chance; (2) through the agency of the goddess Fortune

44 SD. **Touchstone:** the name of a stone used to test the quality of precious metals (See longer note, page 208.)

45. **wit:** i.e., the intelligence (See longer note, page 208.)

CELIA You know my father hath no child but I, nor
none is like to have; and truly, when he dies, thou
shalt be his heir, for what he hath taken away from
thy father perforce, I will render thee again in
affection. By mine honor I will, and when I break   20
that oath, let me turn monster. Therefore, my sweet
Rose, my dear Rose, be merry.

ROSALIND From henceforth I will, coz, and devise
sports. Let me see—what think you of falling in
love?   25

CELIA Marry, I prithee do, to make sport withal; but
love no man in good earnest, nor no further in
sport neither than with safety of a pure blush thou
mayst in honor come off again.

ROSALIND What shall be our sport, then?   30

CELIA Let us sit and mock the good housewife Fortune
from her wheel, that her gifts may henceforth be
bestowed equally.

ROSALIND I would we could do so, for her benefits are
mightily misplaced, and the bountiful blind woman   35
doth most mistake in her gifts to women.

CELIA 'Tis true, for those that she makes fair she scarce
makes honest, and those that she makes honest she
makes very ill-favoredly.

ROSALIND Nay, now thou goest from Fortune's office to   40
Nature's. Fortune reigns in gifts of the world, not in
the lineaments of nature.

CELIA No? When Nature hath made a fair creature,
may she not by fortune fall into the fire?

Enter ⌈Touchstone.⌉

Though Nature hath given us wit to flout at Fortune,   45
hath not Fortune sent in this fool to cut off the
argument?

48. **too hard for:** (1) more than a match for; (2) too cruel for

49. **natural:** half-wit (Lines 49–55 play on **natural** as "produced by nature" and as "idiot.")

50. **wit:** cleverness

51. **Peradventure:** perhaps; **neither:** i.e., either

52. **wits:** mental faculties

53. **reason of:** discuss

55. **the wits:** clever or learned persons

56. **wit, whither wander you:** a play on the proverbial "Wit, whither wilt?" usually addressed to someone whose tongue is carrying him/her away, but here used more literally

65. **naught:** worthless, bad; **stand to it:** insist, maintain

67. **forsworn:** perjured (by swearing to a false statement)

75. **if you swear:** i.e., if one swears

A Fool in motley. (2.7.13)
From August Casimir Redel, *Apophtegmata symbolica* . . . [n.d.].

ROSALIND   Indeed, there is Fortune too hard for Nature, when Fortune makes Nature's natural the
cutter-off of Nature's wit.   50

CELIA   Peradventure this is not Fortune's work neither,
but Nature's, who perceiveth our natural wits too
dull to reason of such goddesses, ⌈and⌉ hath sent
this natural for our whetstone, for always the dull-
ness of the fool is the whetstone of the wits. ⌈*To*   55
Touchstone.⌉ How now, wit, whither wander you?

TOUCHSTONE   Mistress, you must come away to your
father.

CELIA   Were you made the messenger?

TOUCHSTONE   No, by mine honor, but I was bid to come   60
for you.

ROSALIND   Where learned you that oath, fool?

TOUCHSTONE   Of a certain knight that swore by his
honor they were good pancakes, and swore by his
honor the mustard was naught. Now, I'll stand to it,   65
the pancakes were naught and the mustard was
good, and yet was not the knight forsworn.

CELIA   How prove you that in the great heap of your
knowledge?

ROSALIND   Ay, marry, now unmuzzle your wisdom.   70

TOUCHSTONE   Stand you both forth now: stroke your
chins, and swear by your beards that I am a knave.

CELIA   By our beards (if we had them), thou art.

TOUCHSTONE   By my knavery (if I had it), then I were.
But if you swear by that that is not, you are not   75
forsworn. No more was this knight swearing by his
honor, for he never had any, or if he had, he had
sworn it away before ever he saw those pancakes or
that mustard.

CELIA   Prithee, who is 't that thou mean'st?   80

TOUCHSTONE   One that old Frederick, your father, loves.

⌈CELIA⌉   My father's love is enough to honor him.

84. **taxation:** i.e., attacking people

88. **wit:** wisdom

90. **Le Beau:** The name means, literally, "the beautiful."

92. **put on:** force on

94. **news-crammed:** wordplay on the practice of fattening fowl for the table

96. **Bonjour:** good day

99. **color:** kind

101. **wit:** cleverness

102. **destinies:** in Greek mythology, the goddesses who control the course of one's life (also called the Fates); **decrees:** i.e., decree

106. **amaze:** perplex, bewilder

111. **to do:** i.e., to be done

115. **tale:** perhaps with a pun on "tail," or ending

An orchard. (1.1.41)
From Octavio Boldoni, *Theatrum temporaneum* . . . (1636).

Enough. Speak no more of him; you'll be whipped
for taxation one of these days.

TOUCHSTONE   The more pity that fools may not speak   85
wisely what wise men do foolishly.

CELIA   By my troth, thou sayest true. For, since the little
wit that fools have was silenced, the little foolery
that wise men have makes a great show. Here
comes Monsieur ⌜Le⌝ Beau.   90

Enter Le Beau.

ROSALIND   With his mouth full of news.

CELIA   Which he will put on us as pigeons feed their
young.

ROSALIND   Then shall we be news-crammed.

CELIA   All the better. We shall be the more   95
marketable.—*Bonjour,* Monsieur Le Beau. What's
the news?

LE BEAU   Fair princess, you have lost much good sport.

CELIA   Sport? Of what color?

LE BEAU   What color, madam? How shall I answer you?   100

ROSALIND   As wit and fortune will.

TOUCHSTONE   Or as the destinies decrees.

CELIA   Well said. That was laid on with a trowel.

TOUCHSTONE   Nay, if I keep not my rank—

ROSALIND   Thou losest thy old smell.   105

LE BEAU   You amaze me, ladies. I would have told you of
good wrestling, which you have lost the sight of.

ROSALIND   Yet tell us the manner of the wrestling.

LE BEAU   I will tell you the beginning, and if it please
your Ladyships, you may see the end, for the best is   110
yet to do, and here, where you are, they are coming
to perform it.

CELIA   Well, the beginning that is dead and buried.

LE BEAU   There comes an old man and his three sons—

CELIA   I could match this beginning with an old tale.   115

116. **proper:** fine-looking, well-proportioned

118. **bills:** labels or written documents

118–19. **Be . . . presents:** the opening formula of legal documents

122. **that:** so that

125. **dole:** dolor, sorrow

135. **any else longs:** i.e., anyone else who longs

135–36. **broken music:** wordplay on **rib-breaking** (literally, **broken music** was music written in parts for different instruments)

142 SD. **Flourish:** a fanfare of trumpets to announce the approach of someone important

143–44. **Since . . . forwardness:** i.e., since Orlando will not be dissuaded from wrestling, let him experience whatever danger (**peril**) his over-eagerness brings on him   **entreated:** persuaded by pleading

147. **looks successfully:** i.e., seems likely to succeed

A "cross." (2.4.11)
From Edward Hawkins, *The silver coins of England . . .* (1841).

LE BEAU   Three proper young men of excellent growth
     and presence.
ROSALIND   With bills on their necks: "Be it known unto
     all men by these presents."
LE BEAU   The eldest of the three wrestled with Charles,   120
     the Duke's wrestler, which Charles in a moment
     threw him and broke three of his ribs, that there is
     little hope of life in him. So he served the second,
     and so the third. Yonder they lie, the poor old man
     their father making such pitiful dole over them that   125
     all the beholders take his part with weeping.
ROSALIND   Alas!
TOUCHSTONE   But what is the sport, monsieur, that the
     ladies have lost?
LE BEAU   Why, this that I speak of.   130
TOUCHSTONE   Thus men may grow wiser every day. It is
     the first time that ever I heard breaking of ribs was
     sport for ladies.
CELIA   Or I, I promise thee.
ROSALIND   But is there any else longs to see this broken   135
     music in his sides? Is there yet another dotes upon
     rib-breaking? Shall we see this wrestling, cousin?
LE BEAU   You must if you stay here, for here is the place
     appointed for the wrestling, and they are ready to
     perform it.   140
CELIA   Yonder sure they are coming. Let us now stay
     and see it.

     Flourish. Enter Duke ⌈Frederick,⌉ Lords, Orlando,
                 Charles, and Attendants.

DUKE FREDERICK   Come on. Since the youth will not be
     entreated, his own peril on his forwardness.
ROSALIND, ⌈*to Le Beau*⌉   Is yonder the man?   145
LE BEAU   Even he, madam.
CELIA   Alas, he is too young. Yet he looks successfully.

152. **odds:** superiority; **the man:** i.e., Charles
153. **fain:** gladly
157. **by:** i.e., nearby
163–64. **He is . . . challenger:** i.e., he has issued a challenge to all comers
164. **come but in:** i.e., come in only or merely
168. **If you . . . eyes:** perhaps, if you imagined how you look
169. **fear:** dreadfulness, formidableness
170. **to a more equal enterprise:** i.e., to find an undertaking at your level of strength or achievement
174. **suit:** petition
175. **might:** i.e., may
177. **wherein:** i.e., though; **much:** very; **to deny:** in denying
180. **wherein:** in the course of which; **foiled:** overthrown; disgraced
181. **gracious:** favored, popular

DUKE FREDERICK How now, daughter and cousin? Are
    you crept hither to see the wrestling?
ROSALIND Ay, my liege, so please you give us leave.   150
DUKE FREDERICK You will take little delight in it, I can
    tell you, there is such odds in the man. In pity of the
    challenger's youth, I would fain dissuade him, but
    he will not be entreated. Speak to him, ladies; see if
    you can move him.   155
CELIA Call him hither, good Monsieur Le Beau.
DUKE FREDERICK Do so. I'll not be by.
                                    ⌜*He steps aside.*⌝
LE BEAU ⌜*to Orlando*⌝ Monsieur the challenger, the
    Princess calls for you.
ORLANDO I attend them with all respect and duty.   160
ROSALIND Young man, have you challenged Charles the
    wrestler?
ORLANDO No, fair princess. He is the general challeng-
    er. I come but in as others do, to try with him the
    strength of my youth.   165
CELIA Young gentleman, your spirits are too bold for
    your years. You have seen cruel proof of this man's
    strength. If you saw yourself with your eyes or knew
    yourself with your judgment, the fear of your adven-
    ture would counsel you to a more equal enterprise.   170
    We pray you for your own sake to embrace your
    own safety and give over this attempt.
ROSALIND Do, young sir. Your reputation shall not
    therefore be misprized. We will make it our suit to
    the Duke that the wrestling might not go forward.   175
ORLANDO I beseech you, punish me not with your hard
    thoughts, wherein I confess me much guilty to deny
    so fair and excellent ladies anything. But let your
    fair eyes and gentle wishes go with me to my trial,
    wherein, if I be foiled, there is but one shamed that   180
    was never gracious; if killed, but one dead that is
    willing to be so. I shall do my friends no wrong, for

184–85. **Only . . . place:** i.e., I merely fill a place in the world

189. **eke out:** supplement

195. **will:** desire (including sexual desire, in response to the sexual implication of Charles' expression **lie with**)

196. **working:** action, doing

199. **warrant:** assure, promise

202–3. **You . . . before:** Proverbial: "Do not triumph before the victory." **You:** i.e., if you **after:** i.e., afterward **before:** i.e., beforehand

203. **come your ways:** come on

204. **Hercules:** a mythological hero of great strength, one of whose feats was the defeat of Antaeus, son of Earth (or Gaea), at wrestling; **speed:** helper

205. **would:** wish

209. **should down:** i.e., should go down, or be thrown

211–12. **well breathed:** i.e., exercised, warmed up

I have none to lament me; the world no injury, for
in it I have nothing. Only in the world I fill up a
place which may be better supplied when I have 185
made it empty.

ROSALIND The little strength that I have, I would it
were with you.

CELIA And mine, to eke out hers.

ROSALIND Fare you well. Pray heaven I be deceived in 190
you.

CELIA Your heart's desires be with you.

CHARLES Come, where is this young gallant that is so
desirous to lie with his mother earth?

ORLANDO Ready, sir; but his will hath in it a more 195
modest working.

DUKE FREDERICK, ⌜*coming forward*⌝ You shall try but
one fall.

CHARLES No, I warrant your Grace you shall not entreat him to a second, that have so mightily per- 200
suaded him from a first.

ORLANDO You mean to mock me after, you should not
have mocked me before. But come your ways.

ROSALIND Now Hercules be thy speed, young man!

CELIA I would I were invisible, to catch the strong 205
fellow by the leg.

⌜*Orlando and Charles*⌝ *wrestle.*

ROSALIND O excellent young man!

CELIA If I had a thunderbolt in mine eye, I can tell who
should down.

⌜*Orlando throws Charles.*⌝ *Shout.*

DUKE FREDERICK No more, no more. 210

ORLANDO Yes, I beseech your Grace. I am not yet well
breathed.

DUKE FREDERICK How dost thou, Charles?

LE BEAU He cannot speak, my lord.

DUKE FREDERICK Bear him away. 215

⌜*Charles is carried off by Attendants.*⌝

What is thy name, young man?

219. **some man else:** some other man
221. **still:** always
224. **house:** family
229. **calling:** name; station in life
233. **man his:** i.e., man was his
234. **unto:** in addition to
235. **Ere:** before
238. **envious:** malicious, spiteful
239. **Sticks . . . heart:** i.e., stabs me to the heart
241. **But justly:** i.e., exactly, precisely
242. **happy:** fortunate
244. **out of suits with fortune:** i.e., out of Fortune's favor (The image may be related to the livery [uniform, **suits**] that a member of Fortune's retinue would wear; or it may relate to the petitions [**suits**] that Fortune will no longer hear.)

ORLANDO Orlando, my liege, the youngest son of Sir
  Rowland de Boys.

DUKE FREDERICK
  I would thou hadst been son to some man else.
  The world esteemed thy father honorable,   220
  But I did find him still mine enemy.
  Thou shouldst have better pleased me with this
    deed
  Hadst thou descended from another house.
  But fare thee well. Thou art a gallant youth.   225
  I would thou hadst told me of another father.
                   Duke exits ⌐*with Touchstone, Le Beau,*
                              Lords, and Attendants.⌐

CELIA, ⌐*to Rosalind*⌐
  Were I my father, coz, would I do this?

ORLANDO
  I am more proud to be Sir Rowland's son,
  His youngest son, and would not change that calling
  To be adopted heir to Frederick.   230

ROSALIND, ⌐*to Celia*⌐
  My father loved Sir Rowland as his soul,
  And all the world was of my father's mind.
  Had I before known this young man his son,
  I should have given him tears unto entreaties
  Ere he should thus have ventured.   235

CELIA   Gentle cousin,
  Let us go thank him and encourage him.
  My father's rough and envious disposition
  Sticks me at heart.—Sir, you have well deserved.
  If you do keep your promises in love   240
  But justly, as you have exceeded all promise,
  Your mistress shall be happy.

ROSALIND, ⌐*giving Orlando a chain from her neck*⌐
                              Gentleman,
  Wear this for me—one out of suits with fortune,

245. **could:** i.e., would gladly

249. **parts:** qualities, abilities, talents

251. **quintain:** wooden post used for jousting practice or in rural games

257. **Have with you:** i.e., I'm coming

259. **conference:** conversation

261. **Or . . . or:** i.e., either . . . or

265. **condition:** disposition, state of mind

266. **misconsters:** misconstrues, misunderstands (accented miscónsters)

267. **humorous:** moody, capricious

267–68. **What he . . . of:** i.e., it is more suitable for you to understand what he is than for me to say

Fortune and her wheel. (1.2.31–32)
From Gregor Reisch, *Margarita philosophica* . . . [1503].

32

That could give more but that her hand lacks   245
    means.—
Shall we go, coz?

CELIA   Ay.—Fare you well, fair gentleman.

ORLANDO, ⌜*aside*⌝
    Can I not say "I thank you"? My better parts
    Are all thrown down, and that which here stands up   250
    Is but a quintain, a mere lifeless block.

ROSALIND, ⌜*to Celia*⌝
    He calls us back. My pride fell with my fortunes.
    I'll ask him what he would.—Did you call, sir?
    Sir, you have wrestled well and overthrown
    More than your enemies.   255

CELIA   Will you go, coz?

ROSALIND   Have with you. ⌜*To Orlando.*⌝ Fare you well.
                        ⌜*Rosalind and Celia*⌝ *exit.*

ORLANDO
    What passion hangs these weights upon my tongue?
    I cannot speak to her, yet she urged conference.
    O poor Orlando! Thou art overthrown.   260
    Or Charles or something weaker masters thee.

                Enter Le Beau.

LE BEAU
    Good sir, I do in friendship counsel you
    To leave this place. Albeit you have deserved
    High commendation, true applause, and love,
    Yet such is now the Duke's condition   265
    That he misconsters all that you have done.
    The Duke is humorous. What he is indeed
    More suits you to conceive than I to speak of.

ORLANDO
    I thank you, sir, and pray you tell me this:
    Which of the two was daughter of the duke   270
    That here was at the wrestling?

273. **smaller:** See longer note, page 209.

276–77. **whose loves / Are:** i.e., the love of Rosalind and Celia for each other is

278. **of late:** recently

280. **argument:** evidence, cause

284. **suddenly:** very soon

286. **knowledge:** personal acquaintance

287. **bounden:** bound, obligated

288. **must I:** i.e., must I go; **smother:** suffocating smoke (Proverbial: "Shunning the smoke he fell into the fire.")

289. **tyrant:** (1) usurping; (2) cruel, violent, wicked

1.3 Duke Frederick suddenly decides to banish Rosalind. His daughter Celia, determined to go with Rosalind into exile, suggests that they seek the banished duke in the Forest of Arden, and that, for safety on their journey, they disguise themselves as a country girl and her brother. They agree to ask the court Fool, Touchstone, to go with them.

---

1. **Cupid:** the god of love in Roman mythology

3. **Not one . . . dog:** proverbial

6. **reasons:** i.e., talk

9. **any:** i.e., any reason(s), sanity (Rosalind is playing with the traditional opposition of madness to reason.)

LE BEAU
   Neither his daughter, if we judge by manners,
   But yet indeed the ⌜smaller⌝ is his daughter.
   The other is daughter to the banished duke,
   And here detained by her usurping uncle   275
   To keep his daughter company, whose loves
   Are dearer than the natural bond of sisters.
   But I can tell you that of late this duke
   Hath ta'en displeasure 'gainst his gentle niece,
   Grounded upon no other argument   280
   But that the people praise her for her virtues
   And pity her for her good father's sake;
   And, on my life, his malice 'gainst the lady
   Will suddenly break forth. Sir, fare you well.
   Hereafter, in a better world than this,   285
   I shall desire more love and knowledge of you.
ORLANDO
   I rest much bounden to you. Fare you well.
                       ⌜*Le Beau exits.*⌝
   Thus must I from the smoke into the smother,
   From tyrant duke unto a tyrant brother.
   But heavenly Rosalind!   290
                           He exits.

Scene 3
Enter Celia and Rosalind.

CELIA   Why, cousin! Why, Rosalind! Cupid have mercy,
    not a word?
ROSALIND   Not one to throw at a dog.
CELIA   No, thy words are too precious to be cast away
    upon curs. Throw some of them at me. Come, lame   5
    me with reasons.
ROSALIND   Then there were two cousins laid up, when
    the one should be lamed with reasons, and the
    other mad without any.

15. **petticoats:** skirts

18. **Hem:** cough

24. **try:** test (yourself)

24–25. **in despite of:** i.e., despite; or, perhaps, in defiance of

25. **fall:** (1) a **fall** (or a bout) in wrestling; (2) a sexual encounter (In *Romeo and Juliet,* Juliet's future womanhood is pictured in the words: "Thou wilt fall backward when thou hast more wit" [1.3.46].)

25–26. **turning . . . out of service:** i.e., dismissing . . . as our servants

26–27. **on such a sudden:** i.e., so suddenly

30. **ensue:** follow logically

31. **chase:** pursuit (**Chase** is linked to **ensue** by a shared sense of "follow[ing].")

32. **dearly:** direly; intensely, keenly

34. **faith:** a mild oath (also found as "by my faith," "in faith," etc.)

35. **deserve well:** i.e., deserve to be **hated** (See line 32, above.) Rosalind responds as if Celia meant "deserve good things."

36. **for that:** i.e., because he deserves well

40. **dispatch you:** leave quickly; **with your safest haste:** i.e., with **haste,** which offers your best chance for safety

CELIA But is all this for your father? 10

ROSALIND No, some of it is for my child's father. O, how full of briers is this working-day world!

CELIA They are but burs, cousin, thrown upon thee in holiday foolery. If we walk not in the trodden paths, our very petticoats will catch them. 15

ROSALIND I could shake them off my coat. These burs are in my heart.

CELIA Hem them away.

ROSALIND I would try, if I could cry "hem" and have him. 20

CELIA Come, come, wrestle with thy affections.

ROSALIND O, they take the part of a better wrestler than myself.

CELIA O, a good wish upon you. You will try in time, in despite of a fall. But turning these jests out of 25 service, let us talk in good earnest. Is it possible on such a sudden you should fall into so strong a liking with old Sir Rowland's youngest son?

ROSALIND The Duke my father loved his father dearly.

CELIA Doth it therefore ensue that you should love his 30 son dearly? By this kind of chase I should hate him, for my father hated his father dearly. Yet I hate not Orlando.

ROSALIND No, faith, hate him not, for my sake.

CELIA Why should I not? Doth he not deserve well? 35

ROSALIND Let me love him for that, and do you love him because I do.

Enter Duke ⌜Frederick⌝ with Lords.

Look, here comes the Duke.

CELIA With his eyes full of anger.

DUKE FREDERICK, ⌜*to Rosalind*⌝
Mistress, dispatch you with your safest haste, 40
And get you from our court.

ROSALIND Me, uncle?

43. **cousin:** i.e., niece

49. **intelligence:** communication

51. **frantic:** insane

54. **offend:** wrong

56. **their purgation:** clearing themselves of suspicion

57. **grace:** (1) divine grace; (2) virtue

60. **whereon . . . depends:** i.e., the grounds on which the probability (of my guilt) is based

65. **friends:** relatives

67–68. **mistake me not so much / To think:** i.e., do not have such a wrong view of me as to think

70. **stayed:** detained

71. **Else:** otherwise

73. **remorse:** compassion

Men wearing doublets and hose.
(2.4.6; 3.2.200, 223–24; 4.1.215)
From [Robert Greene,] *A quip for an vpstart courtier . . .* (1620).

DUKE FREDERICK   You, cousin.
  Within these ten days if that thou beest found
  So near our public court as twenty miles,   45
  Thou diest for it.

ROSALIND   I do beseech your Grace,
  Let me the knowledge of my fault bear with me.
  If with myself I hold intelligence
  Or have acquaintance with mine own desires,   50
  If that I do not dream or be not frantic—
  As I do trust I am not—then, dear uncle,
  Never so much as in a thought unborn
  Did I offend your Highness.

DUKE FREDERICK   Thus do all traitors.   55
  If their purgation did consist in words,
  They are as innocent as grace itself.
  Let it suffice thee that I trust thee not.

ROSALIND
  Yet your mistrust cannot make me a traitor.
  Tell me whereon the ⌈likelihood⌉ depends.   60

DUKE FREDERICK
  Thou art thy father's daughter. There's enough.

ROSALIND
  So was I when your Highness took his dukedom.
  So was I when your Highness banished him.
  Treason is not inherited, my lord,
  Or if we did derive it from our friends,   65
  What's that to me? My father was no traitor.
  Then, good my liege, mistake me not so much
  To think my poverty is treacherous.

CELIA   Dear sovereign, hear me speak.

DUKE FREDERICK
  Ay, Celia, we stayed her for your sake;   70
  Else had she with her father ranged along.

CELIA
  I did not then entreat to have her stay.
  It was your pleasure and your own remorse.

74. **that time:** i.e., at that time

76. **still:** always

77. **Rose . . . instant:** i.e., risen at the same moment; **eat:** i.e., eaten

78. **Juno's swans:** The image is of a pair of birds yoked together pulling the chariot of Juno, queen of the gods. See longer note, page 209.

87. **doom:** judgment

92. **the time:** i.e., your time limit of ten days

95. **change:** i.e., exchange

96. **charge:** order, command

Jove, as an eagle, abducting Ganymede. (1.3.131–32)
From Gabriele Simeoni, *La vita . . . d'Ouidio* (1559).

I was too young that time to value her,
But now I know her. If she be a traitor,   75
Why, so am I. We still have slept together,
Rose at an instant, learned, played, eat together,
And, wheresoe'er we went, like Juno's swans
Still we went coupled and inseparable.

DUKE FREDERICK
She is too subtle for thee, and her smoothness,   80
Her very silence, and her patience
Speak to the people, and they pity her.
Thou art a fool. She robs thee of thy name,
And thou wilt show more bright and seem more
    virtuous   85
When she is gone. Then open not thy lips.
Firm and irrevocable is my doom
Which I have passed upon her. She is banished.

CELIA
Pronounce that sentence then on me, my liege.
I cannot live out of her company.   90

DUKE FREDERICK
You are a fool.—You, niece, provide yourself.
If you outstay the time, upon mine honor
And in the greatness of my word, you die.
                              Duke ⌐and Lords⌐ exit.

CELIA
O my poor Rosalind, whither wilt thou go?
Wilt thou change fathers? I will give thee mine.   95
I charge thee, be not thou more grieved than I am.

ROSALIND   I have more cause.

CELIA   Thou hast not, cousin.
Prithee, be cheerful. Know'st thou not the Duke
Hath banished me, his daughter?   100

ROSALIND   That he hath not.

CELIA
No, hath not? Rosalind lacks then the love
Which teacheth thee that thou and I am one.

108. **take . . . you:** i.e., endure your reversal of fortune by yourself

117. **mean:** shabby

119. **The like do you:** i.e., you do the same kind of thing; **pass along:** proceed on our way

120. **stir:** provoke

122. **more . . . tall:** i.e., unusually tall (for a woman)

123. **suit me:** dress myself; **all points:** i.e., completely, from head to toe

124. **curtal-ax:** cutlass

125. **boar-spear:** a spear used in hunting wild boar

126. **what:** i.e., whatever

128. **mannish cowards:** i.e., cowards who ape manhood

129. **outface it:** boldly brazen it out

131. **Jove's own page:** i.e., the beautiful boy **Ganymede,** whom Jove loved (See longer note, pages 209–10, and illustration, page 40.)

132. **look you:** make sure you

Shall we be sundered? Shall we part, sweet girl?
No, let my father seek another heir. 105
Therefore devise with me how we may fly,
Whither to go, and what to bear with us,
And do not seek to take your change upon you,
To bear your griefs yourself and leave me out.
For, by this heaven, now at our sorrows pale, 110
Say what thou canst, I'll go along with thee.

ROSALIND   Why, whither shall we go?

CELIA

To seek my uncle in the Forest of Arden.

ROSALIND

Alas, what danger will it be to us,
Maids as we are, to travel forth so far? 115
Beauty provoketh thieves sooner than gold.

CELIA

I'll put myself in poor and mean attire,
And with a kind of umber smirch my face.
The like do you. So shall we pass along
And never stir assailants. 120

ROSALIND   Were it not better,
Because that I am more than common tall,
That I did suit me all points like a man?
A gallant curtal-ax upon my thigh,
A boar-spear in my hand, and in my heart 125
Lie there what hidden woman's fear there will,
We'll have a swashing and a martial outside—
As many other mannish cowards have
That do outface it with their semblances.

CELIA

What shall I call thee when thou art a man? 130

ROSALIND

I'll have no worse a name than Jove's own page,
And therefore look you call me Ganymede.
But what will you ⌈be⌉ called?

134. **state:** condition
135. **Aliena:** i.e., alien, outsider
136. **assayed:** attempted
137. **fool:** professional jester
140. **Leave me alone:** i.e., leave it to me; **woo:** invite, tempt
142. **fittest:** most appropriate
144. **content:** contentment, pleasure

"Thrice-crownèd queen of night." (3.2.2)
From Ottavio Rossi, *Le memorie bresciane . . .* (1616).

44

CELIA
 Something that hath a reference to my state:
 No longer Celia, but Aliena.   135
ROSALIND
 But, cousin, what if we assayed to steal
 The clownish fool out of your father's court?
 Would he not be a comfort to our travel?
CELIA
 He'll go along o'er the wide world with me.
 Leave me alone to woo him. Let's away   140
 And get our jewels and our wealth together,
 Devise the fittest time and safest way
 To hide us from pursuit that will be made
 After my flight. Now go ⌜we in⌝ content
 To liberty, and not to banishment.   145

 They exit.

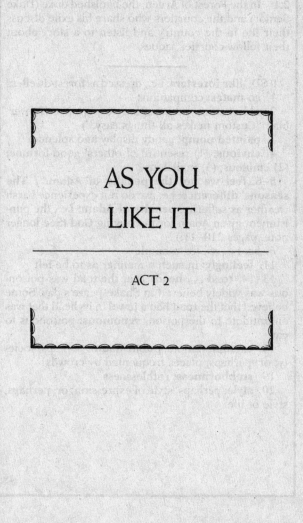

AS YOU
LIKE IT

ACT 2

2.1 In the Forest of Arden, the banished duke (Duke Senior) and the courtiers who share his exile discuss their life in the country and listen to a story about their fellow-courtier Jaques.

---

0 SD. **like foresters:** i.e., dressed as forest-dwellers

1. **co-mates:** companions

2. **old custom:** perhaps, long experience (Proverbial: "Custom makes all things easy.")

3. **painted pomp:** gaudy display and splendor

4. **envious:** (1) resentful of others' good fortune; (2) emulous; (3) malicious

5–6. **feel we not the penalty of Adam, / The seasons' difference:** i.e., we do not experience harsh weather as suffering **penalty of Adam:** i.e., the punishment given Adam for disobeying God (See longer note, pages 210–11.)

6. **as:** i.e., as, for example

11. **feelingly:** in such a manner as to be felt

13–14. **toad . . . head:** That the toad was poisonous was widely believed in Shakespeare's day. Some believed that the **toad** had a **jewel** in its head that was an antidote to the poison. **venomous:** poisonous to eat

15. **exempt:** remote; **public haunt:** perhaps, society; or, perhaps, places frequented by crowds

19. **stubbornness:** ruthlessness

20. **style:** perhaps, style of expression; or, perhaps, style of life

ACT 2

Scene 1

*Enter Duke Senior, Amiens, and two or three Lords, like
foresters.*

DUKE SENIOR
Now, my co-mates and brothers in exile,
Hath not old custom made this life more sweet
Than that of painted pomp? Are not these woods
More free from peril than the envious court?
Here feel we not the penalty of Adam,   5
The seasons' difference, as the icy fang
And churlish chiding of the winter's wind,
Which when it bites and blows upon my body
Even till I shrink with cold, I smile and say
"This is no flattery. These are counselors   10
That feelingly persuade me what I am."
Sweet are the uses of adversity,
Which, like the toad, ugly and venomous,
Wears yet a precious jewel in his head.
And this our life, exempt from public haunt,   15
Finds tongues in trees, books in the running brooks,
Sermons in stones, and good in everything.
AMIENS
I would not change it. Happy is your Grace,
That can translate the stubbornness of fortune
Into so quiet and so sweet a style.   20

49

22. **fools:** an expression of pity or endearment

23. **desert:** uninhabited

24. **forkèd heads:** i.e., barbed arrowheads

27. **melancholy:** suffering from an excess of black bile (In the medicine of Shakespeare's time, the body was regarded as filled with four fluids, or "humors": blood, phlegm, yellow bile, and black bile. The nature of one's disposition was determined by the relative proportions of the humors in one's body.); **Jaques:** For pronunciation, see note to 1.1.5.

28. **And . . . kind:** i.e., by killing the deer native to the forest **kind:** i.e., way

28–29. **you . . . brother:** i.e., you are a greater usurper than your brother

31. **lay along:** stretched out

32. **antique:** (1) old; (2) perhaps, antic or grotesque (accented án-tique)

33. **brawls:** flows noisily

34. **sequestered stag:** i.e., a stag separated from the herd (See page 182.)

39. **big round tears:** There was a common belief in Shakespeare's day that deer weep as they die. (See illustration, page 106.)

42. **markèd of:** observed by

46. **moralize:** draw a moral from

48. **his:** i.e., its; **needless stream:** i.e., stream that needed no more moisture

49. **quoth:** says

49–51. **thou . . . much:** i.e., like worldly people, you make a will in which you bequeath yet more money to those who already have too much **worldlings:** those devoted to things of the world

(continued)

DUKE SENIOR
  Come, shall we go and kill us venison?
  And yet it irks me the poor dappled fools,
  Being native burghers of this desert city,
  Should in their own confines with forkèd heads
  Have their round haunches gored.   25
FIRST LORD   Indeed, my lord,
  The melancholy Jaques grieves at that,
  And in that kind swears you do more usurp
  Than doth your brother that hath banished you.
  Today my Lord of Amiens and myself   30
  Did steal behind him as he lay along
  Under an oak, whose antique root peeps out
  Upon the brook that brawls along this wood;
  To the which place a poor sequestered stag
  That from the hunter's aim had ta'en a hurt   35
  Did come to languish. And indeed, my lord,
  The wretched animal heaved forth such groans
  That their discharge did stretch his leathern coat
  Almost to bursting, and the big round tears
  Coursed one another down his innocent nose   40
  In piteous chase. And thus the hairy fool,
  Much markèd of the melancholy Jaques,
  Stood on th' extremest verge of the swift brook,
  Augmenting it with tears.
DUKE SENIOR   But what said Jaques?   45
  Did he not moralize this spectacle?
FIRST LORD
  O yes, into a thousand similes.
  First, for his weeping into the needless stream:
  "Poor deer," quoth he, "thou mak'st a testament
  As worldlings do, giving thy sum of more   50
  To that which had too ⌜much.⌝" Then, being there
    alone,
  Left and abandoned of his velvet ⌜friends:⌝
  " 'Tis right," quoth he. "Thus misery doth part

51. **being:** i.e., the deer being

53. **of:** i.e., by; **velvet:** (1) i.e., the texture of a deer's coat or, perhaps, the skin enveloping the antlers; (2) by extension, the lavish garments of the worldlings to whom Jaques has just compared the deer

54–55. **misery . . . company:** Proverbial: "Poverty parts friends." **flux:** stream, flood

55. **Anon:** soon; **careless:** carefree, free of anxiety

56. **Full:** i.e., having fed to the full; **by:** past

57. **stays:** stops

58. **greasy:** fat and ready for killing (a hunting term)

59. **Wherefore:** why

61. **invectively:** with bitter denunciation

64. **mere:** absolute; **what's:** i.e., whatever is

65. **up:** i.e., off

71. **cope:** meet with; contend with

72. **matter:** sense, substance

73. **straight:** straightway, immediately

2.2 Duke Frederick, discovering Celia's disappearance, suspects Orlando. He sends servants to bring Orlando to court.

———————

3 **Are . . . this:** i.e., agreed to this and allowed it to happen

5. **ladies . . . chamber:** i.e., ladies-in-waiting, who are both personal attendants and confidantes

7. **untreasured:** i.e., emptied of the treasure

The flux of company." Anon a careless herd,   55
Full of the pasture, jumps along by him
And never stays to greet him. "Ay," quoth Jaques,
"Sweep on, you fat and greasy citizens.
'Tis just the fashion. Wherefore do you look
Upon that poor and broken bankrupt there?"   60
Thus most invectively he pierceth through
The body of country, city, court,
Yea, and of this our life, swearing that we
Are mere usurpers, tyrants, and what's worse,
To fright the animals and to kill them up   65
In their assigned and native dwelling place.

DUKE SENIOR
And did you leave him in this contemplation?

SECOND LORD
We did, my lord, weeping and commenting
Upon the sobbing deer.

DUKE SENIOR   Show me the place.   70
I love to cope him in these sullen fits,
For then he's full of matter.

FIRST LORD   I'll bring you to him straight.

They exit.

Scene 2
Enter Duke ⌜Frederick⌝ with Lords.

DUKE FREDERICK
Can it be possible that no man saw them?
It cannot be. Some villains of my court
Are of consent and sufferance in this.

FIRST LORD
I cannot hear of any that did see her.
The ladies her attendants of her chamber   5
Saw her abed, and in the morning early
They found the bed untreasured of their mistress.

8. **roinish:** scabby, scurvy, base; **clown:** low comic or rustic simpleton (a contemptuous term for Touchstone, whose role is that of a professional jester, or Fool)

13. **parts:** qualities, abilities; **graces:** virtues

17. **Send . . . brother:** i.e., send someone to his brother's; **that gallant:** i.e., Orlando

19. **him . . . him:** i.e., Oliver . . . Orlando; **suddenly:** immediately

20. **quail:** fail

21. **again:** back

2.3 Orlando learns from Adam, an old servant, that Oliver plans to kill Orlando. Adam and Orlando decide to go in search of a new life.

_____

2. **What:** an interjection that here introduces an exclamation

3. **memory:** memorial

4. **what make you:** i.e., what are you doing

7. **fond to:** foolish as to

8. **bonny:** perhaps, large, or sturdy: **prizer:** champion, prizefighter; **humorous:** peevish

12. **No more do yours:** i.e., so do yours

13. **sanctified:** sanctimonious

SECOND LORD

My lord, the roinish clown at whom so oft
Your Grace was wont to laugh is also missing.
Hisperia, the Princess' gentlewoman,   10
Confesses that she secretly o'erheard
Your daughter and her cousin much commend
The parts and graces of the wrestler
That did but lately foil the sinewy Charles,
And she believes wherever they are gone   15
That youth is surely in their company.

DUKE FREDERICK

Send to his brother. Fetch that gallant hither.
If he be absent, bring his brother to me.
I'll make him find him. Do this suddenly,
And let not search and inquisition quail   20
To bring again these foolish runaways.

They exit.

Scene 3
Enter Orlando and Adam, ⌜meeting.⌝

ORLANDO   Who's there?

ADAM

What, my young master, O my gentle master,
O my sweet master, O you memory
Of old Sir Rowland! Why, what make you here?
Why are you virtuous? Why do people love you?   5
And wherefore are you gentle, strong, and valiant?
Why would you be so fond to overcome
The bonny prizer of the humorous duke?
Your praise is come too swiftly home before you.
Know you not, master, to ⌜some⌝ kind of men   10
Their graces serve them but as enemies?
No more do yours. Your virtues, gentle master,
Are sanctified and holy traitors to you.

15. **Envenoms:** poisons

18. **Within this roof:** i.e., under this roof

23. **your praises:** i.e., others' praise of you

24. **use:** are accustomed

26. **cut you off:** kill you

27. **practices:** treacherous schemes

28. **no place:** (1) no place for you; (2) no house or residence; **butchery:** place of torture or of torment; literally, slaughterhouse

29. **Abhor it:** shrink back from it with horror

31. **so:** i.e., so long as

32–35. **wouldst . . . do:** See longer note, page 211.

33. **boist'rous:** rough, strong

36. **do how I can:** i.e., whatever I do

38. **a diverted blood:** i.e., an estranged kinship; **bloody:** bloodthirsty

40. **thrifty hire:** i.e., carefully conserved wages

42. **service:** the ability to perform a servant's duties

43. **unregarded:** disregarded, disrespected

44. **that:** i.e., the five hundred crowns; **He that . . . feed:** See Luke 12.24: "Consider the ravens, for they neither sow nor reap . . . and (notwithstanding) God feedeth them."

45. **providently . . . sparrow:** See Matthew 6.26, which says "fowls of the air" where Luke 12.24 says "ravens"; see also Matthew 10.29: "Are not two little sparrows sold for a farthing? And one of them shall not light on the ground without your father [i.e., your father's consent]." **providently:** with providing care and foresight

 O, what a world is this when what is comely
 Envenoms him that bears it!   15
⌜ORLANDO⌝ Why, what's the matter?
ADAM O unhappy youth,
 Come not within these doors. Within this roof
 The enemy of all your graces lives.
 Your brother—no, no brother—yet the son— 20
 Yet not the son, I will not call him son—
 Of him I was about to call his father,
 Hath heard your praises, and this night he means
 To burn the lodging where you use to lie,
 And you within it. If he fail of that,   25
 He will have other means to cut you off.
 I overheard him and his practices.
 This is no place, this house is but a butchery.
 Abhor it, fear it, do not enter it.
⌜ORLANDO⌝
 Why, whither, Adam, wouldst thou have me go? 30
ADAM
 No matter whither, so you come not here.
ORLANDO
 What, wouldst thou have me go and beg my food,
 Or with a base and boist'rous sword enforce
 A thievish living on the common road?
 This I must do, or know not what to do;   35
 Yet this I will not do, do how I can.
 I rather will subject me to the malice
 Of a diverted blood and bloody brother.
ADAM
 But do not so. I have five hundred crowns,
 The thrifty hire I saved under your father, 40
 Which I did store to be my foster nurse
 When service should in my old limbs lie lame,
 And unregarded age in corners thrown.
 Take that, and He that doth the ravens feed,
 Yea, providently caters for the sparrow,   45

48. **lusty:** healthy, vigorous

51. **unbashful forehead:** i.e., impudent disregard for decency; **woo:** solicit

54. **kindly:** agreeable, pleasant

58. **constant:** steadfast, loyal; **antique:** ancient

59. **service . . . duty:** i.e., servants exerted themselves (sweated) out of a sense of duty; **meed:** reward, wages

62–63. **having . . . having:** i.e., once promotion is granted, performance of duties ceases (**Choke their service up** is perhaps a gardening metaphor.)

66. **In lieu of:** in return for; **husbandry:** thrift, economy

67. **come thy ways:** i.e., come on

68. **youthful wages:** i.e., wages saved since your youth

69. **settled low content:** sober, humble state of contentment

75. **too late a week:** i.e., too late a time

Be comfort to my age. Here is the gold.
All this I give you. Let me be your servant.
Though I look old, yet I am strong and lusty,
For in my youth I never did apply
Hot and rebellious liquors in my blood,   50
Nor did not with unbashful forehead woo
The means of weakness and debility.
Therefore my age is as a lusty winter,
Frosty but kindly. Let me go with you.
I'll do the service of a younger man   55
In all your business and necessities.

ORLANDO
O good old man, how well in thee appears
The constant service of the antique world,
When service sweat for duty, not for meed.
Thou art not for the fashion of these times,   60
Where none will sweat but for promotion,
And having that do choke their service up
Even with the having. It is not so with thee.
But, poor old man, thou prun'st a rotten tree
That cannot so much as a blossom yield   65
In lieu of all thy pains and husbandry.
But come thy ways. We'll go along together,
And ere we have thy youthful wages spent,
We'll light upon some settled low content.

ADAM
Master, go on, and I will follow thee   70
To the last gasp with truth and loyalty.
From ⌜seventeen⌝ years till now almost fourscore
Here livèd I, but now live here no more.
At seventeen years, many their fortunes seek,
But at fourscore, it is too late a week.   75
Yet fortune cannot recompense me better
Than to die well, and not my master's debtor.
                                                They exit.

2.4 Rosalind, Celia, and Touchstone reach the Forest of Arden. Rosalind is in disguise as a boy named Ganymede and Celia as a country girl named Aliena. They overhear a conversation between an old shepherd (Corin) and a lovelorn young shepherd (Silvius). "Ganymede" and "Aliena" persuade Corin to help them buy a cottage.

---

0 SD. **for:** i.e., disguised as; **alias:** otherwise called
1. **Jupiter:** in Roman mythology, king of the gods
6. **weaker vessel:** proverbial for "woman," from its use in 1 Peter 3.7; **doublet and hose:** close-fitting jacket and breeches—that is, typical male attire (See page 38.)
7. **petticoat:** skirt—that is, typical female attire
9. **no:** i.e., any
11. **cross:** wordplay on a familiar biblical verse ("whosoever doth not **bear** his **cross** and come after me cannot be my disciple," Luke 14.27) and on **cross** as a coin stamped with a cross (See page 24.)
19. **Look you:** an expression to call attention to something
22. **that:** i.e., if only

Scene 4

Enter Rosalind for Ganymede, Celia for Aliena, and Clown, alias Touchstone.

ROSALIND
O Jupiter, how ⌜weary⌝ are my spirits!

TOUCHSTONE   I care not for my spirits, if my legs were not weary.

ROSALIND   I could find in my heart to disgrace my man's apparel and to cry like a woman, but I must   5 comfort the weaker vessel, as doublet and hose ought to show itself courageous to petticoat. Therefore courage, good Aliena.

CELIA   I pray you bear with me. I cannot go no further.

TOUCHSTONE   For my part, I had rather bear with you   10 than bear you. Yet I should bear no cross if I did bear you, for I think you have no money in your purse.

ROSALIND   Well, this is the Forest of Arden.

TOUCHSTONE   Ay, now am I in Arden, the more fool I.   15 When I was at home I was in a better place, but travelers must be content.

ROSALIND   Ay, be so, good Touchstone.

Enter Corin and Silvius.

Look you who comes here, a young man and an old in solemn talk.   20

⌜*Rosalind, Celia, and Touchstone step aside and eavesdrop.*⌝

CORIN, ⌜*to Silvius*⌝
That is the way to make her scorn you still.

SILVIUS
O Corin, that thou knew'st how I do love her!

CORIN
I partly guess, for I have loved ere now.

27-28. **if thy love . . . so:** i.e., if your love was ever like mine—as certainly it cannot have been, since I think no man ever loved the way I do

30. **fantasy:** desire

37. **Wearing:** wearying, tiring out; **in:** i.e., with

39. **broke:** i.e., broken

43. **searching of:** probing

44. **by hard adventure:** by cruel chance

46. **him:** i.e., the stone

47. **a-night:** at night

48. **batler:** The meaning of this word is unknown, since it is not recorded elsewhere. One guess is that a batler was a wooden paddle for beating clothes in the wash.

49. **chopped:** chapped (See picture, page 172.)

50-53. **wooing . . . sake:** perhaps a reference to the use of the peapod as a rustic love token; perhaps also an obscene joke, in which **cods** refers to "testicles"

SILVIUS
  No, Corin, being old, thou canst not guess,
  Though in thy youth thou wast as true a lover   25
  As ever sighed upon a midnight pillow.
  But if thy love were ever like to mine—
  As sure I think did never man love so—
  How many actions most ridiculous
  Hast thou been drawn to by thy fantasy?   30
CORIN
  Into a thousand that I have forgotten.
SILVIUS
  O, thou didst then never love so heartily.
  If thou rememb'rest not the slightest folly
  That ever love did make thee run into,
  Thou hast not loved.   35
  Or if thou hast not sat as I do now,
  Wearing thy hearer in thy mistress' praise,
  Thou hast not loved.
  Or if thou hast not broke from company
  Abruptly, as my passion now makes me,   40
  Thou hast not loved.
  O Phoebe, Phoebe, Phoebe!   *He exits.*
ROSALIND
  Alas, poor shepherd, searching of ⌜thy wound,⌝
  I have by hard adventure found mine own.
TOUCHSTONE And I mine. I remember when I was in   45
  love I broke my sword upon a stone and bid him
  take that for coming a-night to Jane Smile; and I
  remember the kissing of her batler, and the cow's
  dugs that her pretty chopped hands had milked;
  and I remember the wooing of a peascod instead of   50
  her, from whom I took two cods and, giving her
  them again, said with weeping tears "Wear these for
  my sake." We that are true lovers run into strange
  capers. But as all is mortal in nature, so is all nature
  in love mortal in folly.   55

56. **ware:** i.e., aware

57–58. **I . . . it:** Touchstone perhaps plays with the proverb "Fools set stools for wise men to break their shins." **ware:** wary, cautious

60. **upon:** i.e., after

61. **something:** somewhat

65. **clown:** peasant

66. **not thy kinsman:** i.e., not a low comic, or **clown,** like you

69. **Else:** otherwise

70. **even:** i.e., afternoon

74. **desert:** uninhabited; **entertainment:** food and shelter

77. **faints:** grows weak; **succor:** i.e., lack of aid or assistance

82. **fleeces:** i.e., sheep

83. **churlish:** stingy, grudging

84. **little recks:** cares little

86. **cote:** perhaps, cottage; perhaps, sheepcote (a shelter for sheep); **bounds of feed:** pasture land

A civet cat. (3.2.63)
From Edward Topsell, *The historie of foure-footed beastes . . .* (1607).

ROSALIND   Thou speak'st wiser than thou art ware of.

TOUCHSTONE   Nay, I shall ne'er be ware of mine own
 wit till I break my shins against it.

ROSALIND
 Jove, Jove, this shepherd's passion
 Is much upon my fashion.   60

TOUCHSTONE   And mine, but it grows something stale
 with me.

CELIA   I pray you, one of you question yond man, if he
 for gold will give us any food. I faint almost to death.

TOUCHSTONE, ⌈*to Corin*⌉   Holla, you clown!   65

ROSALIND   Peace, fool. He's not thy kinsman.

CORIN   Who calls?

TOUCHSTONE   Your betters, sir.

CORIN   Else are they very wretched.

ROSALIND, ⌈*to Touchstone*⌉
 Peace, I say. ⌈*As Ganymede, to Corin.*⌉ Good even to 70
 ⌈you,⌉ friend.

CORIN
 And to you, gentle sir, and to you all.

ROSALIND, ⌈*as Ganymede*⌉
 I prithee, shepherd, if that love or gold
 Can in this desert place buy entertainment,
 Bring us where we may rest ourselves and feed. 75
 Here's a young maid with travel much oppressed,
 And faints for succor.

CORIN   Fair sir, I pity her
 And wish for her sake more than for mine own
 My fortunes were more able to relieve her.   80
 But I am shepherd to another man
 And do not shear the fleeces that I graze.
 My master is of churlish disposition
 And little recks to find the way to heaven
 By doing deeds of hospitality.   85
 Besides, his cote, his flocks, and bounds of feed
 Are now on sale, and at our sheepcote now,

89. **will feed on:** i.e., would wish to eat; **what is:** i.e., what's there

90. **in my voice:** i.e., as far as I have any say

91. **What:** i.e., who

92. **swain:** country gallant or lover; **but erewhile:** i.e., just now

94. **stand with honesty:** i.e., is in accord with integrity

96. **have . . . us:** i.e., have what is needed to pay for it from us

97. **mend:** raise

98. **waste:** spend

100. **upon report:** i.e., on further report (on receiving more information)

102. **feeder:** servant

103. **right suddenly:** immediately

2.5 Amiens' song celebrating life in the woods is mocked by Jaques' parody of the song.

1–8. **Under . . . weather:** Amiens' invitation to lie **under the greenwood tree** seems to play on the phrase "To go the greenwood," which means to become an outlaw. For Amiens' song in relation to the Robin Hood ballads, see longer note to Robin Hood, 1.1.115.

2. **Who:** i.e., anyone who

3–4. **turn . . . throat:** perhaps, compose his melody in accord with the bird's song **note:** tune, melody **throat:** voice

By reason of his absence, there is nothing
That you will feed on. But what is, come see,
And in my voice most welcome shall you be.   90
ROSALIND, ⌜*as Ganymede*⌝
What is he that shall buy his flock and pasture?
CORIN
That young swain that you saw here but erewhile,
That little cares for buying anything.
ROSALIND, ⌜*as Ganymede*⌝
I pray thee, if it stand with honesty,
Buy thou the cottage, pasture, and the flock,   95
And thou shalt have to pay for it of us.
CELIA, ⌜*as Aliena*⌝
And we will mend thy wages. I like this place,
And willingly could waste my time in it.
CORIN
Assuredly the thing is to be sold.
Go with me. If you like upon report   100
The soil, the profit, and this kind of life,
I will your very faithful feeder be
And buy it with your gold right suddenly.

They exit.

Scene 5
Enter Amiens, Jaques, and others.

Song.

⌜AMIENS *sings*⌝
    Under the greenwood tree
    Who loves to lie with me
    And turn his merry note
    Unto the sweet bird's throat,
Come hither, come hither, come hither.   5
      Here shall he see
      No enemy
    But winter and rough weather.
JAQUES   More, more, I prithee, more.

15. **ragged:** harsh, discordant, rough

17. **stanzo:** i.e., stanza (This word had come into English from Italian only in the decade or so before *As You Like It;* there was then no "correct" spelling of the new word, **stanzo** being as acceptable as our "stanza.")

19. **What you will:** i.e., whatever you like

20–21. **I care . . . nothing:** i.e., I am interested in names only if they are the names of people who owe me money (Jaques plays on the word *name,* which in its Latin form [*nomen*] could be used to mean "debtor.")

24. **that:** i.e., that which; **compliment:** formal civility, politeness

25. **dog-apes:** perhaps, dog-faced baboons (See page 148.)

27. **the beggarly thanks:** i.e., the excessive thanks of a beggar who has been given alms

29. **end:** finish; **cover the while:** meanwhile, lay the cloth (in preparation for a meal) See longer note, pages 211–12.

31. **look:** search for

33. **disputable:** perhaps, disputatious, argumentative

36 SP. ALL **together here:** i.e., as a chorus (These words are set in the margin in the Folio. Some editors move them to late in the song, believing that the first five lines are for a soloist, with the chorus joining in with the line *"Here shall he see."*)

37. **i' th' sun:** perhaps, free of care and sorrow; or, perhaps, with no shelter (Proverbial: "Out of God's blessing into the warm sun.")

AMIENS It will make you melancholy, Monsieur   10
   Jaques.
JAQUES I thank it. More, I prithee, more. I can suck
   melancholy out of a song as a weasel sucks eggs.
   More, I prithee, more.
AMIENS My voice is ragged. I know I cannot please you.   15
JAQUES I do not desire you to please me. I do desire
   you to sing. Come, more, another stanzo. Call you
   'em "stanzos"?
AMIENS What you will, Monsieur Jaques.
JAQUES Nay, I care not for their names. They owe me   20
   nothing. Will you sing?
AMIENS More at your request than to please myself.
JAQUES Well then, if ever I thank any man, I'll thank
   you. But that they call "compliment" is like th'
   encounter of two dog-apes. And when a man thanks   25
   me heartily, methinks I have given him a penny and
   he renders me the beggarly thanks. Come, sing. And
   you that will not, hold your tongues.
AMIENS Well, I'll end the song.—Sirs, cover the while;
   the Duke will drink under this tree.—He hath been   30
   all this day to look you.
JAQUES And I have been all this day to avoid him. He is
   too disputable for my company. I think of as many
   matters as he, but I give heaven thanks and make no
   boast of them. Come, warble, come.   35

                    Song.

ALL *together here.*
          Who doth ambition shun
          And loves to live i' th' sun,
          Seeking the food he eats
          And pleased with what he gets,
      Come hither, come hither, come hither.   40
          Here shall he see
          No enemy
      But winter and rough weather.

44. **note:** tune, melody

45. **in despite of my invention:** perhaps, in defiance of my intellect and imagination; or, perhaps, despite my lack of imagination

52. **Ducdame:** probably a nonsense word; pronounced with three syllables (See longer note, page 212.)

57. **Greek:** i.e., unintelligible, meaningless (See longer note to **Ducdame**, 2.5.52.)

57–58. **to call fools into a circle:** Many productions stage this moment as a joke that Jaques plays on his companions, who have formed **a circle** around him as he sings.

59. **first-born of Egypt:** See Exodus 12.29–30: "The Lord smote all the first-born in the land of Egypt . . . and there was a great cry in Egypt."

60. **banquet:** light meal of fruit and wine

2.6 Orlando leaves Adam, near starvation, under a tree and goes off determined to find food.

1–2. **for food:** i.e., for lack of food

5. **comfort:** perhaps, take comfort

6. **uncouth:** unknown, strange

8. **conceit:** imagination (of your condition)

9. **comfortable:** cheerful

9–10. **at the arm's end:** i.e., at arm's length

10. **presently:** immediately

JAQUES I'll give you a verse to this note that I made
yesterday in despite of my invention.   45
AMIENS And I'll sing it.
⌈JAQUES⌉ Thus it goes:
> *If it do come to pass*
> *That any man turn ass,*
> *Leaving his wealth and ease*   50
> *A stubborn will to please,*
> *Ducdame, ducdame, ducdame.*
> *Here shall he see*
> *Gross fools as he,*
> *An if he will come to me.*   55
AMIENS What's that "ducdame"?
JAQUES 'Tis a Greek invocation to call fools into a
circle. I'll go sleep if I can. If I cannot, I'll rail
against all the first-born of Egypt.
AMIENS And I'll go seek the Duke. His banquet is   60
prepared.

They exit.

Scene 6
Enter Orlando and Adam.

ADAM Dear master, I can go no further. O, I die for
food. Here lie I down and measure out my grave.
Farewell, kind master.   ⌈*He lies down.*⌉
ORLANDO Why, how now, Adam? No greater heart in
thee? Live a little, comfort a little, cheer thyself a   5
little. If this uncouth forest yield anything savage, I
will either be food for it or bring it for food to thee.
Thy conceit is nearer death than thy powers. For my
sake, be comfortable. Hold death awhile at the
arm's end. I will here be with thee presently, and if   10
I bring thee not something to eat, I will give thee
leave to die. But if thou diest before I come, thou art

13. **Well said:** i.e., well done

14. **cheerly:** i.e., cheerful (In line 17, **cheerly** is used as a word of encouragement.)

17. **desert:** uninhabited place

2.7 As Duke Senior and his companions sit down to eat, Orlando enters, demanding food. Welcomed by the duke, he brings Adam to join them.

---

0 SD. **like:** i.e., dressed as

2. **like a man:** i.e., in the form of a man

3. **is but even:** i.e., has just

4. **hearing of:** i.e., hearing

5. **compact of jars:** made up of discords

6. **spheres:** The stars and planets were thought to move within transparent spheres, which, in turning, produced music of perfect harmony, the so-called music of the **spheres.**

7. **would:** want to

10. **woo:** solicit

11. **merrily:** merry

12. **fool:** professional jester

13. **motley fool:** probably, a Fool dressed in the multicolored garments distinctive of his profession (See page 20.)

15 **him:** i.e., himself

16. **on:** i.e., against; **Lady Fortune:** See illustration, page 32.

a mocker of my labor. Well said. Thou look'st
cheerly, and I'll be with thee quickly. Yet thou liest
in the bleak air. Come, I will bear thee to some   15
shelter, and thou shalt not die for lack of a dinner if
there live anything in this desert. Cheerly, good
Adam.

They exit.

Scene 7
Enter Duke Senior and ⌜*Lords,*⌝ *like outlaws.*

DUKE SENIOR
  I think he be transformed into a beast,
  For I can nowhere find him like a man.
FIRST LORD
  My lord, he is but even now gone hence.
  Here was he merry, hearing of a song.
DUKE SENIOR
  If he, compact of jars, grow musical,   5
  We shall have shortly discord in the spheres.
  Go seek him. Tell him I would speak with him.

Enter Jaques.

FIRST LORD
  He saves my labor by his own approach.
DUKE SENIOR, ⌜*to Jaques*⌝
  Why, how now, monsieur? What a life is this
  That your poor friends must woo your company?   10
  What, you look merrily.
JAQUES
  A fool, a fool, I met a fool i' th' forest,
  A motley fool. A miserable world!
  As I do live by food, I met a fool,
  Who laid him down and basked him in the sun   15
  And railed on Lady Fortune in good terms,

17. **In good set terms:** i.e., in deliberately composed language (not in spontaneous expressions)

19–20. **Call . . . fortune:** Here Touchstone plays with the proverb "Fortune favors fools" or "Fools have the best luck."

21. **dial:** perhaps a watch, or perhaps a small sundial; **poke:** pouch or pocket

24. **wags:** goes; staggers, waddles

30. **moral:** make a moral application

32. **deep-contemplative:** i.e., profoundly meditative

33. **sans:** without

35. **only:** best

40. **dry as the remainder biscuit:** i.e., extremely dry (Sea biscuits, or hardtack, were proverbially dry even at the beginning of a voyage.) **remainder:** leftover (A **dry** brain was, perhaps, stupid but retentive, although there is evidence that dryness could be associated with learning: Robert Burton in his 1626 *Anatomy of Melancholy* wrote: "Saturn and Mercury, the Patrons of Learning, are both dry Planets.")

41. **places:** perhaps, topics or subjects of discourse; perhaps, literally, "places in his brain"

42. **observation:** i.e., things learned through observing or through experience

46–63, 72–90. **It is . . . man:** See longer note, pages 212–13.

46. **suit:** (1) petition; (2) apparel

48. **rank:** excessively large

49–51. **liberty . . . please:** i.e., freedom to satirize whomever I choose **Withal:** i.e., along with my suit of motley **large:** extensive **charter:** license

In good set terms, and yet a motley fool.
"Good morrow, fool," quoth I. "No, sir," quoth he,
"Call me not 'fool' till heaven hath sent me
    fortune."   20
And then he drew a dial from his poke
And, looking on it with lack-luster eye,
Says very wisely "It is ten o'clock.
Thus we may see," quoth he, "how the world wags.
'Tis but an hour ago since it was nine,   25
And after one hour more 'twill be eleven.
And so from hour to hour we ripe and ripe,
And then from hour to hour we rot and rot,
And thereby hangs a tale." When I did hear
The motley fool thus moral on the time,   30
My lungs began to crow like chanticleer
That fools should be so deep-contemplative,
And I did laugh sans intermission
An hour by his dial. O noble fool!
A worthy fool! Motley's the only wear.   35

DUKE SENIOR   What fool is this?

JAQUES
O worthy fool!—One that hath been a courtier,
And says "If ladies be but young and fair,
They have the gift to know it." And in his brain,
Which is as dry as the remainder biscuit   40
After a voyage, he hath strange places crammed
With observation, the which he vents
In mangled forms. O, that I were a fool!
I am ambitious for a motley coat.

DUKE SENIOR
Thou shalt have one.   45

JAQUES   It is my only suit,
Provided that you weed your better judgments
Of all opinion that grows rank in them
That I am wise. I must have liberty
Withal, as large a charter as the wind,   50

52. **folly:** perhaps, satire

54. **plain:** i.e., as obvious (because of the church steeple); **way:** i.e., the way; **parish:** i.e., a parish

55. **hit:** i.e., satirize

56. **Doth:** i.e., acts; **he:** i.e., the person under attack

57. **Not to seem senseless of:** i.e., not to ignore, as if having no sense of; **bob:** taunt, jibe

58. **anatomized:** dissected, laid open

59. **squand'ring glances:** straying or randomly directed satirical attacks

60. **Invest . . . motley:** (1) clothe me in my Fool's costume; (2) endow me with the authority of a Fool

62. **Cleanse:** purge

63. **they:** i.e., the world

65. **for a counter:** i.e., in exchange for something which (like your opinion) has no intrinsic value (a **counter**)

66–71. **Most . . . world:** See longer note, page 213. **mischievous:** harmful

68. **brutish sting:** carnal appetite or impulse

69. **embossèd:** bulging, swollen; **headed evils:** i.e., wickedness, or possibly diseases, that have come to a head, like boils

70. **foot:** i.e., movement

72. **on:** against; **pride:** splendid adornment

73. **tax:** accuse; **private party:** i.e., particular person

74. **it:** i.e., conspicuous display, adornment

75. **Till . . . ebb:** i.e., until the wealth that supports it (its **very means**), becoming **weary** or exhausted, begins to ebb

76. **What woman:** i.e., what particular woman

(continued)

76

To blow on whom I please, for so fools have.
And they that are most gallèd with my folly,
They most must laugh. And why, sir, must they so?
The "why" is plain as way to parish church:
He that a fool doth very wisely hit   55
Doth very foolishly, although he smart,
⌜Not to⌝ seem senseless of the bob. If not,
The wise man's folly is anatomized
Even by the squand'ring glances of the fool.
Invest me in my motley. Give me leave   60
To speak my mind, and I will through and through
Cleanse the foul body of th' infected world,
If they will patiently receive my medicine.

DUKE SENIOR
Fie on thee! I can tell what thou wouldst do.

JAQUES
What, for a counter, would I do but good?   65

DUKE SENIOR
Most mischievous foul sin in chiding ⌜sin;⌝
For thou thyself hast been a libertine,
As sensual as the brutish sting itself,
And all th' embossèd sores and headed evils
That thou with license of free foot hast caught   70
Wouldst thou disgorge into the general world.

JAQUES   Why, who cries out on pride
That can therein tax any private party?
Doth it not flow as hugely as the sea
Till that the weary very means do ebb?   75
What woman in the city do I name
When that I say the city-woman bears
The cost of princes on unworthy shoulders?
Who can come in and say that I mean her,
When such a one as she such is her neighbor?   80
Or what is he of basest function
That says his bravery is not on my cost,
Thinking that I mean him, but therein suits

77. **city-woman:** woman from the merchant class

78. **The cost of princes:** i.e., a costly garment appropriate only for royalty (See longer note on 2.7.46–63, 72–90.)

79. **come in:** perhaps, interrupt; or, perhaps, **come in** as a complainant against me

80. **When . . . neighbor:** i.e., when her neighbor is just like her

81. **function:** calling, occupation

82. **bravery:** fine apparel; **is not on my cost:** i.e., costs me nothing

83–84. **therein . . . speech:** i.e., in taking my attack personally, he shows that my attack fits him

87. **do him right:** i.e., does him justice, gives him his due

88. **free:** guiltless

89. **taxing:** accusation, satire

90. **of:** by

95. **Of what . . . of:** i.e., what kind of fighting cock is this?

96. **boldened:** made bold, given courage

99. **vein:** state of mind

100. **show:** appearance

101. **inland bred:** raised in the interior of the country, rather than in its wild, outlying districts

102. **nurture:** (good) breeding

104. **answerèd:** satisfied

105. **An:** i.e., if; **reason:** perhaps with a pun on *raisin*, or grape

107–8. **Your gentleness . . . gentleness:** wordplay on **gentleness** as (1) behavior appropriate for a gentleman, and (2) kindness, compassion

109. **for food:** i.e., for lack of food

His folly to the mettle of my speech?
There then. How then, what then? Let me see   85
  wherein
My tongue hath wronged him. If it do him right,
Then he hath wronged himself. If he be free,
Why then my taxing like a wild goose flies
Unclaimed of any man.   90

Enter Orlando, ⌐*brandishing a sword.*⌐

                              But who ⌐comes⌐ here?
ORLANDO   Forbear, and eat no more.
JAQUES   Why, I have eat none yet.
ORLANDO
  Nor shalt not till necessity be served.
JAQUES   Of what kind should this cock come of?   95
DUKE SENIOR, ⌐*to Orlando*⌐
  Art thou thus boldened, man, by thy distress,
  Or else a rude despiser of good manners,
  That in civility thou seem'st so empty?
ORLANDO
  You touched my vein at first. The thorny point
  Of bare distress hath ta'en from me the show   100
  Of smooth civility, yet am I inland bred
  And know some nurture. But forbear, I say.
  He dies that touches any of this fruit
  Till I and my affairs are answerèd.
JAQUES   An you will not be answered with reason, I   105
  must die.
DUKE SENIOR, ⌐*to Orlando*⌐
  What would you have? Your gentleness shall force
  More than your force move us to gentleness.
ORLANDO
  I almost die for food, and let me have it.
DUKE SENIOR
  Sit down and feed, and welcome to our table.   110

113. **countenance:** look

116. **melancholy:** gloomy, dismal

119. **knolled:** tolled, summoned

123. **enforcement:** i.e., force (literally, the action of bringing force to bear)

130–31. **take . . . ministered:** i.e., you may command our help to supply your needs **wanting:** lack, need **ministered:** supplied

136. **sufficed:** provided for

137. **weak evils:** i.e., weaknesses (literally, evils that make him weak)

140. **waste:** consume

A good man's feast. (2.7.120)
From T[homas] F[ella], *A book of diverse devices . . .*
(1585–1622).

ORLANDO
Speak you so gently? Pardon me, I pray you.
I thought that all things had been savage here,
And therefore put I on the countenance
Of stern commandment. But whate'er you are
That in this desert inaccessible,   115
Under the shade of melancholy boughs,
Lose and neglect the creeping hours of time,
If ever you have looked on better days,
If ever been where bells have knolled to church,
If ever sat at any good man's feast,   120
If ever from your eyelids wiped a tear
And know what 'tis to pity and be pitied,
Let gentleness my strong enforcement be,
In the which hope I blush and hide my sword.
                    ⌈*He sheathes his sword.*⌉

DUKE SENIOR
True is it that we have seen better days,   125
And have with holy bell been knolled to church,
And sat at good men's feasts and wiped our eyes
Of drops that sacred pity hath engendered.
And therefore sit you down in gentleness,
And take upon command what help we have   130
That to your wanting may be ministered.

ORLANDO
Then but forbear your food a little while
Whiles, like a doe, I go to find my fawn
And give it food. There is an old poor man
Who after me hath many a weary step   135
Limped in pure love. Till he be first sufficed,
Oppressed with two weak evils, age and hunger,
I will not touch a bit.

DUKE SENIOR   Go find him out,
And we will nothing waste till you return.   140

ORLANDO
I thank you; and be blessed for your good comfort.
                    ⌈*He exits.*⌉

142. **unhappy:** unfortunate

144. **pageants:** shows, spectacles; **scene:** drama, play

145. **play in:** i.e., play

150. **His acts being seven ages:** The idea that human life can be pictured as occurring in stages is an ancient one. Shakespeare's use of the word **acts** associates the traditional figuration interestingly with the theater. (See page xii.)

151. **nurse's:** i.e., wet nurse's (See page 84.)

157. **pard:** panther or leopard

158. **Jealous in honor:** i.e., suspicious of possible affronts to his **honor; sudden:** rash, impetuous

160. **justice:** justice of the peace, judge

163. **modern:** ordinary, commonplace

165. **pantaloon:** feeble old man (*Pantalone* was originally a stock character in Italian comedy. See page 110.)

166. **pouch:** purse

167. **youthful hose:** breeches he wore when he was young

168. **shrunk shank:** shrunken or withered leg(s)

169. **Turning again:** returning

170. **his:** its

171. **history:** drama

172. **mere oblivion:** utter obliviousness

173. **Sans:** without

DUKE SENIOR
  Thou seest we are not all alone unhappy.
  This wide and universal theater
  Presents more woeful pageants than the scene
  Wherein we play in.   145
JAQUES   All the world's a stage,
  And all the men and women merely players.
  They have their exits and their entrances,
  And one man in his time plays many parts,
  His acts being seven ages. At first the infant,   150
  Mewling and puking in the nurse's arms.
  Then the whining schoolboy with his satchel
  And shining morning face, creeping like snail
  Unwillingly to school. And then the lover,
  Sighing like furnace, with a woeful ballad   155
  Made to his mistress' eyebrow. Then a soldier,
  Full of strange oaths and bearded like the pard,
  Jealous in honor, sudden and quick in quarrel,
  Seeking the bubble reputation
  Even in the cannon's mouth. And then the justice, 160
  In fair round belly with good capon lined,
  With eyes severe and beard of formal cut,
  Full of wise saws and modern instances;
  And so he plays his part. The sixth age shifts
  Into the lean and slippered pantaloon   165
  With spectacles on nose and pouch on side,
  His youthful hose, well saved, a world too wide
  For his shrunk shank, and his big manly voice,
  Turning again toward childish treble, pipes
  And whistles in his sound. Last scene of all,   170
  That ends this strange eventful history,
  Is second childishness and mere oblivion,
  Sans teeth, sans eyes, sans taste, sans everything.

Enter Orlando, ⌜*carrying*⌝ *Adam.*

178. **scarce:** i.e., scarcely

181. **cousin:** a formal way for a sovereign to address one of his nobles

183. **unkind:** (1) unnatural; (2) inconsiderate

187. **rude:** rough, boisterous

195. **warp:** perhaps, freeze; perhaps, ruffle

197. **friend remembered not:** i.e., the failure of one friend to remember another

"The infant . . . in the nurse's arms." (2.7.150–51)
From Desiderius Erasmus, *Morias enkomion* [transl.]
Stultitiae laus . . . (1676).

DUKE SENIOR
  Welcome. Set down your venerable burden,
  And let him feed.   175
ORLANDO   I thank you most for him.
ADAM   So had you need.—
  I scarce can speak to thank you for myself.
DUKE SENIOR
  Welcome. Fall to. I will not trouble you
  As yet to question you about your fortunes.—   180
  Give us some music, and, good cousin, sing.

⌜*The Duke and Orlando continue their conversation,*
                  apart.⌝

                  Song.

⌜AMIENS *sings*⌝
      Blow, blow, thou winter wind.
      Thou art not so unkind
        As man's ingratitude.
      Thy tooth is not so keen,   185
      Because thou art not seen,
        Although thy breath be rude.
    Heigh-ho, sing heigh-ho, unto the green holly.
    Most friendship is feigning, most loving mere folly.
        ⌜*Then*⌝ *heigh-ho, the holly.*   190
      This life is most jolly.

      Freeze, freeze, thou bitter sky,
      That dost not bite so nigh
        As benefits forgot.
      Though thou the waters warp,   195
      Thy sting is not so sharp
        As friend remembered not.
    Heigh-ho, sing heigh-ho, unto the green holly.
    Most friendship is feigning, most loving mere folly.
        ⌜*Then*⌝ *heigh-ho, the holly.*   200
      This life is most jolly.

203. **faithfully:** convincingly

204. **effigies:** likeness, image (accent on second syllable)

207. **residue . . . fortune:** i.e., the rest of what has happened to you

209. **right:** i.e., as truly

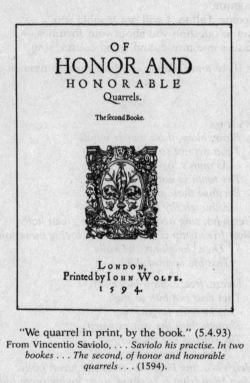

OF
HONOR AND
HONORABLE
Quarrels.

The second Booke.

LONDON,
Printed by IOHN WOLFE.
1594.

"We quarrel in print, by the book." (5.4.93)
From Vincentio Saviolo, . . . *Saviolo his practise. In two bookes . . . The second, of honor and honorable quarrels . . .* (1594).

DUKE SENIOR, ⌜*to Orlando*⌝
    If that you were the good Sir Rowland's son,
    As you have whispered faithfully you were,
    And as mine eye doth his effigies witness
    Most truly limned and living in your face,   205
    Be truly welcome hither. I am the duke
    That loved your father. The residue of your fortune
    Go to my cave and tell me.—Good old man,
    Thou art right welcome as thy ⌜master⌝ is.
    ⌜*To Lords.*⌝ Support him by the arm. ⌜*To Orlando.*⌝   210
        Give me your hand,
    And let me all your fortunes understand.
                                        They exit.

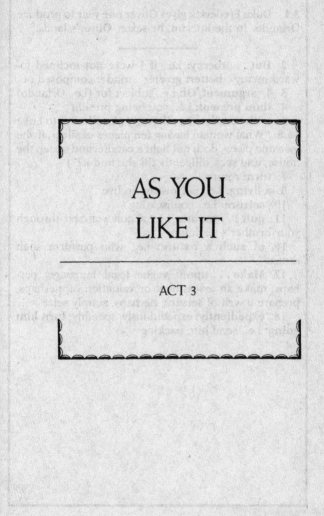

AS YOU
LIKE IT

ACT 3

3.1   Duke Frederick gives Oliver one year to produce Orlando. In the interim, he seizes Oliver's lands.

————————

2. **But . . . mercy:** i.e., if I were not inclined to-ward mercy   **better:** greater   **made:** composed of

3–4. **argument/Of:** i.e., subject for (i.e., Orlando)

4. **thou present:** i.e., you being present

6. **with candle:** i.e., diligently (An allusion to Luke 15.8: "What woman having ten pieces of silver, if she lose one piece, doth not light a candle, and sweep the house, and seek diligently till she find it?")

7. **turn:** return

8. **a living:** i.e., permission to live

10. **seizure:** i.e., confiscating

11. **quit . . . mouth:** i.e., acquit yourself through your brother's testimony

16. **of such a nature:** i.e., who perform such duties

17. **Make . . . upon:** vague legal language: per-haps, make an assessment or valuation of; perhaps, prepare a writ of seizure; perhaps, simply seize

18. **expediently:** expeditiously, speedily; **turn him going:** i.e., send him packing

ACT 3

Scene 1
Enter Duke ⌜Frederick,⌝ Lords, and Oliver.

DUKE FREDERICK, ⌜*to Oliver*⌝
Not see him since? Sir, sir, that cannot be.
But were I not the better part made mercy,
I should not seek an absent argument
Of my revenge, thou present. But look to it:
Find out thy brother wheresoe'er he is.   5
Seek him with candle. Bring him, dead or living,
Within this twelvemonth, or turn thou no more
To seek a living in our territory.
Thy lands and all things that thou dost call thine,
Worth seizure, do we seize into our hands   10
Till thou canst quit thee by thy brother's mouth
Of what we think against thee.

OLIVER
O, that your Highness knew my heart in this:
I never loved my brother in my life.

DUKE FREDERICK
More villain thou.—Well, push him out of doors,   15
And let my officers of such a nature
Make an extent upon his house and lands.
Do this expediently, and turn him going.
                                                          They exit.

3.2 Orlando hangs poems in praise of Rosalind on trees in the forest, where Rosalind and Celia find them. In disguise as Ganymede, Rosalind meets Orlando and tells him she can cure his lovesickness if he will pretend that she is Rosalind and come every day to court her. Orlando agrees.

---

1. **verse:** i.e., poem
2. **thrice-crownèd . . . night:** the mythological goddess who had three forms: Luna, the moon goddess; Diana, goddess of chastity; and Proserpina, goddess of the underworld (See page 44.)
3. **pale sphere:** either the transparent sphere within which the moon was thought to orbit the earth (see note on line 2.7.6), or the moon itself
4. **Thy huntress' name:** i.e., the name of Rosalind (here figured as one of the virgin-huntresses who, in mythology, form Diana's train); **my full life doth sway:** controls my entire life
6. **character:** inscribe
7. **That:** i.e., so that
8. **virtue:** superiority, merit, excellence
10. **fair:** beautiful; **unexpressive:** inexpressible
13. **in respect of:** i.e., as to, with regard to
14. **in respect that:** i.e., considering that
15. **naught:** worthless
16. **private:** secluded (i.e., solitary)
19. **spare:** frugal
20. **humor:** temperament
21. **stomach:** (1) inclination; (2) belly
24. **wants:** lacks
25. **content:** contentment
29. **wit:** knowledge; **art:** education

Scene 2
Enter Orlando, ⌈with a paper.⌉

ORLANDO
Hang there, my verse, in witness of my love.
  And thou, thrice-crownèd queen of night, survey
With thy chaste eye, from thy pale sphere above,
  Thy huntress' name that my full life doth sway.
O Rosalind, these trees shall be my books,   5
  And in their barks my thoughts I'll character,
That every eye which in this forest looks
  Shall see thy virtue witnessed everywhere.
Run, run, Orlando, carve on every tree
The fair, the chaste, and unexpressive she.   10
                                        He exits.

Enter Corin and ⌈Touchstone.⌉

CORIN And how like you this shepherd's life, Master
  Touchstone?
TOUCHSTONE Truly, shepherd, in respect of itself, it is a
  good life; but in respect that it is a shepherd's life, it
  is naught. In respect that it is solitary, I like it very   15
  well; but in respect that it is private, it is a very vile
  life. Now in respect it is in the fields, it pleaseth me
  well; but in respect it is not in the court, it is
  tedious. As it is a spare life, look you, it fits my
  humor well; but as there is no more plenty in it, it   20
  goes much against my stomach. Hast any philosophy in thee, shepherd?
CORIN No more but that I know the more one sickens,
  the worse at ease he is, and that he that wants
  money, means, and content is without three good   25
  friends; that the property of rain is to wet, and fire
  to burn; that good pasture makes fat sheep; and that
  a great cause of the night is lack of the sun; that he
  that hath learned no wit by nature nor art may

30. **complain of:** i.e., lament the lack of; **breeding:** upbringing

32. **a natural philosopher:** (1) a "born" philosopher; (2) a philosopher whose subject is nature, a scientist (since what has become "science" was then called "natural philosophy"); (3) a half-witted philosopher (See 1.2.49.)

36. **hope:** i.e., hope not

37–38. **ill-roasted:** badly cooked

38. **all on one side:** i.e., cooked only on one side

42. **manners . . . wicked:** (1) behavior must be very bad; (2) morals must be evil

44. **parlous:** i.e., perilous, dangerous

48. **mockable:** deserving of scorn

48–49. **salute . . . but:** i.e., whenever you greet (each other) at court

51. **Instance:** (1) evidence, proof (if **instance** is a noun); (2) provide proof (if a verb)

52. **still:** constantly

53. **fells:** fleeces (See page 134.)

54. **your courtier's:** i.e., courtiers'

55. **mutton:** sheep

60. **sounder:** i.e., sound

61. **they:** i.e., shepherds' hands; **tarred . . . surgery:** i.e., covered with the tar used in treating cuts on the hides **surgery:** the practice of treating injuries

63. **civet:** i.e., perfume (derived, as Touchstone points out, from the anal pouch of civet cats) See page 64.

64. **worms' meat:** i.e., piece of maggoty flesh

64–65. **in respect of:** in comparison to

65. **Learn of:** i.e., learn from

complain of good breeding or comes of a very dull   30
kindred.

TOUCHSTONE   Such a one is a natural philosopher. Wast
ever in court, shepherd?

CORIN   No, truly.

TOUCHSTONE   Then thou art damned.   35

CORIN   Nay, I hope.

TOUCHSTONE   Truly, thou art damned, like an ill-
roasted egg, all on one side.

CORIN   For not being at court? Your reason.

TOUCHSTONE   Why, if thou never wast at court, thou   40
never saw'st good manners; if thou never saw'st
good manners, then thy manners must be wicked,
and wickedness is sin, and sin is damnation. Thou
art in a parlous state, shepherd.

CORIN   Not a whit, Touchstone. Those that are good   45
manners at the court are as ridiculous in the
country as the behavior of the country is most
mockable at the court. You told me you salute not at
the court but you kiss your hands. That courtesy
would be uncleanly if courtiers were shepherds.   50

TOUCHSTONE   Instance, briefly. Come, instance.

CORIN   Why, we are still handling our ewes, and their
fells, you know, are greasy.

TOUCHSTONE   Why, do not your courtier's hands sweat?
And is not the grease of a mutton as wholesome as   55
the sweat of a man? Shallow, shallow. A better
instance, I say. Come.

CORIN   Besides, our hands are hard.

TOUCHSTONE   Your lips will feel them the sooner. Shallow again. A more sounder instance. Come.   60

CORIN   And they are often tarred over with the surgery
of our sheep; and would you have us kiss tar? The
courtier's hands are perfumed with civet.

TOUCHSTONE   Most shallow man. Thou worms' meat in
respect of a good piece of flesh, indeed. Learn of the   65

67. **flux:** discharge; **Mend:** improve

69. **wit:** intelligence; **rest:** cease (Touchstone replies as if **rest** means "be at ease.")

71–72. **God . . . raw:** See longer note, page 213.

72. **raw:** crude, unfinished, uncultivated

73. **true:** trustworthy; **that:** i.e., what; **get:** earn

75. **content . . . harm:** i.e., resigned to any misfortune

78. **simple sin:** perhaps, sin arising from your simplicity, ignorance, or rusticity

79–80. **offer . . . living:** presume to make your livelihood

80. **bawd:** go-between in a sexual intrigue

81. **bell-wether:** male sheep that leads the flock

82. **crooked-pated . . . ram:** i.e., an old horned male sheep (For **cuckoldly,** see longer note to **hornbeasts,** 3.3.49. See also page 178.)

82–83. **out . . . match:** i.e., outside the bounds of appropriate mating

84. **will have no:** i.e., wants no

85. **else:** otherwise

88. **Ind:** i.e., Indies

92. **fairest lined:** (1) most beautifully delineated; (2) drawn in the lightest colors

93. **black to:** i.e., black in comparison to (By the standards of Shakespeare's time, **black** was the opposite of beautiful or "fair.")

95. **fair:** beauty

96. **rhyme you so:** i.e., rhyme in the same way; **together:** without intermission

98. **the right . . . market:** i.e., perhaps, exactly the (monotonous) jog-trot of dairy-women taking butter to market

wise and perpend: civet is of a baser birth than tar,
the very uncleanly flux of a cat. Mend the instance,
shepherd.

CORIN   You have too courtly a wit for me. I'll rest.

TOUCHSTONE   Wilt thou rest damned? God help thee,   70
shallow man. God make incision in thee; thou art
raw.

CORIN   Sir, I am a true laborer. I earn that I eat, get that
I wear, owe no man hate, envy no man's happiness,
glad of other men's good, content with my harm,   75
and the greatest of my pride is to see my ewes graze
and my lambs suck.

TOUCHSTONE   That is another simple sin in you, to bring
the ewes and the rams together and to offer to get
your living by the copulation of cattle; to be bawd to   80
a bell-wether and to betray a she-lamb of a twelvemonth to a crooked-pated old cuckoldly ram, out of
all reasonable match. If thou be'st not damned for
this, the devil himself will have no shepherds. I
cannot see else how thou shouldst 'scape.   85

Enter Rosalind, ⌐as Ganymede.⌐

CORIN   Here comes young Master Ganymede, my new
mistress's brother.

ROSALIND, ⌐*as Ganymede, reading a paper*⌐
        From the east to western Ind
        No jewel is like Rosalind.
        Her worth being mounted on the wind,   90
        Through all the world bears Rosalind.
        All the pictures fairest lined
        Are but black to Rosalind.
        Let no face be kept in mind
        But the fair of Rosalind.   95

TOUCHSTONE   I'll rhyme you so eight years together,
dinners and suppers and sleeping hours excepted.
It is the right butter-women's rank to market.

99. **Out:** an expression of reproach

103. **cat will after kind:** proverbial, referring to following one's instincts (but often specifically sexual instincts)

105. **Wintered garments:** i.e., clothes worn in winter; **lined:** provided with lining (With reference to dogs, **lined** means "copulated with.")

107. **sheaf and bind:** i.e., bind into sheaves

108. **cart:** Women who transgressed community standards were shamed by being paraded through the streets in open carts.

111–12. **sweetest rose . . . prick:** Proverbial: "No rose without a prickle." **rose:** a form of the name Rosalind **find:** suffer, undergo as pain or punishment **prick:** with probable wordplay on the sexual meaning

113. **false gallop:** literally, a canter (with wordplay on **false** as "defective")

117. **tree . . . fruit:** Compare Matthew 7.18: "A good tree cannot bring forth bad fruit."

118. **you:** perhaps with wordplay on "yew"

119. **medlar:** (1) tree bearing a small apple-shaped fruit; (2) meddler; (3) prostitute

120–22. **earliest fruit . . . medlar:** Proverbial: "Medlars are never good till they be rotten." See longer note, page 213.

128. **For:** i.e., because

130. **civil:** (1) civilized; (2) grave, solemn

131. **brief:** i.e., briefly

132. **his erring:** i.e., its wandering

ROSALIND, ⌐*as Ganymede*⌐ Out, fool.

TOUCHSTONE For a taste: 100
    If a hart do lack a hind,
    Let him seek out Rosalind.
    If the cat will after kind,
    So be sure will Rosalind.
    Wintered garments must be lined; 105
    So must slender Rosalind.
    They that reap must sheaf and bind;
    Then to cart with Rosalind.
    Sweetest nut hath sourest rind;
    Such a nut is Rosalind. 110
    He that sweetest rose will find
    Must find love's prick, and Rosalind.
This is the very false gallop of verses. Why do you
infect yourself with them?

ROSALIND, ⌐*as Ganymede*⌐ Peace, you dull fool. I found 115
them on a tree.

TOUCHSTONE Truly, the tree yields bad fruit.

ROSALIND, ⌐*as Ganymede*⌐ I'll graft it with you, and
then I shall graft it with a medlar. Then it will be
the earliest fruit i' th' country, for you'll be rotten 120
ere you be half ripe, and that's the right virtue of
the medlar.

TOUCHSTONE You have said, but whether wisely or no,
let the forest judge.

    Enter Celia, ⌐*as Aliena,*⌐ *with a writing.*

ROSALIND, ⌐*as Ganymede*⌐ Peace. Here comes my sister 125
reading. Stand aside.

CELIA, ⌐*as Aliena, reads*⌐
    Why should this ⌐*a*⌐ *desert be?*
      For it is unpeopled? No.
    Tongues I'll hang on every tree
      That shall civil sayings show.
    Some how brief the life of man 130
      Runs his erring pilgrimage,

133–34. **That . . . age:** i.e., so that a handspan encloses his whole life (Compare Psalm 39.5 in the Book of Common Prayer: "Thou hast made my days as it were a span long.")

136. **'Twixt:** i.e., between

141. **sprite:** i.e., spirit

142. **would . . . show:** i.e., wanted to show in human form (Literally, **in little** means "in miniature.")

145. **graces:** virtues; **wide-enlarged:** distributed widely among many women; or, perhaps, enlarged to their full extent (within Rosalind)

147. **cheek:** i.e., beauty; **heart:** (lack of) fidelity (See longer note, pages 213–14.)

148. **Cleopatra's majesty:** Cleopatra was an Egyptian queen (69–30 BC) who attracted, in succession, both Julius Caesar and Mark Antony. (See Shakespeare's *Antony and Cleopatra*.)

149. **Atalanta's . . . part:** See longer note, page 214.

150. **Sad:** grave, sober; **Lucretia's modesty:** i.e., Lucrece's scrupulous chastity (See longer note, page 214, and woodcut, page 166.)

151. **parts:** qualities, attributes; ingredients

152. **heavenly synod:** (1) assembly of gods; (2) conjunction of planets

154. **touches dearest prized:** i.e., the most highly esteemed qualities

155. **Heaven would:** i.e., it was heaven's will

156. **I to:** i.e., that I should

157–60. **O . . . people:** Rosalind playfully addresses Celia as if the latter had just delivered a boring sermon on love to a church congregation. **withal:** with

(continued)

That the stretching of a span
  Buckles in his sum of age;
Some of violated vows   135
  'Twixt the souls of friend and friend.
But upon the fairest boughs,
  Or at every sentence end,
Will I "Rosalinda" write,
  Teaching all that read to know   140
The quintessence of every sprite
  Heaven would in little show.
Therefore heaven nature charged
  That one body should be filled
With all graces wide-enlarged.   145
  Nature presently distilled
Helen's cheek, but not ⌈her⌉ heart,
  Cleopatra's majesty,
Atalanta's better part,
  Sad Lucretia's modesty.   150
Thus Rosalind of many parts
  By heavenly synod was devised
Of many faces, eyes, and hearts
  To have the touches dearest prized.
Heaven would that she these gifts should have   155
And I to live and die her slave.

ROSALIND, ⌈as Ganymede⌉ O most gentle Jupiter, what
  tedious homily of love have you wearied your pa-
  rishioners withal, and never cried "Have patience,
  good people."   160

CELIA, ⌈as Aliena⌉ How now?—Back, friends. Shepherd, go off a little.—Go with him, sirrah.

TOUCHSTONE Come, shepherd, let us make an honorable retreat, though not with bag and baggage, yet
  with scrip and scrippage.   165
                   ⌈*Touchstone and Corin*⌉ *exit.*

CELIA Didst thou hear these verses?

ROSALIND O yes, I heard them all, and more too, for

161. **How now:** an interjection, elliptical for "how is it now?"; **Back:** i.e., get back, withdraw

164–65. **retreat . . . scrippage:** wordplay on the military phrase "to march out with **bag and baggage**" (i.e., to make an **honorable retreat**) **bag and baggage:** all the army's possessions **scrip:** a small bag carried by shepherds or beggars **scrippage:** a word made up to parallel **baggage**

166. **these verses:** stanzas of verse (but taken by Rosalind to mean complete metrical lines)

168–73. **some of them . . . in the verse:** elaborate wordplay on **feet** (as divisions of a verse), **bear** (as "allow" and "carry"), **lame** (as "crippled" and "metrically defective"), and **without** ("in the absence of" and "outside of")

175. **should be:** i.e., came to be

177. **nine days:** an allusion to the proverb "a wonder lasts but nine days"

180. **berhymed:** celebrated in rhyme; **Pythagoras:** ancient Greek philosopher who taught the transmigration of souls

181. **that:** i.e., when; **Irish rat:** Proverbial: "To rhyme to death [i.e., destroy by magic spells], as they do rats in Ireland."

183. **Trow you:** i.e., can you guess

185. **And a chain:** i.e., and with a chain

188–90. **it is . . . encounter:** Proverbial: "Friends may meet, but mountains never greet."

197. **out of all whooping:** i.e., beyond the limits of expressions of wonder

198. **Good my complexion:** a mild oath or expression of impatience, with (perhaps) some reference to her own nature or disposition

(continued)
102

some of them had in them more feet than the verses would bear.

CELIA   That's no matter. The feet might bear the verses.   170

ROSALIND   Ay, but the feet were lame and could not bear themselves without the verse, and therefore stood lamely in the verse.

CELIA   But didst thou hear without wondering how thy name should be hanged and carved upon these   175 trees?

ROSALIND   I was seven of the nine days out of the wonder before you came, for look here what I found on a palm tree. ⌜*She shows the paper she read.*⌝ I was never so berhymed since Pythagoras'   180 time that I was an Irish rat, which I can hardly remember.

CELIA   Trow you who hath done this?

ROSALIND   Is it a man?

CELIA   And a chain, that you once wore, about his neck.   185 Change you color?

ROSALIND   I prithee, who?

CELIA   O Lord, Lord, it is a hard matter for friends to meet, but mountains may be removed with earthquakes and so encounter.   190

ROSALIND   Nay, but who is it?

CELIA   Is it possible?

ROSALIND   Nay, I prithee now, with most petitionary vehemence, tell me who it is.

CELIA   O wonderful, wonderful, and most wonderful   195 wonderful, and yet again wonderful, and after that out of all whooping!

ROSALIND   Good my complexion, dost thou think though I am caparisoned like a man, I have a doublet and hose in my disposition? One inch of   200 delay more is a South Sea of discovery. I prithee, tell me who is it quickly, and speak apace. I would thou couldst stammer, that thou might'st pour this

199. **caparisoned:** decked out

200. **inch:** tiny bit

201. **a South . . . discovery:** a much-debated phrase that seems to refer to tedious voyages of exploration in the South Pacific

208. **So . . . belly:** Celia may be playing with a sexual meaning of **drink** (i.e., to have intercourse). If so, **belly** would mean "womb" as well as "stomach."

209. **of God's making:** i.e., a normal human being (proverbial)

214. **stay:** wait for

218. **the devil take mocking:** a mild curse on those who mock or deride

218–19. **sad brow and true maid:** i.e., with a serious face and as an honorable virgin

224. **What did he:** i.e., what was he doing

225. **Wherein:** in what (clothing)

226. **makes he:** i.e., is he doing

229. **Gargantua's mouth:** Gargantua was a folk-tale giant who, in Rabelais' version of the story, swallowed five pilgrims in a salad.

232. **catechism:** the series of questions and answers used by the church to teach basic religious principles (See page xxix.)

234. **freshly:** i.e., vigorous

236. **atomies:** dust particles in sunlight

236–37. **resolve the propositions:** answer the questions

238. **observance:** observation, attention

concealed man out of thy mouth as wine comes out
of a narrow-mouthed bottle—either too much at 205
once, or none at all. I prithee take the cork out of
thy mouth, that I may drink thy tidings.

CELIA So you may put a man in your belly.

ROSALIND Is he of God's making? What manner of
man? Is his head worth a hat, or his chin worth a 210
beard?

CELIA Nay, he hath but a little beard.

ROSALIND Why, God will send more, if the man will be
thankful. Let me stay the growth of his beard, if
thou delay me not the knowledge of his chin. 215

CELIA It is young Orlando, that tripped up the wrestler's heels and your heart both in an instant.

ROSALIND Nay, but the devil take mocking. Speak sad
brow and true maid.

CELIA I' faith, coz, 'tis he. 220

ROSALIND Orlando?

CELIA Orlando.

ROSALIND Alas the day, what shall I do with my doublet
and hose? What did he when thou saw'st him? What
said he? How looked he? Wherein went he? What 225
makes he here? Did he ask for me? Where remains
he? How parted he with thee? And when shalt thou
see him again? Answer me in one word.

CELIA You must borrow me Gargantua's mouth first.
'Tis a word too great for any mouth of this age's size. 230
To say ay and no to these particulars is more than to
answer in a catechism.

ROSALIND But doth he know that I am in this forest and
in man's apparel? Looks he as freshly as he did the
day he wrestled? 235

CELIA It is as easy to count atomies as to resolve the
propositions of a lover. But take a taste of my
finding him, and relish it with good observance. I
found him under a tree like a dropped acorn.

240. **Jove's tree:** In Virgil and Ovid, the oak is **Jove's tree.**

242. **Give me audience:** listen to me

247. **becomes:** adorns

248–49. **curvets unseasonably:** leaps at the wrong times

249. **furnished like:** i.e., dressed as

251. **burden:** undersong (the bass part sung along with the melody)

255. **bring me out:** i.e., disturb or confuse me

256. **Soft:** an exclamation meaning "wait a minute"

257. **note:** observe

259. **as lief:** i.e., just as soon

260. **for fashion sake:** i.e., for the sake of outward form or ceremony

262. **God be wi' you:** i.e., good-bye

267. **ill-favoredly:** i.e., badly

269. **just:** exactly

A sobbing deer. (2.1.69)
From Edward Topsell, *The historie of foure-footed beastes . . .* (1607).

ROSALIND It may well be called Jove's tree when it   240
   drops forth ⌜such⌝ fruit.

CELIA Give me audience, good madam.

ROSALIND Proceed.

CELIA There lay he, stretched along like a wounded
   knight.   245

ROSALIND Though it be pity to see such a sight, it well
   becomes the ground.

CELIA Cry "holla" to ⌜thy⌝ tongue, I prithee. It curvets
   unseasonably. He was furnished like a hunter.

ROSALIND O, ominous! He comes to kill my heart.   250

CELIA I would sing my song without a burden. Thou
   bring'st me out of tune.

ROSALIND Do you not know I am a woman? When I
   think, I must speak. Sweet, say on.

CELIA You bring me out.   255

Enter Orlando and Jaques.

   Soft, comes he not here?

ROSALIND 'Tis he. Slink by, and note him.
                 ⌜*Rosalind and Celia step aside.*⌝

JAQUES, ⌜*to Orlando*⌝ I thank you for your company,
   but, good faith, I had as lief have been myself alone.

ORLANDO And so had I, but yet, for fashion sake, I   260
   thank you too for your society.

JAQUES God be wi' you. Let's meet as little as we can.

ORLANDO I do desire we may be better strangers.

JAQUES I pray you mar no more trees with writing love
   songs in their barks.   265

ORLANDO I pray you mar no more of my verses with
   reading them ill-favoredly.

JAQUES Rosalind is your love's name?

ORLANDO Yes, just.

JAQUES I do not like her name.   270

ORLANDO There was no thought of pleasing you when
   she was christened.

277. **conned them out of rings:** i.e., memorized them from the mottoes inscribed in gold rings

278. **right:** true, genuine; **painted cloth:** i.e., wall hangings painted with pictures and mottoes

281. **Atalanta's heels:** See longer note to 3.2.149.

300. **under that habit:** i.e., in that role; **play the knave:** (1) act the part of a boy; (2) deceive him

A shepherd. (2.4.43, 3.2.11–85)
From *Hortus sanitatis . . .* (1536).

JAQUES   What stature is she of?

ORLANDO   Just as high as my heart.

JAQUES   You are full of pretty answers. Have you not 275
    been   acquainted   with   goldsmiths'   wives   and
    conned them out of rings?

ORLANDO   Not so. But I answer you right painted cloth,
    from whence you have studied your questions.

JAQUES   You have a nimble wit. I think 'twas made of 280
    Atalanta's heels. Will you sit down with me? And we
    two will rail against our mistress the world and all
    our misery.

ORLANDO   I will chide no breather in the world but
    myself, against whom I know most faults. 285

JAQUES   The worst fault you have is to be in love.

ORLANDO   'Tis a fault I will not change for your best
    virtue. I am weary of you.

JAQUES   By my troth, I was seeking for a fool when I
    found you. 290

ORLANDO   He is drowned in the brook. Look but in, and
    you shall see him.

JAQUES   There I shall see mine own figure.

ORLANDO   Which I take to be either a fool or a cipher.

JAQUES   I'll tarry no longer with you. Farewell, good 295
    Signior Love.

ORLANDO   I am glad of your departure. Adieu, good
    Monsieur Melancholy.   ⌜*Jaques exits.*⌝

ROSALIND, ⌜*aside to Celia*⌝ I will speak to him like a
    saucy lackey, and under that habit play the knave 300
    with him. ⌜*As Ganymede.*⌝ Do you hear, forester?

ORLANDO   Very well. What would you?

ROSALIND, ⌜*as Ganymede*⌝ I pray you, what is 't
    o'clock?

ORLANDO   You should ask me what time o' day. There's 305
    no clock in the forest.

ROSALIND, ⌜*as Ganymede*⌝ Then there is no true lover
    in the forest; else sighing every minute and

309. **detect:** reveal

314. **divers paces:** various gaits (From this line through line 339, **time** is imaged as a horse carrying **divers persons.**)

315–16. **ambles . . . trots . . . gallops:** different gaits of a horse; **withal:** i.e., with

319. **hard:** at an uneasy pace

320. **contract of her marriage:** formal agreement to marry; betrothal

322. **se'nnight:** i.e., sevennight, week

325. **lacks:** i.e., can't read

329. **lean:** unremunerative; **wasteful:** debilitating

330. **heavy:** dreadful, burdensome

334. **softly:** slowly (The phrase is proverbial.)

337–38. **vacation:** the period each year when the law-courts in London do not sit, the time **between term and term**

342. **skirts:** edge or outskirts

"The lean and slippered pantaloon." (2.7.165)
From Otto van Veen, *Quinti Horatii Flacci emblemata . . .* (1612).

groaning every hour would detect the lazy foot of
time as well as a clock.   310
ORLANDO   And why not the swift foot of time? Had not
that been as proper?
ROSALIND, ⌜*as Ganymede*⌝ By no means, sir. Time
travels in divers paces with divers persons. I'll tell
you who time ambles withal, who time trots withal,   315
who time gallops withal, and who he stands still
withal.
ORLANDO   I prithee, who doth he trot withal?
ROSALIND, ⌜*as Ganymede*⌝ Marry, he trots hard with a
young maid between the contract of her marriage   320
and the day it is solemnized. If the interim be but a
se'nnight, time's pace is so hard that it seems the
length of seven year.
ORLANDO   Who ambles time withal?
ROSALIND, ⌜*as Ganymede*⌝ With a priest that lacks Latin   325
and a rich man that hath not the gout, for the one
sleeps easily because he cannot study, and the other
lives merrily because he feels no pain—the one
lacking the burden of lean and wasteful learning,
the other knowing no burden of heavy tedious   330
penury. These time ambles withal.
ORLANDO   Who doth he gallop withal?
ROSALIND, ⌜*as Ganymede*⌝ With a thief to the gallows,
for though he go as softly as foot can fall, he thinks
himself too soon there.   335
ORLANDO   Who stays it still withal?
ROSALIND, ⌜*as Ganymede*⌝ With lawyers in the vacation, for they sleep between term and term, and
then they perceive not how time moves.
ORLANDO   Where dwell you, pretty youth?   340
ROSALIND, ⌜*as Ganymede*⌝ With this shepherdess, my
sister, here in the skirts of the forest, like fringe
upon a petticoat.
ORLANDO   Are you native of this place?

346. **kindled:** i.e., born

348. **purchase:** acquire; **removed:** remote

349. **of:** i.e., by

351. **inland:** See note to 2.7.101.

352. **courtship:** (1) wooing, courting; (2) courtly behavior; **there:** i.e., at court

353. **read many lectures:** deliver many admonitory speeches

354. **touched:** infected, tainted

356. **taxed:** accused, charged

361. **his:** its

365. **physic:** medicine, remedies

368. **elegies:** love poems

370. **fancy-monger:** A **monger** is a seller or promoter; **fancy,** here, is love or desire.

371. **quotidian:** quotidian fever, chills and fevers that recur daily

373. **love-shaked:** i.e., suffering with love's chills and fevers

377. **cage:** prison; **rushes:** stalks of the rush plant, used for making baskets

Grafting trees. (3.2.118)
From Marco Bussato, *Giardino di agricoltura . . .* (1599).

ROSALIND, ⌜*as Ganymede*⌝ As the cony that you see 345
dwell where she is kindled.

ORLANDO Your accent is something finer than you
could purchase in so removed a dwelling.

ROSALIND, ⌜*as Ganymede*⌝ I have been told so of many.
But indeed an old religious uncle of mine taught 350
me to speak, who was in his youth an inland man,
one that knew courtship too well, for there he fell in
love. I have heard him read many lectures against it,
and I thank God I am not a woman, to be touched
with so many giddy offenses as he hath generally 355
taxed their whole sex withal.

ORLANDO Can you remember any of the principal evils
that he laid to the charge of women?

ROSALIND, ⌜*as Ganymede*⌝ There were none principal.
They were all like one another as halfpence are, 360
every one fault seeming monstrous till his fellow
fault came to match it.

ORLANDO I prithee recount some of them.

ROSALIND, ⌜*as Ganymede*⌝ No, I will not cast away my
physic but on those that are sick. There is a man 365
haunts the forest that abuses our young plants with
carving "Rosalind" on their barks, hangs odes upon
hawthorns and elegies on brambles, all, forsooth,
⌜deifying⌝ the name of Rosalind. If I could meet
that fancy-monger, I would give him some good 370
counsel, for he seems to have the quotidian of love
upon him.

ORLANDO I am he that is so love-shaked. I pray you tell
me your remedy.

ROSALIND, ⌜*as Ganymede*⌝ There is none of my uncle's 375
marks upon you. He taught me how to know a man
in love, in which cage of rushes I am sure you ⌜are⌝
not prisoner.

ORLANDO What were his marks?

ROSALIND, ⌜*as Ganymede*⌝ A lean cheek, which you 380

381. **blue eye:** i.e., eyes discolored from exhaustion or weeping

382. **unquestionable:** i.e., unsociable, unwilling to talk

384. **simply . . . beard:** i.e., what you have in the way of a beard

385. **younger brother's revenue:** i.e., small, like such a revenue

386. **bonnet unbanded:** hat missing its hatband

389. **point-device:** scrupulously neat

390. **accouterments:** apparel; **as:** i.e., as if; **than:** i.e., rather than

397. **in the which:** i.e., in which; **still:** always

398. **give the lie to:** i.e., contradict; **their consciences:** i.e., what they know in their hearts; **in good sooth:** i.e., truly

405. **Neither rhyme nor reason:** proverbial

408–9. **a dark house and a whip:** standard Elizabethan treatment for insanity

409. **they:** i.e., lovers

410. **the lunacy:** i.e., lovesickness

416. **set him:** i.e., assigned him, gave him the task

have not; a blue eye and sunken, which you have
not; an unquestionable spirit, which you have not; a
beard neglected, which you have not—but I pardon
you for that, for simply your having in beard is a
younger brother's revenue. Then your hose should 385
be ungartered, your bonnet unbanded, your sleeve
unbuttoned, your shoe untied, and everything
about you demonstrating a careless desolation. But
you are no such man. You are rather point-device in
your accouterments, as loving yourself than seem- 390
ing the lover of any other.

ORLANDO Fair youth, I would I could make thee believe
I love.

ROSALIND, ⌜*as Ganymede*⌝ Me believe it? You may as
soon make her that you love believe it, which I 395
warrant she is apter to do than to confess she does.
That is one of the points in the which women still
give the lie to their consciences. But, in good sooth,
are you he that hangs the verses on the trees
wherein Rosalind is so admired? 400

ORLANDO I swear to thee, youth, by the white hand of
Rosalind, I am that he, that unfortunate he.

ROSALIND, ⌜*as Ganymede*⌝ But are you so much in love
as your rhymes speak?

ORLANDO Neither rhyme nor reason can express how 405
much.

ROSALIND, ⌜*as Ganymede*⌝ Love is merely a madness,
and, I tell you, deserves as well a dark house and a
whip as madmen do; and the reason why they are
not so punished and cured is that the lunacy is so 410
ordinary that the whippers are in love too. Yet I
profess curing it by counsel.

ORLANDO Did you ever cure any so?

ROSALIND, ⌜*as Ganymede*⌝ Yes, one, and in this manner. He was to imagine me his love, his mistress, 415
and I set him every day to woo me; at which time

417. **moonish:** fickle, changeable

419. **apish:** affected, silly

422. **cattle of this color:** wordplay on the proverb "a horse of that color," substituting the contemptuous term **cattle**

423. **entertain:** accept, receive

425. **drave:** i.e., drove

425–26. **mad . . . madness:** i.e., insane infatuation to actual madness

426–28. **forswear . . . monastic:** i.e., give up the world for the monastic life (**The world** is here pictured as a **full stream** and the monastery is like a **nook,** a small or sheltered creek.) **merely:** completely

429. **liver:** thought to be the seat of love

430. **that:** i.e., so that

435. **cote:** cottage

439. **by the way:** i.e., along the way

3.3 Touchstone, desiring a goat-keeper named Audrey, has arranged for a country priest to marry them in the woods. Jaques persuades Touchstone to wait until he can have a real wedding in a church.

---

3. **feature:** appearance, shape

would I, being but a moonish youth, grieve, be
effeminate, changeable, longing and liking, proud,
fantastical, apish, shallow, inconstant, full of tears,
full of smiles; for every passion something, and for   420
no passion truly anything, as boys and women are,
for the most part, cattle of this color; would now
like him, now loathe him; then entertain him, then
forswear him; now weep for him, then spit at him,
that I drave my suitor from his mad humor of love   425
to a living humor of madness, which was to forswear the full stream of the world and to live in a
nook merely monastic. And thus I cured him, and
this way will I take upon me to wash your liver as
clean as a sound sheep's heart, that there shall not   430
be one spot of love in 't.

ORLANDO I would not be cured, youth.

ROSALIND, ⌜*as Ganymede*⌝ I would cure you if you
would but call me Rosalind and come every day to
my cote and woo me.   435

ORLANDO Now, by the faith of my love, I will. Tell me
where it is.

ROSALIND, ⌜*as Ganymede*⌝ Go with me to it, and I'll
show it you; and by the way you shall tell me where
in the forest you live. Will you go?   440

ORLANDO With all my heart, good youth.

ROSALIND, ⌜*as Ganymede*⌝ Nay, you must call me
Rosalind.—Come, sister, will you go?

They exit.

Scene 3
Enter ⌜*Touchstone and*⌝ *Audrey,* ⌜*followed by*⌝ *Jaques.*

TOUCHSTONE Come apace, good Audrey. I will fetch up
your goats, Audrey. And how, Audrey? Am I the
man yet? Doth my simple feature content you?

4. **warrant:** protect

6-8. **I . . . Goths:** See longer note, page 214. **capricious:** fanciful, witty **honest:** a vague adjective of praise used to refer to an alleged inferior in a patronizing way

9. **ill-inhabited:** badly housed

10. **Jove in a thatched house:** In classical mythology, **Jove,** king of the Roman gods, was entertained unawares by a poor couple in their thatched hut.

11-12. **verses cannot be understood:** This was Ovid's complaint against the Getae. (See longer note to 3.3.6-8.)

12. **seconded with:** supported or encouraged by

13. **forward:** precocious

14. **great reckoning:** large bill (See longer note to 3.3.13-14, pages 214-15.)

17. **a true:** an honorable, an upright (Touchstone, in line 18, puns on **true** as "genuine.")

19. **feigning:** (1) imaginative, inventive; (2) deceitful, untrue

25. **honest:** chaste (Throughout this conversation with Audrey, the words **honest** and **honesty** mean "chaste" and "chastity," the common meanings in Shakespeare when the words are applied to women.)

26. **feign:** i.e., lie

27. **have me honest:** i.e., have me be chaste

28. **hard-favored:** i.e., ugly

31. **material:** (1) full of good sense or information; (2) earthy, coarse

32. **fair:** beautiful

(continued)

AUDREY Your features, Lord warrant us! What features?   5

TOUCHSTONE I am here with thee and thy goats, as the
most capricious poet, honest Ovid, was among the
Goths.

JAQUES, ⌈*aside*⌉ O knowledge ill-inhabited, worse than
Jove in a thatched house.   10

TOUCHSTONE When a man's verses cannot be understood, nor a man's good wit seconded with the
forward child, understanding, it strikes a man more
dead than a great reckoning in a little room. Truly, I
would the gods had made thee poetical.   15

AUDREY I do not know what "poetical" is. Is it honest
in deed and word? Is it a true thing?

TOUCHSTONE No, truly, for the truest poetry is the most
feigning, and lovers are given to poetry, and what
they swear in poetry may be said as lovers they do   20
feign.

AUDREY Do you wish, then, that the gods had made me
poetical?

TOUCHSTONE I do, truly, for thou swear'st to me thou
art honest. Now if thou wert a poet, I might have   25
some hope thou didst feign.

AUDREY Would you not have me honest?

TOUCHSTONE No, truly, unless thou wert hard-favored;
for honesty coupled to beauty is to have honey a
sauce to sugar.   30

JAQUES, ⌈*aside*⌉ A material fool.

AUDREY Well, I am not fair, and therefore I pray the
gods make me honest.

TOUCHSTONE Truly, and to cast away honesty upon a
foul slut were to put good meat into an unclean   35
dish.

AUDREY I am not a slut, though I thank the gods I am
foul.

TOUCHSTONE Well, praised be the gods for thy foulness;

35. **foul slut:** dirty or slovenly woman (Audrey's use of **slut,** line 37, may carry the meaning of "woman of loose morals," as Touchstone's does in line 40.); **meat:** food

38. **foul:** unattractive

40. **hereafter:** at a future time, later

42. **Sir Oliver Martext:** See longer note, page 215; **vicar:** parish priest

45. **fain:** gladly

48. **stagger:** hesitate, begin to doubt; **attempt:** undertaking

49. **assembly:** congregation; **horn-beasts:** i.e., Audrey's **goats** and the forest's deer (For the connection between **horns** and cuckoldry, see longer note, pages 215–16. See also page 184.)

50. **what though:** i.e., what does it matter

51. **necessary:** inevitable, determined by natural law

51–52. **Many . . . goods:** Proverbial (to describe a very wealthy man): "He knows no end of his goods."

54. **getting:** earning

56. **rascal:** (1) young, lean, or inferior deer; (2) rabble, persons of the lowest class

60. **defense:** (1) fortification; (2) the art of self-defense

62. **want:** be without, lack

64. **dispatch us:** perhaps, finish the business (of marrying us) and send us on our way

66–67. **give the woman:** a reference to the question in the marriage ceremony, "Who giveth this woman . . . ?"

sluttishness may come hereafter. But be it as it may   40
be, I will marry thee; and to that end I have been
with Sir Oliver Martext, the vicar of the next village,
who hath promised to meet me in this place of the
forest and to couple us.

JAQUES, ⌜*aside*⌝ I would fain see this meeting.   45

AUDREY   Well, the gods give us joy.

TOUCHSTONE   Amen. A man may, if he were of a fearful
heart, stagger in this attempt, for here we have no
temple but the wood, no assembly but horn-beasts.
But what though? Courage. As horns are odious,   50
they are necessary. It is said "Many a man knows no
end of his goods." Right: many a man has good
horns and knows no end of them. Well, that is the
dowry of his wife; 'tis none of his own getting.
Horns? Even so. Poor men alone? No, no. The   55
noblest deer hath them as huge as the rascal. Is the
single man therefore blessed? No. As a walled town
is more worthier than a village, so is the forehead of
a married man more honorable than the bare brow
of a bachelor. And by how much defense is better   60
than no skill, by so much is a horn more precious
than to want.

Enter Sir Oliver Martext.

Here comes Sir Oliver.—Sir Oliver Martext, you are
well met. Will you dispatch us here under this tree,
or shall we go with you to your chapel?   65

OLIVER MARTEXT   Is there none here to give the
woman?

TOUCHSTONE   I will not take her on gift of any man.

OLIVER MARTEXT   Truly, she must be given, or the
marriage is not lawful.   70

JAQUES, ⌜*coming forward*⌝ Proceed, proceed. I'll give
her.

73–74. **What-you-call-'t:** One pronunciation of the name **Jaques** was "jakes," the name given a privy. Touchstone may be ostentatiously avoiding this word—or else calling attention to it.

74–75. **God 'ild you:** i.e., thank you (literally, God yield [reward] you)

75. **last:** most recent

76. **toy in hand:** trifle to be attended to

76–77. **pray be covered:** i.e., put your hat back on (usually said by a person of higher rank to an inferior who has removed his hat as a sign of respect)

78. **motley:** See note to **motley fool** at 2.7.13.

79–80. **bow, curb, bells:** devices used to control domesticated animals **bow:** yoke **her bells:** i.e., bells tied to the falcon's legs to make her easier to find (Shakespeare uses **her** because the **falcon** is female; the male of the species is called a "tercel.")

86–87. **join you together:** marry you (See longer note to 3.3.83–87, page 216.)

87. **join:** construct by putting different parts together

90. **I am not in the mind but:** i.e., I am in the mind (i.e., of the opinion) that

91. **of:** i.e., by; **like:** i.e., likely

97. **bawdry:** immorality

99–105. **O sweet Oliver . . . with thee:** These two ballad stanzas may be parts of the same ballad, or they may come from separate ballads. The sixteenth-century music to "O sweet Oliver" has been found, but not the lyrics. **brave:** worthy, excellent, handsome **Wind:** go

TOUCHSTONE Good even, good Monsieur What-you-call-'t. How do you, sir? You are very well met. God 'ild you for your last company. I am very glad to see 75 you. Even a toy in hand here, sir. Nay, pray be covered.

JAQUES Will you be married, motley?

TOUCHSTONE As the ox hath his bow, sir, the horse his curb, and the falcon her bells, so man hath his 80 desires; and as pigeons bill, so wedlock would be nibbling.

JAQUES And will you, being a man of your breeding, be married under a bush like a beggar? Get you to church, and have a good priest that can tell you 85 what marriage is. This fellow will but join you together as they join wainscot. Then one of you will prove a shrunk panel and, like green timber, warp, warp.

TOUCHSTONE I am not in the mind but I were better to 90 be married of him than of another, for he is not like to marry me well, and not being well married, it will be a good excuse for me hereafter to leave my wife.

JAQUES Go thou with me, and let me counsel thee. 95
⌜TOUCHSTONE⌝ Come, sweet Audrey. We must be married, or we must live in bawdry.—Farewell, good Master Oliver, not
      O sweet Oliver,
      O brave Oliver, 100
    Leave me not behind thee,
But
      Wind away,
      Begone, I say,
    I will not to wedding with thee. 105
      ⌜*Audrey, Touchstone, and Jaques exit.*⌝

OLIVER MARTEXT 'Tis no matter. Ne'er a fantastical knave of them all shall flout me out of my calling.
      ⌜*He exits.*⌝

3.4 Corin invites "Ganymede" and "Aliena" to observe the lovelorn Silvius as Silvius courts the disdainful Phoebe.

---

8. **Judas's:** Judas Iscariot was the apostle in the New Testament who betrayed Jesus, and thus the name **Judas** became synonymous with treachery. (The dialogue in lines 7–8 about Orlando's **hair** may allude to legends about Judas's red hair, called by the French "dissembling hair.")

9. **kisses are Judas's own children:** To identify Jesus to his enemies, Judas kissed him. (See Matthew 26.48–49.)

11. **Your chestnut:** i.e., chestnut

14. **holy bread:** bread consecrated by the priest (communion wafers), or, less likely, bread blessed by the priest and distributed to those who did not receive communion

15. **cast:** cast-off, discarded; **of:** from, or, belonging to; **Diana:** goddess of chastity

22. **pickpurse:** pickpocket

24. **concave:** hollow; **covered goblet:** perhaps, a goblet covered because it is empty; or, perhaps, a goblet with a rounded, ornamental cover

30–31. **They . . . reckonings:** i.e., a barman **(tapster)** confirms (attests to) the accuracy of excessive tavern bills **(false reckonings);** a lover confirms (encourages) **false** expectations (or **reckonings)**

31–32. **attends . . . on:** serves as an attendant to

Scene 4

Enter Rosalind, ⌐dressed as Ganymede,⌐ and Celia,
⌐dressed as Aliena.⌐

ROSALIND Never talk to me. I will weep.

CELIA Do, I prithee, but yet have the grace to consider
that tears do not become a man.

ROSALIND But have I not cause to weep?

CELIA As good cause as one would desire. Therefore   5
weep.

ROSALIND His very hair is of the dissembling color.

CELIA Something browner than Judas's. Marry, his
kisses are Judas's own children.

ROSALIND I' faith, his hair is of a good color.   10

CELIA An excellent color. Your chestnut was ever the
only color.

ROSALIND And his kissing is as full of sanctity as the
touch of holy bread.

CELIA He hath bought a pair of cast lips of Diana. A   15
nun of winter's sisterhood kisses not more reli-
giously. The very ice of chastity is in them.

ROSALIND But why did he swear he would come this
morning, and comes not?

CELIA Nay, certainly, there is no truth in him.   20

ROSALIND Do you think so?

CELIA Yes, I think he is not a pickpurse nor a horse-
stealer, but for his verity in love, I do think him as
concave as a covered goblet or a worm-eaten nut.

ROSALIND Not true in love?   25

CELIA Yes, when he is in, but I think he is not in.

ROSALIND You have heard him swear downright he
was.

CELIA "Was" is not "is." Besides, the oath of ⌐a⌐ lover is
no stronger than the word of a tapster. They are   30
both the confirmer of false reckonings. He attends
here in the forest on the Duke your father.

34. **question:** conversation

38. **brave:** a general word of praise meaning worthy, excellent

40. **traverse, athwart:** terms from the sport of jousting that describe the unskillful or cowardly act of hitting the opponent across the chest with the lance

41. **puny:** unskilled, inferior

41–42. **spurs . . . side:** in jousting, a cowardly action that avoids meeting the opponent head-on

42. **goose:** i.e., fool

46. **complained of:** lamented

51. **pageant:** theatrical scene (here, a debate between the passions of **love** and **disdain**)

52. **pale complexion:** The lover's sighs were thought to drain blood from his heart, leaving him **pale.**

55. **mark:** watch

56. **remove:** go (to this other place)

The phoenix. (4.3.18)
From Conrad Lycosthenes, *Prodigiorum . . .* [1557].

ROSALIND I met the Duke yesterday and had much
question with him. He asked me of what parentage
I was. I told him, of as good as he. So he laughed   35
and let me go. But what talk we of fathers when
there is such a man as Orlando?
CELIA O, that's a brave man. He writes brave verses,
speaks brave words, swears brave oaths, and breaks
them bravely, quite traverse, athwart the heart of   40
his lover, as a puny tilter that spurs his horse but on
one side breaks his staff like a noble goose; but all's
brave that youth mounts and folly guides.

Enter Corin.

Who comes here?
CORIN
Mistress and master, you have oft inquired   45
After the shepherd that complained of love,
Who you saw sitting by me on the turf,
Praising the proud disdainful shepherdess
That was his mistress.
CELIA, ⌜*as Aliena*⌝ Well, and what of him?   50
CORIN
If you will see a pageant truly played
Between the pale complexion of true love
And the red glow of scorn and proud disdain,
Go hence a little, and I shall conduct you
If you will mark it.   55
ROSALIND, ⌜*aside to Celia*⌝ O come, let us remove.
The sight of lovers feedeth those in love.
⌜*As Ganymede, to Corin.*⌝ Bring us to this sight, and
you shall say
I'll prove a busy actor in their play.   60
                                            They exit.

3.5 "Ganymede" intervenes to try to help Silvius prevail over Phoebe and win her love. Instead, Phoebe falls in love with "Ganymede."

———————————

3. **bitterness:** hostility, acrimony
6. **Falls not the axe:** i.e., does not let the ax fall
12. **pretty:** i.e., proper, ingenious; **sure:** i.e., surely
18. **counterfeit:** pretend
22. **but:** merely
23. **Lean:** i.e., if you merely lean
24. **cicatrice:** scarlike mark or impression; **capable:** perhaps, perceptible; **impressure:** impression
27. **Nor I am sure:** i.e., I am sure

An executioner. (3.5.3–7)
From [Richard Verstegen,] *Theatre des cruautez des hereticques . . .* (1607).

Scene 5
Enter Silvius and Phoebe.

SILVIUS
  Sweet Phoebe, do not scorn me. Do not, Phoebe.
  Say that you love me not, but say not so
  In bitterness. The common executioner,
  Whose heart th' accustomed sight of death makes
    hard,   5
  Falls not the axe upon the humbled neck
  But first begs pardon. Will you sterner be
  Than he that dies and lives by bloody drops?

Enter, ⌐unobserved,⌐ Rosalind ⌐as Ganymede,⌐ Celia ⌐as
  Aliena,⌐ and Corin.

PHOEBE
  I would not be thy executioner.
  I fly thee, for I would not injure thee.   10
  Thou tell'st me there is murder in mine eye.
  'Tis pretty, sure, and very probable
  That eyes, that are the frail'st and softest things,
  Who shut their coward gates on atomies,
  Should be called tyrants, butchers, murderers.   15
  Now I do frown on thee with all my heart,
  And if mine eyes can wound, now let them kill thee.
  Now counterfeit to swoon, why, now fall down;
  Or if thou canst not, O, for shame, for shame,
  Lie not, to say mine eyes are murderers.   20
  Now show the wound mine eye hath made in thee.
  Scratch thee but with a pin, and there remains
  Some scar of it. Lean upon a rush,
  The cicatrice and capable impressure
  Thy palm some moment keeps. But now mine eyes,   25
  Which I have darted at thee, hurt thee not;
  Nor I am sure there is no force in eyes
  That can do hurt.

31. **fancy:** i.e., desire, love

33. **love's keen arrows:** Cupid, the god of love, is traditionally represented as causing a person to fall in love by shooting him or her with an arrow. (See page 150.)

40. **and all at once:** i.e., all at the same time

41. **What though:** i.e., even though

47–48. **ordinary / Of nature's sale-work:** i.e., the ordinary products made by nature for general sale

48. **'Od's my little life:** an exclamation of surprise **'Od's:** i.e., God save

49. **tangle my eyes:** an allusion to the belief that beams come from eyes, and that falling in love involves the entangling of the lovers' eye-beams

51. **inky, black:** By Elizabethan standards of beauty, only fair hair and fair skin are beautiful.

52. **bugle:** i.e., black and shiny (Bugles were glass beads, usually black.); **cheek of cream:** i.e., cream-colored (yellowish-white) cheek

53. **entame:** tame, subdue

55. **south:** i.e., south wind

56. **properer:** i.e., more proper, more handsome or fine

58. **ill-favored:** i.e., ugly

59. **glass:** looking-glass, mirror

60. **out of you:** i.e., from her image as reflected in you; **proper:** i.e., beautiful

61. **lineaments:** features; **show her:** i.e., reveal her to be, display her

SILVIUS   O dear Phoebe,
  If ever—as that ever may be near—   30
  You meet in some fresh cheek the power of fancy,
  Then shall you know the wounds invisible
  That love's keen arrows make.
PHOEBE   But till that time
  Come not thou near me. And when that time   35
    comes,
  Afflict me with thy mocks, pity me not,
  As till that time I shall not pity thee.
ROSALIND, ⌈*as Ganymede, coming forward*⌉
  And why, I pray you? Who might be your mother,
  That you insult, exult, and all at once,   40
  Over the wretched? What though you have no
    beauty—
  As, by my faith, I see no more in you
  Than without candle may go dark to bed—
  Must you be therefore proud and pitiless?   45
  Why, what means this? Why do you look on me?
  I see no more in you than in the ordinary
  Of nature's sale-work.—'Od's my little life,
  I think she means to tangle my eyes, too.—
  No, faith, proud mistress, hope not after it.   50
  'Tis not your inky brows, your black silk hair,
  Your bugle eyeballs, nor your cheek of cream
  That can entame my spirits to your worship.—
  You foolish shepherd, wherefore do you follow her,
  Like foggy south puffing with wind and rain?   55
  You are a thousand times a properer man
  Than she a woman. 'Tis such fools as you
  That makes the world full of ill-favored children.
  'Tis not her glass but you that flatters her,
  And out of you she sees herself more proper   60
  Than any of her lineaments can show her.—
  But, mistress, know yourself. Down on your knees
  And thank heaven, fasting, for a good man's love,

66. Cry the man mercy: i.e., beg the man's pardon, ask his forgiveness

67. Foul is most foul, being foul to be a scoffer: wordplay on **foul** as (1) ugly and (2) wicked (The general sense is that ugliness compounded with mockery is especially ugly and wicked.)

68. take her to thee: i.e., take charge, or take care, of her

69. a year together: i.e., for a full year without intermission

74. sauce her: i.e., rebuke her stingingly

78. in wine: i.e., when drunk

79–80. If . . . hard by: Editors hazard a variety of guesses—none very persuasive—as to why Rosalind gives this information to Phoebe. **olives:** i.e., olive trees; **hard by:** i.e., nearby

81. ply her hard: i.e., keep urging her

83. could see: i.e., could look at you

84. abused in sight: i.e., deceived in what he sees

86–87. Dead shepherd . . . sight: The quotation (line 87) is from Christopher Marlowe's *Hero and Leander*. Marlowe, who had died in 1593, is called **shepherd** perhaps because of his famous poem, "The passionate shepherd to his love," or because, in the tradition of pastoral poetry, poets often referred to themselves and fellow-poets as shepherds.

91. gentle: a complimentary epithet meaning "kind, courteous"

92. Wherever sorrow is, relief would be: i.e., one who feels sorry for another would want to relieve his suffering

For I must tell you friendly in your ear,
Sell when you can; you are not for all markets.   65
Cry the man mercy, love him, take his offer.
Foul is most foul, being foul to be a scoffer.—
So take her to thee, shepherd. Fare you well.

PHOEBE
Sweet youth, I pray you chide a year together.
I had rather hear you chide than this man woo.   70

ROSALIND, ⸢*as Ganymede*⸣   He's fall'n in love with your
foulness. (⸢*To Silvius.*⸣) And she'll fall in love with
my anger. If it be so, as fast as she answers thee with
frowning looks, I'll sauce her with bitter words. (⸢*To
Phoebe.*⸣) Why look you so upon me?   75

PHOEBE   For no ill will I bear you.

ROSALIND, ⸢*as Ganymede*⸣
I pray you, do not fall in love with me,
For I am falser than vows made in wine.
Besides, I like you not. If you will know my house,
'Tis at the tuft of olives, here hard by.—   80
Will you go, sister?—Shepherd, ply her hard.—
Come, sister.—Shepherdess, look on him better,
And be not proud. Though all the world could see,
None could be so abused in sight as he.—
Come, to our flock.   85

                    She exits, ⸢*with Celia and Corin.*⸣

PHOEBE, ⸢*aside*⸣
Dead shepherd, now I find thy saw of might:
"Who ever loved that loved not at first sight?"

SILVIUS
Sweet Phoebe—

PHOEBE   Ha, what sayst thou, Silvius?

SILVIUS   Sweet Phoebe, pity me.   90

PHOEBE
Why, I am sorry for thee, gentle Silvius.

SILVIUS
Wherever sorrow is, relief would be.

95. **extermined:** exterminated

100. **yet it is not:** i.e., the time has not yet come

102. **erst:** previously

107. **I in such a poverty of grace:** i.e., I am so poor in gifts from fortune or fate

109. **glean the broken ears:** This image of a poor person gathering ears of grain left behind in the fields after the harvest appears twice in the Bible. (See longer note, pages 216–17.) In line 111, Phoebe's **smile** becomes the **broken** (i.e., **scattered**) **ears** of grain that poor Silvius will live on.

114. **bounds:** lands

115. **carlot:** churl, peasant

120. **pretty:** fine, gallant

"We are still handling our ewes, and their fells . . . are greasy." (3.2.52–53)
From Pietro de Crescenzi, [Ruralia commoda, 1561].

If you do sorrow at my grief in love,
By giving love your sorrow and my grief
Were both extermined. 95

PHOEBE
Thou hast my love. Is not that neighborly?

SILVIUS
I would have you.

PHOEBE   Why, that were covetousness.
Silvius, the time was that I hated thee;
And yet it is not that I bear thee love, 100
But since that thou canst talk of love so well,
Thy company, which erst was irksome to me,
I will endure, and I'll employ thee too.
But do not look for further recompense
Than thine own gladness that thou art employed. 105

SILVIUS
So holy and so perfect is my love,
And I in such a poverty of grace,
That I shall think it a most plenteous crop
To glean the broken ears after the man
That the main harvest reaps. Loose now and then 110
A scattered smile, and that I'll live upon.

PHOEBE
Know'st thou the youth that spoke to me erewhile?

SILVIUS
Not very well, but I have met him oft,
And he hath bought the cottage and the bounds
That the old carlot once was master of. 115

PHOEBE
Think not I love him, though I ask for him.
'Tis but a peevish boy—yet he talks well—
But what care I for words? Yet words do well
When he that speaks them pleases those that hear.
It is a pretty youth—not very pretty— 120
But sure he's proud—and yet his pride becomes
  him.

132. **mingled damask:** probably an allusion to the damask rose, in which, in some varieties, red and white are **mingled** to produce pale red or pink

133. **marked:** observed

135. **In parcels:** i.e., in detail

139. **what had he to do:** i.e., what business did he have

141. **I am remembered:** i.e., that I remember; **scorned at:** i.e., mocked, jeered at

142. **answered not again:** i.e., did not answer back

143. **that's all one:** i.e., it doesn't matter; **omittance is no quittance:** i.e., omissions can yet be remedied (The proverb means, literally, that omitting to demand the repayment of a debt does not cancel the debt.)

147. **straight:** i.e., straightway, immediately

148. **The matter's in:** i.e., what I want to say is in

149. **passing short:** very curt or abrupt

He'll make a proper man. The best thing in him
Is his complexion; and faster than his tongue
Did make offense, his eye did heal it up.   125
He is not very tall—yet for his years he's tall.
His leg is but so-so—and yet 'tis well.
There was a pretty redness in his lip,
A little riper and more lusty red
Than that mixed in his cheek: 'twas just the   130
    difference
Betwixt the constant red and mingled damask.
There be some women, Silvius, had they marked
    him
In parcels as I did, would have gone near   135
To fall in love with him; but for my part
I love him not nor hate him not; and yet
⌜I⌝ have more cause to hate him than to love him.
For what had he to do to chide at me?
He said mine eyes were black and my hair black,   140
And now I am remembered, scorned at me.
I marvel why I answered not again.
But that's all one: omittance is no quittance.
I'll write to him a very taunting letter,
And thou shalt bear it. Wilt thou, Silvius?   145

SILVIUS
Phoebe, with all my heart.

PHOEBE   I'll write it straight.
The matter's in my head and in my heart.
I will be bitter with him and passing short.
Go with me, Silvius.   150

They exit.

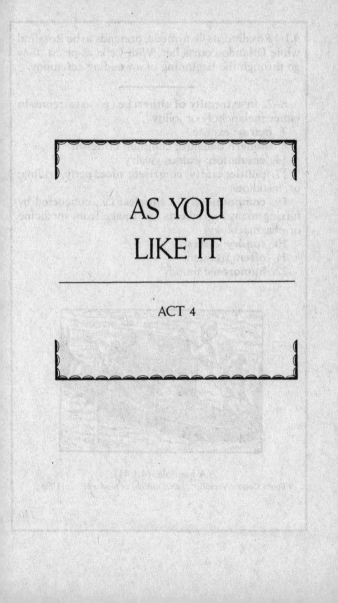

AS YOU
LIKE IT

ACT 4

4.1 Rosalind, as Ganymede, pretends to be Rosalind while Orlando courts her. With Celia as priest, they go through the beginning of a wedding ceremony.

6–7. **in extremity of either:** i.e., go to extremes in either melancholy or jollity

7. **betray:** expose

8. **modern censure:** common criticism

14. **emulation:** jealous rivalry

17. **politic:** crafty, contrived; **nice:** petty, trifling; or, fastidious

19. **compounded . . . simples:** i.e., concocted by mixing many ingredients (an image from medicine or pharmacology)

20. **sundry:** diverse

21. **often:** frequent

22. **humorous:** moody

A gondola. (4.1.41)
From Cesare Vecellio, *Habiti antichi et moderni* . . . [1598].

have great reason to be sad. I fear you have sold
your own lands to see other men's. Then to have   25
seen much and to have nothing is to have rich eyes
and poor hands.

JAQUES   Yes, I have gained my experience.

ROSALIND, ⌜*as Ganymede*⌝ And your experience makes
you sad. I had rather have a fool to make me merry   30
than experience to make me sad—and to travel for
it too.

Enter Orlando.

ORLANDO
Good day and happiness, dear Rosalind.

JAQUES   Nay then, God be wi' you, an you talk in blank
verse.   35

ROSALIND, ⌜*as Ganymede*⌝ Farewell, Monsieur Travel-
ler. Look you lisp and wear strange suits, disable all
the benefits of your own country, be out of love with
your nativity, and almost chide God for making you
that countenance you are, or I will scarce think you   40
have swam in a gondola.
⌜*Jaques exits.*⌝
Why, how now, Orlando, where have you been all
this while? You a lover? An you serve me such
another trick, never come in my sight more.

ORLANDO   My fair Rosalind, I come within an hour of   45
my promise.

ROSALIND, ⌜*as Ganymede*⌝ Break an hour's promise in
love? He that will divide a minute into a thousand
parts and break but a part of the thousand part of a
minute in the affairs of love, it may be said of him   50
that Cupid hath clapped him o' th' shoulder, but I'll
warrant him heart-whole.

ORLANDO   Pardon me, dear Rosalind.

ROSALIND, ⌜*as Ganymede*⌝ Nay, an you be so tardy,

55. **as lief:** i.e., just as soon; **of:** i.e., by

60. **jointure:** property to be used jointly by husband and wife

63. **horns:** See picture, page 142, and longer note to **horn-beasts,** 3.3.49.

64. **fain:** obliged; **beholding:** beholden, indebted

65. **prevents:** forestalls

66. **slander:** disgrace

71. **leer:** countenance, appearance

73. **like:** i.e., likely

77. **you were better:** i.e., you had better

78. **gravelled:** i.e., stuck, embarrassed

79. **matter:** i.e., something to say

80. **out:** at a loss from failure of memory, speechless

81. **warn:** protect, defend

81–82. **cleanliest shift:** cleverest device (The humor of Rosalind's speech is heightened by the fact that **matter** could mean not only "something to say" but also "fluids of the body"—i.e., something to spit.)

88. **that should you:** i.e., you would be (**out,** speechless)

89. **honesty:** While the word **honesty,** when applied to women, always meant "chastity," here Rosalind is speaking as Ganymede, and the word seems to mean "straightforwardness.")

90. **ranker:** greater, more abundant

come no more in my sight. I had as lief be wooed of   55
a snail.

ORLANDO Of a snail?

ROSALIND, ⌜*as Ganymede*⌝ Ay, of a snail, for though he
comes slowly, he carries his house on his head—a
better jointure, I think, than you make a woman.   60
Besides, he brings his destiny with him.

ORLANDO What's that?

ROSALIND, ⌜*as Ganymede*⌝ Why, horns, which such as
you are fain to be beholding to your wives for. But
he comes armed in his fortune and prevents the   65
slander of his wife.

ORLANDO Virtue is no hornmaker, and my Rosalind is
virtuous.

ROSALIND, ⌜*as Ganymede*⌝ And I am your Rosalind.

CELIA, ⌜*as Aliena*⌝ It pleases him to call you so, but he   70
hath a Rosalind of a better leer than you.

ROSALIND, ⌜*as Ganymede, to Orlando*⌝ Come, woo me,
woo me, for now I am in a holiday humor, and like
enough to consent. What would you say to me now
an I were your very, very Rosalind?   75

ORLANDO I would kiss before I spoke.

ROSALIND, ⌜*as Ganymede*⌝ Nay, you were better speak
first, and when you were gravelled for lack of
matter, you might take occasion to kiss. Very good
orators, when they are out, they will spit; and for   80
lovers lacking—God warn us—matter, the cleanliest shift is to kiss.

ORLANDO How if the kiss be denied?

ROSALIND, ⌜*as Ganymede*⌝ Then she puts you to en-
treaty, and there begins new matter.   85

ORLANDO Who could be out, being before his beloved
mistress?

ROSALIND, ⌜*as Ganymede*⌝ Marry, that should you if I
were your mistress, or I should think my honesty
ranker than my wit.   90

91. **of my suit:** i.e., out of my courtship or wooing

96. **in her person:** as her representative; or, assuming her character

98. **in mine own person:** in person, through my own actions (Rosalind's answer plays with another meaning of the phrase, i.e., "representing myself.")

99. **by attorney:** i.e., by proxy

100. **six thousand years old:** When the history of the world was calculated using the generations listed in the Bible, the date of creation was set at 4004 B.C.

102. **videlicet:** that is to say; **Troilus:** a Trojan prince killed by Achilles after being betrayed by his lover Cressida

105. **Leander:** mythological lover of **Hero of Sestos,** drowned when swimming the **Hellespont** to be with her (See page 168.)

111. **found:** here used in a legal sense, as if the **chroniclers** were on a jury that convicted Hero of Leander's death

114. **right:** true, real

118. **coming-on:** cheerfully obliging

ORLANDO What, of my suit?

ROSALIND, ⌈*as Ganymede*⌉ Not out of your apparel, and
yet out of your suit. Am not I your Rosalind?

ORLANDO I take some joy to say you are because I
would be talking of her.   95

ROSALIND, ⌈*as Ganymede*⌉ Well, in her person I say I
will not have you.

ORLANDO Then, in mine own person I die.

ROSALIND, ⌈*as Ganymede*⌉ No, faith, die by attorney.
The poor world is almost six thousand years old, 100
and in all this time there was not any man died in
his own person, *videlicet*, in a love cause. Troilus
had his brains dashed out with a Grecian club, yet
he did what he could to die before, and he is one of
the patterns of love. Leander, he would have lived 105
many a fair year though Hero had turned nun, if it
had not been for a hot midsummer night, for, good
youth, he went but forth to wash him in the Hellespont and, being taken with the cramp, was
drowned; and the foolish chroniclers of that age 110
found it was Hero of Sestos. But these are all lies.
Men have died from time to time, and worms have
eaten them, but not for love.

ORLANDO I would not have my right Rosalind of this
mind, for I protest her frown might kill me.   115

ROSALIND, ⌈*as Ganymede*⌉ By this hand, it will not kill a
fly. But come; now I will be your Rosalind in a more
coming-on disposition, and ask me what you will, I
will grant it.

ORLANDO Then love me, Rosalind.   120

ROSALIND, ⌈*as Ganymede*⌉ Yes, faith, will I, Fridays and
Saturdays and all.

ORLANDO And wilt thou have me?

ROSALIND, ⌈*as Ganymede*⌉ Ay, and twenty such.

ORLANDO What sayest thou?   125

136. **Go to:** an expression of impatience

145. **commission:** authority, license (See longer note, page 217.)

146. **goes before:** anticipates, acts in advance of (She has given the answer before **"the priest"** put the question.)

158. **Barbary cock-pigeon:** The Barbary pigeon was a variety introduced from the Barbary States in North Africa. The **cock-pigeon** was known for its jealousy, especially as contrasted with the mild-mannered **hen.**

159. **against:** just before; **newfangled:** fond of novelty, easily carried away by anything new

161. **Diana in the fountain:** perhaps one of London's fountains that featured a statue of **Diana** (one was erected in 1596); or, perhaps, an allusion to a popular romance, Montemayor's *Diana,* whose heroine weeps into a fountain

A dog-faced baboon. (2.5.25)
From Edward Topsell, *The historie of foure-footed beastes . . .* (1607).

ROSALIND, ⌜*as Ganymede*⌝ Are you not good?

ORLANDO I hope so.

ROSALIND, ⌜*as Ganymede*⌝ Why then, can one desire
too much of a good thing?—Come, sister, you shall
be the priest and marry us.—Give me your hand,   130
Orlando.—What do you say, sister?

ORLANDO, ⌜*to Celia*⌝ Pray thee marry us.

CELIA, ⌜*as Aliena*⌝ I cannot say the words.

ROSALIND, ⌜*as Ganymede*⌝ You must begin "Will you,
Orlando—"   135

CELIA, ⌜*as Aliena*⌝ Go to.—Will you, Orlando, have to
wife this Rosalind?

ORLANDO I will.

ROSALIND, ⌜*as Ganymede*⌝ Ay, but when?

ORLANDO Why now, as fast as she can marry us.   140

ROSALIND, ⌜*as Ganymede*⌝ Then you must say "I take
thee, Rosalind, for wife."

ORLANDO I take thee, Rosalind, for wife.

ROSALIND, ⌜*as Ganymede*⌝ I might ask you for your
commission, but I do take thee, Orlando, for my   145
husband. There's a girl goes before the priest, and
certainly a woman's thought runs before her actions.

ORLANDO So do all thoughts. They are winged.

ROSALIND, ⌜*as Ganymede*⌝ Now tell me how long you   150
would have her after you have possessed her?

ORLANDO Forever and a day.

ROSALIND, ⌜*as Ganymede*⌝ Say "a day" without the
"ever." No, no, Orlando, men are April when they
woo, December when they wed. Maids are May   155
when they are maids, but the sky changes when
they are wives. I will be more jealous of thee than a
Barbary cock-pigeon over his hen, more clamorous
than a parrot against rain, more newfangled than
an ape, more giddy in my desires than a monkey. I 160
will weep for nothing, like Diana in the fountain,

170. **Make:** i.e., make fast, shut

171. **out:** i.e., fly out, escape

173. **Stop:** i.e., close

176. **Wit, whither wilt:** See note to 1.2.56. (Rosalind responds as if the question had its literal meaning of "wit, where do you intend [to go]?")

178. **check for it:** i.e., rebuke for your **wife's wit**

184–5. **her husband's occasion:** i.e., the result of her husband's actions

185. **nurse:** suckle; or, take care of

186. **breed:** bring it up, educate it

189. **lack:** do without

196. **'Tis but one:** i.e., it's only one more (unhappy woman); **cast away:** rejected, abandoned

Blind Cupid. (4.1.226)
From Francesco Petrarca, *Opera . . .* [1508].

and I will do that when you are disposed to be
merry. I will laugh like a hyena, and that when thou
art inclined to sleep.

ORLANDO　But will my Rosalind do so?　　　　　　165

ROSALIND, ⌈*as Ganymede*⌉　By my life, she will do as I
do.

ORLANDO　O, but she is wise.

ROSALIND, ⌈*as Ganymede*⌉　Or else she could not have
the wit to do this. The wiser, the waywarder. Make　170
the doors upon a woman's wit, and it will out at the
casement. Shut that, and 'twill out at the keyhole.
Stop that, 'twill fly with the smoke out at the
chimney.

ORLANDO　A man that had a wife with such a wit, he　175
might say "Wit, whither wilt?"

ROSALIND, ⌈*as Ganymede*⌉　Nay, you might keep that
check for it till you met your wife's wit going to
your neighbor's bed.

ORLANDO　And what wit could wit have to excuse that?　180

ROSALIND, ⌈*as Ganymede*⌉　Marry, to say she came to
seek you there. You shall never take her without her
answer unless you take her without her tongue. O,
that woman that cannot make her fault her husband's occasion, let her never nurse her child　185
herself, for she will breed it like a fool.

ORLANDO　For these two hours, Rosalind, I will leave
thee.

ROSALIND, ⌈*as Ganymede*⌉　Alas, dear love, I cannot lack
thee two hours.　　　　　　190

ORLANDO　I must attend the Duke at dinner. By two
o'clock I will be with thee again.

ROSALIND, ⌈*as Ganymede*⌉　Ay, go your ways, go your
ways. I knew what you would prove. My friends told
me as much, and I thought no less. That flattering　195
tongue of yours won me. 'Tis but one cast away, and
so, come, death. Two o'clock is your hour?

199–200. **By . . . mend me:** mild oaths

200. **pretty:** proper, fine

201. **dangerous:** i.e., profane or blasphemous

202–3. **behind your hour:** i.e., later than the hour (you promised)

203–4. **break-promise:** promise-breaker

206. **gross band:** entire company

209. **religion:** fidelity

212. **let time try:** wordplay on the proverb "Time tries (i.e., tests) all things," with **try** having here the second meaning of "bring to trial, judge"

214. **simply:** absolutely, completely; **misused our sex:** i.e., reviled or misrepresented females

214–15. **love-prate:** love-talk

215. **doublet and hose:** See note to 2.4.6.

216–17. **what the bird hath done to her own nest:** i.e., that (in attacking females) you are like the bird that fouls its own nest (Proverbial: "It is a foul bird that defiles his own nest.")

219. **fathom:** i.e., fathoms

220. **sounded:** measured (as with a fathom-line)

221. **Bay of Portugal:** i.e., the (very deep) sea off the coast of Portugal

222. **that:** i.e., so that

224. **bastard of Venus:** i.e., Cupid, son of **Venus**, perhaps fathered by one of her lovers (See page 160.)

225. **spleen:** impulsiveness, caprice

226. **blind:** Cupid is often pictured as a **blind** (or blindfolded) **boy** (See page 150.); **abuses:** deceives, misuses

230. **shadow:** i.e., place in the shade

ORLANDO Ay, sweet Rosalind.

ROSALIND, ⌈*as Ganymede*⌉ By my troth, and in good
earnest, and so God mend me, and by all pretty   200
oaths that are not dangerous, if you break one jot of
your promise or come one minute behind your
hour, I will think you the most pathetical break-
promise, and the most hollow lover, and the most
unworthy of her you call Rosalind that may be   205
chosen out of the gross band of the unfaithful.
Therefore beware my censure, and keep your
promise.

ORLANDO With no less religion than if thou wert indeed my Rosalind. So, adieu.   210

ROSALIND, ⌈*as Ganymede*⌉ Well, time is the old justice
that examines all such offenders, and let time try.
Adieu.
⌈*Orlando*⌉ *exits.*

CELIA You have simply misused our sex in your love-
prate. We must have your doublet and hose plucked   215
over your head and show the world what the bird
hath done to her own nest.

ROSALIND O coz, coz, coz, my pretty little coz, that thou
didst know how many fathom deep I am in love. But
it cannot be sounded; my affection hath an   220
unknown bottom, like the Bay of Portugal.

CELIA Or rather bottomless, that as fast as you pour
affection in, ⌈it⌉ runs out.

ROSALIND No, that same wicked bastard of Venus, that
was begot of thought, conceived of spleen, and born   225
of madness, that blind rascally boy that abuses
everyone's eyes because his own are out, let him be
judge how deep I am in love. I'll tell thee, Aliena, I
cannot be out of the sight of Orlando. I'll go find a
shadow and sigh till he come.   230

CELIA And I'll sleep.

They exit.

4.2 Duke Senior's courtiers celebrate their having killed a deer.

---

4. **like a Roman conqueror:** See longer note, page 217, and illustration, page 158.

5. **horns:** an allusion to the cuckold's horns (See longer note to **horn-beasts,** 3.3.49.); **branch:** perhaps an allusion to victory wreaths made of branches of laurel (see page 158), with an added allusion to the branches of antlers of the deer

9. **so:** i.e., so long as, if

13 SD. **The rest shall bear this burden:** See longer note, pages 217–18.

14. **Take thou no scorn:** i.e., don't be ashamed

15. **crest:** (1) heraldic device; (2) projection from the head

18. **lusty:** massive, flourishing (with wordplay on "lustful")

4.3 Phoebe sends "Ganymede" a letter offering herself in marriage. As Rosalind and Celia wait for Orlando, they learn that he is late for his appointment with "Ganymede" because he was wounded saving his brother Oliver from attack by a lion.

---

1. **How say you:** i.e., what do you say

2. **much Orlando:** said ironically (i.e., no Orlando)

4–5. **ta'en his bow . . . sleep:** proverbial

Scene 2
Enter Jaques and Lords, ⌜like⌝ foresters.

JAQUES Which is he that killed the deer?

⌜FIRST⌝ LORD Sir, it was I.

JAQUES, ⌜*to the other Lords*⌝ Let's present him to the
   Duke like a Roman conqueror. And it would do well
   to set the deer's horns upon his head for a branch of   5
   victory.—Have you no song, forester, for this purpose?

⌜SECOND⌝ LORD Yes, sir.

JAQUES Sing it. 'Tis no matter how it be in tune, so it
   make noise enough.   10

Music. Song.

⌜SECOND LORD *sings*⌝

   What shall he have that killed the deer?
   His leather skin and horns to wear.
      Then sing him home.

(The rest shall bear this burden:)

   Take thou no scorn to wear the horn.
   It was a crest ere thou wast born.   15
      Thy father's father wore it,
      And thy father bore it.
   The horn, the horn, the lusty horn
   Is not a thing to laugh to scorn.

                                        They exit.

Scene 3
Enter Rosalind ⌜dressed as Ganymede⌝ and Celia
         ⌜dressed as Aliena.⌝

ROSALIND How say you now? Is it not past two o'clock?
   And here much Orlando.

CELIA I warrant you, with pure love and troubled brain
   he hath ta'en his bow and arrows and is gone forth
   to sleep.   5

11. **writing of:** i.e., writing

13. **but as:** i.e., but

14. **startle:** start, be alarmed

15. **play the swaggerer:** i.e., become hostile **play:** behave like **swaggerer:** fighter, quarreler (See longer note to 5.4.49, pages 219–20.); **Bear this, bear all:** proverbial

16. **fair:** attractive, good-looking

17. **and that:** i.e., and says that

18. **Were man:** i.e., if men were; **as rare as phoenix:** proverbial (The **phoenix** was a mythical bird of which there was only one living at any given time. It reproduced itself by reincarnation after burning itself to ashes. See illustration, page 126.); **'Od's my will:** i.e., an expression of impatience **'Od's:** i.e., God save

21. **device:** devising, invention

27. **hand:** here, a reference to Phoebe's actual hand, though the context leads one to expect the word to mean "handwriting," as it does in line 32

28. **freestone-colored:** i.e., the color of sandstone or limestone

30. **huswife's:** i.e., housewife's; or, hussy's (The forms *huswife*, *housewife*, and *hussy* were interchangeable but unstable in the sixteenth century as *housewife* and *hussy* began to move toward their modern, distinct meanings and *huswife* began to merge with *hussy* and then to disappear.)

Enter Silvius.

Look who comes here.

SILVIUS, ⌈*to Rosalind*⌉
My errand is to you, fair youth.
My gentle Phoebe did bid me give you this.
⌈*He gives Rosalind a paper.*⌉
I know not the contents, but as I guess
By the stern brow and waspish action   10
Which she did use as she was writing of it,
It bears an angry tenor. Pardon me.
I am but as a guiltless messenger.
⌈*Rosalind reads the letter.*⌉

ROSALIND, ⌈*as Ganymede*⌉
Patience herself would startle at this letter
And play the swaggerer. Bear this, bear all.   15
She says I am not fair, that I lack manners.
She calls me proud, and that she could not love me
Were man as rare as phoenix. 'Od's my will,
Her love is not the hare that I do hunt.
Why writes she so to me? Well, shepherd, well,   20
This is a letter of your own device.

SILVIUS
No, I protest. I know not the contents.
Phoebe did write it.

ROSALIND, ⌈*as Ganymede*⌉ Come, come, you are a
    fool,   25
And turned into the extremity of love.
I saw her hand. She has a leathern hand,
A freestone-colored hand. I verily did think
That her old gloves were on, but 'twas her hands.
She has a huswife's hand—but that's no matter.   30
I say she never did invent this letter.
This is a man's invention, and his hand.

SILVIUS Sure it is hers.

ROSALIND, ⌈*as Ganymede*⌉
Why, 'tis a boisterous and a cruel style,

37. **giant-rude:** i.e., extremely rude

38. **Ethiop:** i.e., very black (an allusion to black-skinned Africans), with wordplay on "black" as (1) deadly in their **effect,** and (2) the color of the ink, which gives the **words** their look or **countenance**

43. **turned:** transformed

47. **apart:** i.e., aside (in order to become a mortal)

51. **vengeance:** harm

53. **eyne:** eyes

56. **in mild aspect:** i.e., if they looked on me in kindness (**Aspect** is an astrological term, referring to a planet's position and direction as it looks favorably or unfavorably upon the earth. Usually, as he does here, Shakespeare accents the word on the second syllable.)

58. **move:** i.e., affect me

61. **by him seal up thy mind:** perhaps, send by him an answer in a sealed letter

62. **kind:** nature

64. **make:** perhaps, do

65. **deny:** refuse

A laurel wreath of victory. (4.2.3–6)
From Giacomo Lauri, *Antiquae vrbis splendor . . .* (1612–1615).

158

A style for challengers. Why, she defies me   35
Like Turk to Christian. Women's gentle brain
Could not drop forth such giant-rude invention,
Such Ethiop words, blacker in their effect
Than in their countenance. Will you hear the letter?

SILVIUS
So please you, for I never heard it yet,   40
Yet heard too much of Phoebe's cruelty.

ROSALIND, ⌜as Ganymede⌝
She Phoebes me. Mark how the tyrant writes.
(Read.)
       Art thou god to shepherd turned,
       That a maiden's heart hath burned?
  Can a woman rail thus?   45

SILVIUS Call you this railing?

ROSALIND, ⌜as Ganymede⌝
(Read.)
       Why, thy godhead laid apart,
       Warr'st thou with a woman's heart?
  Did you ever hear such railing?
       Whiles the eye of man did woo me,   50
       That could do no vengeance to me.
  Meaning me a beast.
       If the scorn of your bright eyne
       Have power to raise such love in mine,
       Alack, in me what strange effect   55
       Would they work in mild aspect?
       Whiles you chid me, I did love.
       How then might your prayers move?
       He that brings this love to thee
       Little knows this love in me,   60
       And by him seal up thy mind
       Whether that thy youth and kind
       Will the faithful offer take
       Of me, and all that I can make,
       Or else by him my love deny,   65
       And then I'll study how to die.

71. **instrument:** tool (with wordplay on "musical instrument")

73–74. **tame snake:** a term of contempt

75. **charge:** command, order

79. **Pray you:** i.e., please (tell me)

82. **neighbor:** neighboring; **bottom:** valley, dell

83. **rank of osiers:** row of willows

84. **Left:** i.e., that you pass or leave

87. **profit by a tongue:** i.e., derive benefit from speech **by:** i.e., from (as also in line 88)

90. **favor:** appearance; **bestows himself:** behaves

91. **ripe:** mature, i.e., older; **low:** i.e., short

95. **commend him:** offer his greetings

"That same wicked bastard of Venus." (4.1.224)
From Joannes ab Indagine, *The book of palmestry . . .* (1666).

SILVIUS Call you this chiding?

CELIA, ⌐*as Aliena*⌐ Alas, poor shepherd.

ROSALIND, ⌐*as Ganymede*⌐ Do you pity him? No, he
  deserves no pity.—Wilt thou love such a woman?   70
  What, to make thee an instrument and play false
  strains upon thee? Not to be endured. Well, go your
  way to her, for I see love hath made thee a tame
  snake, and say this to her: that if she love me, I
  charge her to love thee; if she will not, I will never   75
  have her unless thou entreat for her. If you be a true
  lover, hence, and not a word, for here comes more
  company.   *Silvius exits.*

Enter Oliver.

OLIVER
  Good morrow, fair ones. Pray you, if you know,
  Where in the purlieus of this forest stands   80
  A sheepcote fenced about with olive trees?

CELIA, ⌐*as Aliena*⌐
  West of this place, down in the neighbor bottom;
  The rank of osiers by the murmuring stream
  Left on your right hand brings you to the place.
  But at this hour the house doth keep itself.   85
  There's none within.

OLIVER
  If that an eye may profit by a tongue,
  Then should I know you by description—
  Such garments, and such years. "The boy is fair,
  Of female favor, and bestows himself   90
  Like a ripe sister; the woman low
  And browner than her brother." Are not you
  The owner of the house I did inquire for?

CELIA, ⌐*as Aliena*⌐
  It is no boast, being asked, to say we are.

OLIVER
  Orlando doth commend him to you both,   95

97. **napkin:** handkerchief

101. **handkercher:** a common early form for "handkerchief"

105. **pacing:** walking, striding

106. **fancy:** love, desire

108. **object:** sight, spectacle

118. **indented:** zigzagging

120. **drawn dry:** emptied (by nursing cubs)

121. **couching:** hiding

123. **royal:** an allusion to the lion as "king of beasts"

"Shall we go and kill us venison?" (2.1.21)
From [George Turberville,] *The noble art
of . . . hunting . . .* (1611).

And to that youth he calls his Rosalind
He sends this bloody napkin. Are you he?
⌜*He shows a stained handkerchief.*⌝
ROSALIND, ⌜*as Ganymede*⌝
I am. What must we understand by this?
OLIVER
Some of my shame, if you will know of me
What man I am, and how, and why, and where   100
This handkercher was stained.
CELIA, ⌜*as Aliena*⌝   I pray you tell it.
OLIVER
When last the young Orlando parted from you,
He left a promise to return again
Within an hour, and pacing through the forest,   105
Chewing the food of sweet and bitter fancy,
Lo, what befell. He threw his eye aside—
And mark what object did present itself:
Under an old oak, whose boughs were mossed with
    age   110
And high top bald with dry antiquity,
A wretched, ragged man, o'ergrown with hair,
Lay sleeping on his back. About his neck
A green and gilded snake had wreathed itself,
Who with her head, nimble in threats, approached   115
The opening of his mouth. But suddenly,
Seeing Orlando, it unlinked itself
And, with indented glides, did slip away
Into a bush, under which bush's shade
A lioness, with udders all drawn dry,   120
Lay couching, head on ground, with catlike watch
When that the sleeping man should stir—for 'tis
The royal disposition of that beast
To prey on nothing that doth seem as dead.
This seen, Orlando did approach the man   125
And found it was his brother, his elder brother.

133. **sucked:** See note to line 120, above.

136. **nature:** natural affection; **his just occasion:** i.e., his sense of being justified in abandoning his brother to the lioness's attack

138. **hurtling:** conflict, clashing

146. **for:** i.e., as for

149. **recountments:** tales (which we recounted)

152. **array:** dress, clothing; **entertainment:** reception as a guest

"Which is he that killed the deer?" (4.2.1)
From [George Turberville,] *The noble art of . . . hunting . . .* (1611).

CELIA, ⌜*as Aliena*⌝
  O, I have heard him speak of that same brother,
  And he did render him the most unnatural
  That lived amongst men.
OLIVER   And well he might so do,   130
  For well I know he was unnatural.
ROSALIND, ⌜*as Ganymede*⌝
  But to Orlando: did he leave him there,
  Food to the sucked and hungry lioness?
OLIVER
  Twice did he turn his back and purposed so,
  But kindness, nobler ever than revenge,   135
  And nature, stronger than his just occasion,
  Made him give battle to the lioness,
  Who quickly fell before him; in which hurtling,
  From miserable slumber I awaked.
CELIA, ⌜*as Aliena*⌝   Are you his brother?   140
ROSALIND, ⌜*as Ganymede*⌝   Was 't you he rescued?
CELIA, ⌜*as Aliena*⌝
  Was 't you that did so oft contrive to kill him?
OLIVER
  'Twas I, but 'tis not I. I do not shame
  To tell you what I was, since my conversion
  So sweetly tastes, being the thing I am.   145
ROSALIND, ⌜*as Ganymede*⌝
  But for the bloody napkin?
OLIVER   By and by.
  When from the first to last betwixt us two
  Tears our recountments had most kindly bathed—
  As how I came into that desert place—   150
  ⌜In⌝ brief, he led me to the gentle duke,
  Who gave me fresh array and entertainment,
  Committing me unto my brother's love;
  Who led me instantly unto his cave,
  There stripped himself, and here upon his arm   155
  The lioness had torn some flesh away,

159. Brief: i.e., in brief; **recovered:** revived

160. some small space: a brief time

176. sirrah: a term of address, usually only to a male social inferior (Here her use of the term may show Rosalind as disoriented and slipping out of her role as Ganymede. While Oliver, as a gentleman, is superior to Ganymede, he is socially inferior to Princess Rosalind.); **a body:** a person

180–81. passion of earnest: i.e., genuine emotion

183. take a good heart: proverbial for "pluck up your courage"

184. be a man: Rosalind (line 185) plays on two senses of this phrase. Oliver means "be manly, courageous."

Sad Lucretia. (3.2.150)
From Silvestro Pietrasanta, . . . *Symbola heroica* . . . (1682).

Which all this while had bled; and now he fainted,
And cried in fainting upon Rosalind.
Brief, I recovered him, bound up his wound,
And after some small space, being strong at heart,   160
He sent me hither, stranger as I am,
To tell this story, that you might excuse
His broken promise, and to give this napkin
Dyed in ⌜his⌝ blood unto the shepherd youth
That he in sport doth call his Rosalind.   165

⌜*Rosalind faints.*⌝

CELIA, ⌜*as Aliena*⌝
    Why, how now, Ganymede, sweet Ganymede?
OLIVER
    Many will swoon when they do look on blood.
CELIA, ⌜*as Aliena*⌝
    There is more in it.—Cousin Ganymede.
OLIVER Look, he recovers.
ROSALIND I would I were at home.   170
CELIA, ⌜*as Aliena*⌝ We'll lead you thither.—I pray you,
    will you take him by the arm?
OLIVER, ⌜*helping Rosalind to rise*⌝ Be of good cheer,
    youth. You a man? You lack a man's heart.
ROSALIND, ⌜*as Ganymede*⌝ I do so, I confess it. Ah,   175
    sirrah, a body would think this was well-counter-
    feited. I pray you tell your brother how well I
    counterfeited. Heigh-ho.
OLIVER This was not counterfeit. There is too great
    testimony in your complexion that it was a passion   180
    of earnest.
ROSALIND, ⌜*as Ganymede*⌝ Counterfeit, I assure you.
OLIVER Well then, take a good heart, and counterfeit to
    be a man.
ROSALIND, ⌜*as Ganymede*⌝ So I do; but i' faith, I should   185
    have been a woman by right.
CELIA, ⌜*as Aliena*⌝ Come, you look paler and paler. Pray
    you draw homewards.—Good sir, go with us.

192. commend: praise

Leander swimming the Hellespont. (4.1.105–11)
From Grammaticus Musaeus, [Hero and Leander] (1538).

168

OLIVER
  That will I, for I must bear answer back
  How you excuse my brother, Rosalind.   190
ROSALIND, ⌜*as Ganymede*⌝ I shall devise something.
  But I pray you commend my counterfeiting to him.
  Will you go?

                                          They exit.

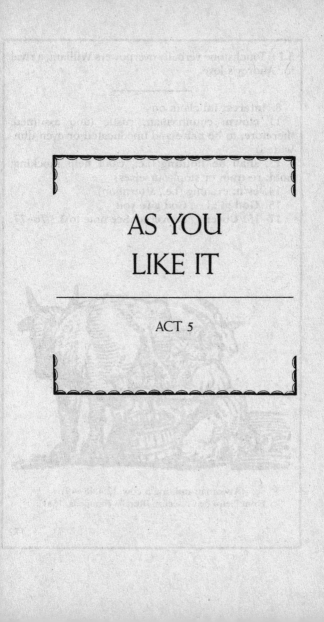

AS YOU
LIKE IT

ACT 5

5.1 Touchstone verbally overpowers William, a rival for Audrey's love.

———

8. **interest in:** claim on

11. **clown:** countryman, rustic (and assumed, therefore, to be naive and uneducated or even dim-witted)

13. **shall be flouting:** i.e., can't help mocking; **hold:** restrain or stop (ourselves)

14. **ev'n:** evening (i.e., afternoon)

15. **God gi':** i.e., God give you

17–18. **Cover . . . covered:** See note to 3.3.76–77.

A woman milking a cow. (2.4.48–49)
From Pietro de Crescenzi, [Ruralia commoda, 1561].

ACT 5

Scene 1
Enter ⌈Touchstone⌉ and Audrey.

TOUCHSTONE We shall find a time, Audrey. Patience, gentle Audrey.

AUDREY Faith, the priest was good enough, for all the old gentleman's saying.

TOUCHSTONE A most wicked Sir Oliver, Audrey, a most 5
vile Martext. But Audrey, there is a youth here in the forest lays claim to you.

AUDREY Ay, I know who 'tis. He hath no interest in me in the world.

Enter William.

Here comes the man you mean. 10

TOUCHSTONE It is meat and drink to me to see a clown. By my troth, we that have good wits have much to answer for. We shall be flouting. We cannot hold.

WILLIAM Good ev'n, Audrey.

AUDREY God gi' good ev'n, William. 15

WILLIAM, ⌈to Touchstone⌉ And good ev'n to you, sir.

TOUCHSTONE Good ev'n, gentle friend. Cover thy head, cover thy head. Nay, prithee, be covered. How old are you, friend?

WILLIAM Five-and-twenty, sir. 20

TOUCHSTONE A ripe age. Is thy name William?

WILLIAM William, sir.

173

29. **a pretty wit:** a fine mind

40–44. **to have . . . am he:** Scholars have traced Touchstone's comic-learned commentary (which says, in effect, "Audrey belongs to me and not to you") to Cicero and Quintilian. **your writers:** i.e., writers **consent:** agree **ipse:** he himself (Latin)

48–50. **vulgar, boorish, common:** Each of these terms, used here as nouns, means the language of the common people, but each carries its adjectival sense, comically insulting those who speak nonlearned language.

52. **to wit:** namely, that is to say

53. **make thee away:** kill you

55. **bastinado:** beating (with a stick or cudgel); **steel:** sword; **bandy:** fight, contend

56. **in faction:** perhaps, as if we were of opposing factions or parties; **policy:** plots, cunning

"If courtiers were shepherds." (3.2.50)
From [Robert Greene,] *A quip for an vpstart courtier . . .* (1592).

174

TOUCHSTONE A fair name. Wast born i' th' forest here?

WILLIAM Ay, sir, I thank God.

TOUCHSTONE "Thank God." A good answer. Art rich?   25

WILLIAM 'Faith sir, so-so.

TOUCHSTONE "So-so" is good, very good, very excellent good. And yet it is not: it is but so-so. Art thou wise?

WILLIAM Ay, sir, I have a pretty wit.

TOUCHSTONE Why, thou sayst well. I do now remember   30
a saying: "The fool doth think he is wise, but the wise man knows himself to be a fool." The heathen philosopher, when he had a desire to eat a grape, would open his lips when he put it into his mouth, meaning thereby that grapes were made to eat and   35
lips to open. You do love this maid?

WILLIAM I do, ⌜sir.⌝

TOUCHSTONE Give me your hand. Art thou learned?

WILLIAM No, sir.

TOUCHSTONE Then learn this of me: to have is to have.   40
For it is a figure in rhetoric that drink, being poured out of a cup into a glass, by filling the one doth empty the other. For all your writers do consent that *ipse* is "he." Now, you are not *ipse*, for I am he.

WILLIAM Which he, sir?   45

TOUCHSTONE He, sir, that must marry this woman. Therefore, you clown, abandon—which is in the vulgar "leave"—the society—which in the boorish is "company"—of this female—which in the common is "woman"; which together is, abandon the   50
society of this female, or, clown, thou perishest; or, to thy better understanding, diest; or, to wit, I kill thee, make thee away, translate thy life into death, thy liberty into bondage. I will deal in poison with thee, or in bastinado, or in steel. I will bandy with   55
thee in faction. I will o'errun thee with ⌜policy.⌝ I will kill thee a hundred and fifty ways. Therefore tremble and depart.

63. **Trip:** move quickly; **I attend:** i.e., I'm coming (literally, I follow or accompany in order to serve)

5.2 Orlando, envious that his brother Oliver and "Aliena," having fallen in love, plan to be married immediately, tells "Ganymede" how bitter he finds his own situation. "Ganymede" tells him that, if Orlando wishes to marry Rosalind, "Ganymede" can, through magic, make Rosalind appear at the wedding. "Ganymede" also exacts a promise from Phoebe: if at the time of the wedding Phoebe refuses to marry "Ganymede," she will marry Silvius.

---

4. **persever:** i.e., persevere (accent on second syllable); **enjoy:** possess; delight in

5. **giddiness:** perhaps, haste (literally, thoughtless folly, fickleness, instability)

5–6. **the poverty of her:** i.e., her poverty

9. **consent with both:** i.e., agree with both (of these statements, or both of us, Aliena and me); **that:** i.e., so that

10. **to your good:** i.e., in your own interest

11–12. **estate upon:** settle on, i.e., give to

14. **all 's:** i.e., all his

18. **brother:** i.e., (future) brother-in-law

19. **sister:** i.e., as Orlando's "Rosalind," Ganymede would be Oliver's (future) sister-in-law

AUDREY Do, good William.
WILLIAM, ⌜*to Touchstone*⌝ God rest you merry, sir.   60
                                                        He exits.

Enter Corin.

CORIN Our master and mistress seeks you. Come away, away.
TOUCHSTONE Trip, Audrey, trip, Audrey.—I attend, I attend.
                                                        They exit.

Scene 2
Enter Orlando, ⌜with his arm in a sling,⌝ and Oliver.

ORLANDO Is 't possible that on so little acquaintance you should like her? That, but seeing, you should love her? And loving, woo? And wooing, she should grant? And will you persever to enjoy her?
OLIVER Neither call the giddiness of it in question, the   5
poverty of her, the small acquaintance, my sudden wooing, nor ⌜her⌝ sudden consenting, but say with me "I love Aliena"; say with her that she loves me; consent with both that we may enjoy each other. It shall be to your good, for my father's house and all   10
the revenue that was old Sir Rowland's will I estate upon you, and here live and die a shepherd.

Enter Rosalind, ⌜as Ganymede.⌝

ORLANDO You have my consent. Let your wedding be tomorrow. Thither will I invite the Duke and all 's contented followers. Go you and prepare Aliena,   15
for, look you, here comes my Rosalind.
ROSALIND, ⌜*as Ganymede, to Oliver*⌝ God save you, brother.
OLIVER And you, fair sister.   ⌜*He exits.*⌝

21. **scarf:** sling

30. **where you are:** i.e., what you mean

32–33. **Caesar's . . . overcame:** The words *veni, vidi, vici,* "I came, I saw, I conquered," were attributed to Julius Caesar as his announcement of a sudden military victory. The phrase had become proverbial to describe swift action.

34–39. **no sooner met . . . marriage:** See longer note, page 218. **degrees:** ascending stages **pair of stairs:** flight of stairs

40–41. **incontinent:** wordplay on the meanings (1) immediately and (2) unchaste, sexually unrestrained

41. **the very wrath:** i.e., the intense grip or passion

52. **serve your turn:** i.e., suffice

"A crooked-pated old cuckoldly ram." (3.2.82)
From Edward Topsell, *The historie of foure-footed beastes . . .* (1607).

ROSALIND, ⌐*as Ganymede*⌐ O my dear Orlando, how it   20
grieves me to see thee wear thy heart in a scarf.

ORLANDO   It is my arm.

ROSALIND, ⌐*as Ganymede*⌐ I thought thy heart had been
wounded with the claws of a lion.

ORLANDO   Wounded it is, but with the eyes of a lady.   25

ROSALIND, ⌐*as Ganymede*⌐ Did your brother tell you
how I counterfeited to swoon when he showed me
your handkercher?

ORLANDO   Ay, and greater wonders than that.

ROSALIND, ⌐*as Ganymede*⌐ O, I know where you are.   30
Nay, 'tis true. There was never anything so sudden
but the fight of two rams, and Caesar's thrasonical
brag of "I came, saw, and ⌐overcame.⌐" For your
brother and my sister no sooner met but they
looked, no sooner looked but they loved, no sooner   35
loved but they sighed, no sooner sighed but they
asked one another the reason, no sooner knew the
reason but they sought the remedy; and in these
degrees have they made a pair of stairs to marriage,
which they will climb incontinent, or else be incon-   40
tinent before marriage. They are in the very wrath
of love, and they will together. Clubs cannot part
them.

ORLANDO   They shall be married tomorrow, and I will
bid the Duke to the nuptial. But O, how bitter a   45
thing it is to look into happiness through another
man's eyes. By so much the more shall I tomorrow
be at the height of heart-heaviness by how much I
shall think my brother happy in having what he
wishes for.   50

ROSALIND, ⌐*as Ganymede*⌐ Why, then, tomorrow I cannot serve your turn for Rosalind?

ORLANDO   I can live no longer by thinking.

ROSALIND, ⌐*as Ganymede*⌐ I will weary you then no
longer with idle talking. Know of me then—for   55

56. **to some purpose:** to the point at issue

57. **conceit:** understanding, intelligence

57–58. **that you:** i.e., so that you

59. **insomuch:** in that

61. **draw a belief from you:** i.e., persuade you to a belief; **to do yourself good:** i.e., which will bring benefit to you

62. **not to grace me:** i.e., not in order to bring honor to myself

63. **strange:** wonderful, exceptional; **year:** i.e., years

64. **conversed with:** associated with, exchanged ideas with

65. **art:** occult learning, magic; **not damnable:** See longer note, pages 218–19.

66. **gesture:** bearing; **cries it out:** proclaims

68. **her:** i.e., Rosalind

70. **inconvenient:** improper (perhaps, because of its connection with magic)

71–72. **human as she is, and without any danger:** See longer note to 5.2.65.

73. **in sober meanings:** i.e., seriously

75. **tender:** regard

77. **if you will be:** if you wish to be

81. **ungentleness:** discourtesy

83. **study:** studied or deliberate effort

84. **ungentle:** unkind

85. **followed:** pursued, attended

now I speak to some purpose—that I know you are
a gentleman of good conceit. I speak not this that
you should bear a good opinion of my knowledge,
insomuch I say I know you ⌜are.⌝ Neither do I labor
for a greater esteem than may in some little mea-   60
sure draw a belief from you to do yourself good, and
not to grace me. Believe then, if you please, that I
can do strange things. I have, since I was three year
old, conversed with a magician, most profound in
his art and yet not damnable. If you do love Rosa-   65
lind so near the heart as your gesture cries it out,
when your brother marries Aliena shall you marry
her. I know into what straits of fortune she is
driven, and it is not impossible to me, if it appear
not inconvenient to you, to set her before your eyes   70
tomorrow, human as she is, and without any
danger.

ORLANDO Speak'st thou in sober meanings?

ROSALIND, ⌜as Ganymede⌝ By my life I do, which I
tender dearly, though I say I am a magician. There-   75
fore put you in your best array, bid your friends; for
if you will be married tomorrow, you shall, and to
Rosalind, if you will.

Enter Silvius and Phoebe.

Look, here comes a lover of mine and a lover of
hers.   80

PHOEBE, ⌜to Rosalind⌝
Youth, you have done me much ungentleness
To show the letter that I writ to you.

ROSALIND, ⌜as Ganymede⌝
I care not if I have. It is my study
To seem despiteful and ungentle to you.
You are there followed by a faithful shepherd.   85
Look upon him, love him; he worships you.

100. **observance:** dutiful service, care

102. **observance:** perhaps a typesetter's error for some other noun (since **observance** repeats line 100)

108. **to love:** i.e., for loving

113. **To her:** i.e., (I speak) to her

A sequestered stag. (2.1.34)
From Nicolaus Reusner, *Emblemata . . .* (1581).

182

PHOEBE, ⌈*to Silvius*⌉
　Good shepherd, tell this youth what 'tis to love.
SILVIUS
　It is to be all made of sighs and tears,
　And so am I for Phoebe.
PHOEBE　And I for Ganymede.　　　　　　　　　　90
ORLANDO　And I for Rosalind.
ROSALIND, ⌈*as Ganymede*⌉　And I for no woman.
SILVIUS
　It is to be all made of faith and service,
　And so am I for Phoebe.
PHOEBE　And I for Ganymede.　　　　　　　　　　95
ORLANDO　And I for Rosalind.
ROSALIND, ⌈*as Ganymede*⌉　And I for no woman.
SILVIUS
　It is to be all made of fantasy,
　All made of passion and all made of wishes,
　All adoration, duty, and observance,　　　　　100
　All humbleness, all patience and impatience,
　All purity, all trial, all observance,
　And so am I for Phoebe.
PHOEBE　And so am I for Ganymede.
ORLANDO　And so am I for Rosalind.　　　　　　105
ROSALIND, ⌈*as Ganymede*⌉　And so am I for no
　woman.
PHOEBE
　If this be so, why blame you me to love you?
SILVIUS
　If this be so, why blame you me to love you?
ORLANDO
　If this be so, why blame you me to love you?　110
ROSALIND, ⌈*as Ganymede*⌉　Why do you speak too,
　"Why blame you me to love you?"
ORLANDO　To her that is not here, nor doth not hear.
ROSALIND, ⌈*as Ganymede*⌉　Pray you, no more of this.

115–16. **against the moon:** i.e., when the moon shines

5.3 Touchstone and Audrey listen while two pages sing.

---

4. **dishonest:** immodest

4–5. **woman of the world:** i.e., married woman (See 1 Corinthians 7.34: "she that is married careth for the things that pertain to the world.")

10. **We are for you:** i.e., we're with you, we're ready

11. **clap into 't roundly:** i.e., start right away

A horned man or cuckold. (3.3.52–53)
From *Bagford Ballads* (printed 1878).

'Tis like the howling of Irish wolves against the 115
moon. (⌜*To Silvius.*⌝) I will help you if I can. (⌜*To
Phoebe.*⌝) I would love you if I could.—Tomorrow
meet me all together. (⌜*To Phoebe.*⌝) I will marry
you if ever I marry woman, and I'll be married
tomorrow. (⌜*To Orlando.*⌝) I will satisfy you if ever I 120
⌜satisfy⌝ man, and you shall be married tomorrow.
(⌜*To Silvius.*⌝) I will content you, if what pleases you
contents you, and you shall be married tomorrow.
(⌜*To Orlando.*⌝) As you love Rosalind, meet. (⌜*To
Silvius.*⌝) As you love Phoebe, meet.—And as I love 125
no woman, I'll meet. So fare you well. I have left
you commands.

SILVIUS   I'll not fail, if I live.

PHOEBE   Nor I.

ORLANDO   Nor I.   130

They exit.

Scene 3
Enter ⌜Touchstone⌝ and Audrey.

TOUCHSTONE   Tomorrow is the joyful day, Audrey. Tomorrow will we be married.

AUDREY   I do desire it with all my heart, and I hope it is
no dishonest desire to desire to be a woman of the
world.   5

Enter two Pages.

Here come two of the banished duke's pages.

FIRST PAGE   Well met, honest gentleman.

TOUCHSTONE   By my troth, well met. Come, sit, sit, and
a song.

SECOND PAGE   We are for you. Sit i' th' middle.   10

⌜*They sit.*⌝

FIRST PAGE   Shall we clap into 't roundly, without

12. **hawking:** clearing our throats loudly

14. **in a tune:** perhaps, keeping time; or, in unison

15. **a horse:** i.e., a single horse

16. **It was a lover and his lass:** See longer note, page 219, and pages xxxvi–xxxvii.

18. **cornfield:** i.e., field of grain

19. **ring time:** i.e., time of exchanging rings

36. **prime:** (1) spring; (2) springtime of life

A sixteenth-century image of the Golden Age. (1.1.117–18)
From Ovid, *Accipe studiose lector . . . Metamorphosin . . .* [1509].

hawking or spitting or saying we are hoarse, which
are the only prologues to a bad voice?
SECOND PAGE   I' faith, i' faith, and both in a tune like
     two gypsies on a horse.   15

                        Song.

⌈PAGES *sing*⌉
     It was a lover and his lass,
          With a hey, and a ho, and a hey-nonny-no,
     That o'er the green cornfield did pass
          In springtime, the only pretty ⌈ring⌉ time,
     When birds do sing, hey ding a ding, ding.   20
     Sweet lovers love the spring.

     Between the acres of the rye,
          With a hey, and a ho, and a hey-nonny-no,
     These pretty country folks would lie
          In springtime, the only pretty ⌈ring⌉ time,   25
     When birds do sing, hey ding a ding, ding.
     Sweet lovers love the spring.

     This carol they began that hour,
          With a hey, and a ho, and a hey-nonny-no,
     How that a life was but a flower   30
          In springtime, the only pretty ⌈ring⌉ time,
     When birds do sing, hey ding a ding, ding.
     Sweet lovers love the spring.

     And therefore take the present time,
          With a hey, and a ho, and a hey-nonny-no,   35
     For love is crownèd with the prime,
          In springtime, the only pretty ⌈ring⌉ time,
     When birds do sing, hey ding a ding, ding.
     Sweet lovers love the spring.

41. **matter:** good sense; **ditty:** lyrics; **note:** music
42. **untunable:** discordant
47. **mend:** improve

5.4 In the presence of Duke Senior and his lords, "Ganymede" reminds Orlando, Silvius, and Phoebe of their promises. "He" and "Aliena" then leave while Touchstone entertains the assembly. Hymen, god of marriage, enters bringing Rosalind and Celia. Duke Senior welcomes his daughter and his niece; Orlando welcomes Rosalind. Phoebe agrees to marry Silvius. As Hymen speaks to each of the four couples, the brother of Orlando and Oliver brings news that Duke Frederick has given up the throne. Duke Senior, now once again in power, returns Oliver's lands to him and establishes Orlando as his heir.

---

4. **As those that:** i.e., in the same way as those people who; **they hope:** i.e., that they merely hope (instead of expect)
5. **compact:** agreement (accent on second syllable); **urged:** presented

TOUCHSTONE Truly, young gentlemen, though there 40
    was no great matter in the ditty, yet the note was
    very untunable.
FIRST PAGE You are deceived, sir. We kept time. We lost
    not our time.
TOUCHSTONE By my troth, yes. I count it but time lost 45
    to hear such a foolish song. God be wi' you, and
    God mend your voices.—Come, Audrey.
                     They ⌜rise and⌝ exit.

Scene 4
Enter Duke Senior, Amiens, Jaques, Orlando, Oliver,
⌜*and*⌝ *Celia* ⌜*as Aliena.*⌝

DUKE SENIOR
  Dost thou believe, Orlando, that the boy
  Can do all this that he hath promisèd?
ORLANDO
  I sometimes do believe and sometimes do not,
  As those that fear they hope, and know they fear.

  Enter Rosalind ⌜*as Ganymede,*⌝ *Silvius, and Phoebe.*

ROSALIND, ⌜*as Ganymede*⌝
  Patience once more whiles our compact is urged. 5
  ⌜*To Duke.*⌝ You say, if I bring in your Rosalind,
  You will bestow her on Orlando here?
DUKE SENIOR
  That would I, had I kingdoms to give with her.
ROSALIND, ⌜*as Ganymede, to Orlando*⌝
  And you say you will have her when I bring her?
ORLANDO
  That would I, were I of all kingdoms king. 10
ROSALIND, ⌜*as Ganymede, to Phoebe*⌝
  You say you'll marry me if I be willing?

15. **So is:** i.e., that is

18. **make . . . even:** i.e., settle (as again at line 26)

28. **lively:** lifelike; **favor:** appearance

30. **Methought:** it seemed to me

33. **desperate:** seriously dangerous (See longer note to **not damnable,** 5.2.65.)

35. **Obscurèd:** hidden, living secretly; **circle:** circuit or compass (with an allusion to the magician's **circle,** inside of which the magician is protected from the spirits he summons)

36. **another flood:** When God destroyed life on the earth with a great **flood,** he had Noah construct an **ark** that would hold Noah's family and one **pair** (male and female) of each kind of living **beasts** (see Genesis 6.5–20); **toward:** about to take place

Noah's ark. (5.4.36–37)
From Vincentius, *The myrrour & dyscrypcyon of the worlde . . .* [1527?].

PHOEBE
 That will I, should I die the hour after.
ROSALIND, ⌜*as Ganymede*⌝
 But if you do refuse to marry me,
 You'll give yourself to this most faithful shepherd?
PHOEBE So is the bargain.   15
ROSALIND, ⌜*as Ganymede, to Silvius*⌝
 You say that you'll have Phoebe if she will?
SILVIUS
 Though to have her and death were both one thing.
ROSALIND, ⌜*as Ganymede*⌝
 I have promised to make all this matter even.
 Keep you your word, O duke, to give your
  daughter,—   20
 You yours, Orlando, to receive his daughter.—
 Keep you your word, Phoebe, that you'll marry me,
 Or else, refusing me, to wed this shepherd.—
 Keep your word, Silvius, that you'll marry her
 If she refuse me. And from hence I go   25
 To make these doubts all even.
                              Rosalind and Celia exit.
DUKE SENIOR
 I do remember in this shepherd boy
 Some lively touches of my daughter's favor.
ORLANDO
 My lord, the first time that I ever saw him
 Methought he was a brother to your daughter.   30
 But, my good lord, this boy is forest-born
 And hath been tutored in the rudiments
 Of many desperate studies by his uncle,
 Whom he reports to be a great magician
 Obscurèd in the circle of this forest.   35

          Enter ⌜*Touchstone*⌝ *and Audrey.*

JAQUES There is sure another flood toward, and these
 couples are coming to the ark. Here comes a pair of

42. **motley-minded:** See note to 2.7.13.

45–46. **put me to my purgation:** i.e., challenge me to prove the truth of what I swore

46. **trod a measure:** danced elegantly

47. **politic:** cunning, crafty

48. **smooth:** flattering; **undone:** (financially) ruined (by not paying my debts)

49. **I have had four quarrels:** This is Touchstone's strongest evidence that he is, in fact, a courtier, since no one below the level of gentleman was entitled to a **quarrel.** (The intricate system by which gentlemen and noblemen defended their honor in sixteenth-century England is parodied by Touchstone in lines 52–107. See longer note, pages 219–20.); **like to have:** i.e., almost

51. **ta'en up:** i.e., taken up, satisfactorily resolved

52. **found:** determined that (a legal term)

53. **cause:** ground of action (a legal term) See lines 71–90 below for Touchstone's elaborate explanation of how **the quarrel was upon the seventh cause.**

57. **God 'ild you:** See note to 3.3.74–75; **you of the like:** i.e., the same from you (the continuation of your good will)

59. **copulatives:** a Latin grammatical term, here used to refer to people wishing to be coupled in marriage (with wordplay on the word "copulation"); **swear:** i.e., promise to be faithful in marriage; **forswear:** i.e., break this promise

60. **blood:** passion, the flesh; **breaks:** i.e., breaks the marriage bond

62. **humor:** whim, inclination

(continued)

very strange beasts, which in all tongues are called
fools.

TOUCHSTONE Salutation and greeting to you all.   40

JAQUES, ⌜*to Duke*⌝ Good my lord, bid him welcome.
This is the motley-minded gentleman that I have so
often met in the forest. He hath been a courtier, he
swears.

TOUCHSTONE If any man doubt that, let him put me to   45
my purgation. I have trod a measure. I have flat-
tered a lady. I have been politic with my friend,
smooth with mine enemy. I have undone three
tailors. I have had four quarrels, and like to have
fought one.   50

JAQUES And how was that ta'en up?

TOUCHSTONE Faith, we met and found the quarrel was
upon the seventh cause.

JAQUES How "seventh cause"?—Good my lord, like
this fellow.   55

DUKE SENIOR I like him very well.

TOUCHSTONE God 'ild you, sir. I desire you of the like. I
press in here, sir, amongst the rest of the country
copulatives, to swear and to forswear, according as
marriage binds and blood breaks. A poor virgin, sir,   60
an ill-favored thing, sir, but mine own. A poor
humor of mine, sir, to take that that no man else
will. Rich honesty dwells like a miser, sir, in a poor
house, as your pearl in your foul oyster.

DUKE SENIOR By my faith, he is very swift and senten-   65
tious.

TOUCHSTONE According to the fool's bolt, sir, and such
dulcet diseases.

JAQUES But for the seventh cause. How did you find the
quarrel on the seventh cause?   70

TOUCHSTONE Upon a lie seven times removed.—Bear
your body more seeming, Audrey.—As thus, sir: I
did dislike the cut of a certain courtier's beard. He

63. **honesty:** chastity

64. **your . . . oyster:** i.e., pearls in ugly oysters

65–66. **swift and sententious:** quick-witted and full of wise sayings (Touchstone replies by alluding to the proverb "A **fool's bolt** [i.e., arrow] is soon [i.e., quickly] shot" [line 67].)

68. **dulcet diseases:** perhaps, sweet disturbances (an echo, perhaps, of technical rhetorical language)

69–70. **find the quarrel:** i.e., determine that **the quarrel** was

71. **a lie:** i.e., an accusation of lying (expressed, in its most direct form, as "you lie" or "I give you the lie") See longer note to 5.4.49.

72. **seeming:** i.e., seemly

73. **did dislike:** i.e., expressed my dislike of

74–75. **if . . . it was:** See longer note, page 220.

75. **in the mind:** i.e., of the opinion

78. **quip:** sharp retort

78–79. **again it was not:** i.e., again I said it was not (See also lines 80 and 82.)

79. **disabled:** disparaged, belittled

83. **countercheck:** rebuff

89. **give me the lie direct:** i.e., directly call me a liar

90. **measured swords:** perhaps, went through the preliminaries of the duel

91. **nominate:** name

93. **in print, by the book:** (1) with exactness; formally; (2) in accord with the printed books designed to teach the code of honorable dueling (There were two such books available in England in the late 1590s. Besides Saviolo's book, there was also William Segar's *The Booke of Honour and Armes*, 1590. Both

(continued)

194

sent me word if I said his beard was not cut well, he
was in the mind it was. This is called "the retort   75
courteous." If I sent him word again it was not well
cut, he would send me word he cut it to please
himself. This is called "the quip modest." If again it
was not well cut, he disabled my judgment. This is
called "the reply churlish." If again it was not well   80
cut, he would answer I spake not true. This is called
"the reproof valiant." If again it was not well cut, he
would say I lie. This is called "the countercheck
quarrelsome," and so to "⌈the⌉ lie circumstantial,"
and "the lie direct."   85

JAQUES And how oft did you say his beard was not well
cut?

TOUCHSTONE I durst go no further than the lie circumstantial, nor he durst not give me the lie direct, and
so we measured swords and parted.   90

JAQUES Can you nominate in order now the degrees of
the lie?

TOUCHSTONE O sir, we quarrel in print, by the book, as
you have books for good manners. I will name you
the degrees: the first, "the retort courteous"; the   95
second, "the quip modest"; the third, "the reply
churlish"; the fourth, "the reproof valiant"; the
fifth, "the countercheck quarrelsome"; the sixth,
"the lie with circumstance"; the seventh, "the lie
direct." All these you may avoid but the lie direct,   100
and you may avoid that too with an "if." I knew
when seven justices could not take up a quarrel, but
when the parties were met themselves, one of them
thought but of an "if," as: "If you said so, then I said
so." And they shook hands and swore brothers.   105
Your "if" is the only peacemaker: much virtue in
"if."

JAQUES, ⌈*to Duke*⌉ Is not this a rare fellow, my lord?
He's as good at anything and yet a fool.

Saviolo and Segar essentially translate Girolamo Muzio's *Il Duello*, 1550. See longer note to 5.4.49 and illustration, page 86.)

94. **books for good manners:** i.e., books of courtesy

100. **avoid:** i.e., make void or empty; extricate oneself from; invalidate (See longer note to 5.4.74–75.)

102. **take up:** satisfactorily resolve

105. **swore brothers:** perhaps, swore to behave as brothers toward each other

106. **virtue:** power

110. **stalking-horse:** a horse (either an old horse or a two- or three-dimensional figure of a horse) behind which a hunter would conceal himself when hunting fowl (See page 198.)

111. **presentation:** display, exhibition

111 SD. **Hymen:** the mythological god of marriage; (See page 202.); **Still music:** i.e., soft music

112–19. **Then . . . bosom is:** This speech has been set to music and is sometimes sung in productions of the play. It is not marked as a song in the Folio.

113. **made even:** i.e., brought into agreement

114. **Atone:** unite, come into harmony

134. **Hymen's bands:** i.e., the bonds of marriage

135. **contents:** (1) substance (i.e., that which is contained); (2) pleasure, joy (See longer note, pages 220–21.)

DUKE SENIOR   He uses his folly like a stalking-horse,   110
and under the presentation of that he shoots his wit.

Enter Hymen, Rosalind, and Celia. Still music.

HYMEN
        Then is there mirth in heaven
        When earthly things made even
          Atone together.
        Good duke, receive thy daughter.   115
        Hymen from heaven brought her,
          Yea, brought her hither,
        That thou mightst join ⌜her⌝ hand with his,
        Whose heart within his bosom is.
ROSALIND, ⌜*to Duke*⌝
To you I give myself, for I am yours.   120
⌜*To Orlando.*⌝ To you I give myself, for I am yours.
DUKE SENIOR
If there be truth in sight, you are my daughter.
ORLANDO
If there be truth in sight, you are my Rosalind.
PHOEBE
If sight and shape be true,
Why then, my love adieu.   125
ROSALIND, ⌜*to Duke*⌝
I'll have no father, if you be not he.
⌜*To Orlando.*⌝ I'll have no husband, if you be not he,
⌜*To Phoebe.*⌝ Nor ne'er wed woman, if you be not
she.
HYMEN
        Peace, ho! I bar confusion.   130
        'Tis I must make conclusion
          Of these most strange events.
        Here's eight that must take hands
        To join in Hymen's bands,
          If truth holds true contents.   135

136. **cross:** adversity, misfortune

138. **accord:** consent

139. **to your lord:** i.e., as your husband

140. **sure:** i.e., joined

143. **Feed:** satisfy

144. **reason wonder may diminish:** i.e., discussion may lessen amazement

146. **Juno's crown:** Juno, sister and wife to Jove, is queen of the gods and protectress of marriage.

147. **board and bed:** i.e., marriage **board:** i.e., dining table

153. **Even daughter:** i.e., just as if you were my daughter; **in no less degree:** i.e., (you are **welcome**) no less than a daughter

154. **eat my word:** proverbial

155. **faith:** constancy; **my fancy to thee doth combine:** i.e., binds my desire to you

A constructed stalking-horse. (5.4.110)
From *The husbandman's jewel . . .* [1695].

⌜*To Rosalind and Orlando.*⌝
  You and you no cross shall part.
⌜*To Celia and Oliver.*⌝
  You and you are heart in heart.
⌜*To Phoebe.*⌝
  You to his love must accord
  Or have a woman to your lord.
⌜*To Audrey and Touchstone.*⌝
  You and you are sure together   140
  As the winter to foul weather.
  ⌜*To All.*⌝
  Whiles a wedlock hymn we sing,
  Feed yourselves with questioning,
  That reason wonder may diminish
  How thus we met, and these things finish.   145

          Song.

  Wedding is great Juno's crown,
    O blessèd bond of board and bed.
  'Tis Hymen peoples every town.
    High wedlock then be honorèd.
  Honor, high honor, and renown   150
    To Hymen, god of every town.

DUKE SENIOR, ⌜*to Celia*⌝
  O my dear niece, welcome thou art to me,
  Even daughter, welcome in no less degree.
PHOEBE, ⌜*to Silvius*⌝
  I will not eat my word. Now thou art mine,
  Thy faith my fancy to thee doth combine.   155

    Enter Second Brother, ⌜*Jaques de Boys.*⌝

SECOND BROTHER
  Let me have audience for a word or two.
  I am the second son of old Sir Rowland,
  That bring these tidings to this fair assembly.

161. **Addressed:** prepared; **power:** army; **on foot:** on the march

162. **In his own conduct:** i.e., under his command

164. **skirts:** outskirts

166. **question:** conversation

168. **crown:** i.e., title

169. **restored . . . again:** i.e., restored

170. **This to be true:** i.e., that this is true

171. **engage:** pledge

173. **offer'st fairly:** bring a fine present

174. **To one his lands withheld:** i.e., to Oliver the lands taken by Frederick; **to the other:** i.e., to Orlando, who, as Rosalind's husband, will inherit the **dukedom**

175. **at large:** in full

176. **do those ends:** accomplish those purposes

178. **after:** i.e., afterward; **every:** i.e., every one

179. **shrewd:** difficult, dangerous

179–80. **us, our:** Duke Senior, restored to his dukedom, now uses the royal "we."

181. **states:** status, rank

182. **new-fall'n:** i.e., newly acquired or awarded

185. **With measure heaped in:** i.e., overflowing with (The image is of a vessel filled to overflowing.); **measures:** dances

188. **pompous:** ceremonious

190. **convertites:** i.e., converts to the religious life

191. **matter:** good sense

Duke Frederick, hearing how that every day
Men of great worth resorted to this forest,   160
Addressed a mighty power, which were on foot
In his own conduct, purposely to take
His brother here and put him to the sword;
And to the skirts of this wild wood he came,
Where, meeting with an old religious man,   165
After some question with him, was converted
Both from his enterprise and from the world,
His crown bequeathing to his banished brother,
And all their lands restored to ⌐them⌐ again
That were with him exiled. This to be true   170
I do engage my life.
DUKE SENIOR   Welcome, young man.
  Thou offer'st fairly to thy brothers' wedding:
  To one his lands withheld, and to the other
  A land itself at large, a potent dukedom.—   175
  First, in this forest let us do those ends
  That here were well begun and well begot,
  And, after, every of this happy number
  That have endured shrewd days and nights with us
  Shall share the good of our returnèd fortune   180
  According to the measure of their states.
  Meantime, forget this new-fall'n dignity,
  And fall into our rustic revelry.—
  Play, music.—And you brides and bridegrooms all,
  With measure heaped in joy to th' measures fall.   185
JAQUES, ⌐to Second Brother⌐
  Sir, by your patience: if I heard you rightly,
  The Duke hath put on a religious life
  And thrown into neglect the pompous court.
SECOND BROTHER   He hath.
JAQUES
  To him will I. Out of these convertites   190
  There is much matter to be heard and learned.

192. **bequeath:** leave

193. **deserves:** i.e., deserve

194–98. **You . . . bed:** See longer note, page 221.

198. **long and well-deservèd:** i.e., well deserved for a long time

201. **victualled:** provided with food

205. **What you would have:** i.e., what you want from me

206. **stay:** wait

Hymen, god of marriage. (5.4.111 SD)
From Vincenzo Cartari, *Imagines deorum . . .* (1581).

⌐*To Duke.*⌐ You to your former honor I bequeath;
Your patience and your virtue well deserves it.
⌐*To Orlando.*⌐ You to a love that your true faith doth
   merit.   195
⌐*To Oliver.*⌐ You to your land, and love, and great
   allies.
⌐*To Silvius.*⌐ You to a long and well-deservèd bed.
⌐*To Touchstone.*⌐ And you to wrangling, for thy
   loving voyage   200
Is but for two months victualled.—So to your
   pleasures.
I am for other than for dancing measures.
DUKE SENIOR   Stay, Jaques, stay.
JAQUES
To see no pastime, I. What you would have   205
I'll stay to know at your abandoned cave.   *He exits.*
DUKE SENIOR
Proceed, proceed. We'll begin these rites,
As we do trust they'll end, in true delights.
                ⌐*Dance. All but Rosalind*⌐ *exit.*

Epilogue

---

1. **the lady:** (1) the heroine; (2) the boy actor who played female parts (In *Hamlet* 2.2.449, Hamlet greets the boy actor of a traveling company as "my young lady and mistress.")

2. **unhandsome:** improper

3–4. **good wine needs no bush:** a proverb in which **bush** means, indirectly, advertisement (A **bush** was the branch of ivy used to identify a vintner or a tavern.)

7. **case:** predicament

8. **insinuate with:** ingratiate myself with

9. **furnished:** costumed

11. **conjure:** earnestly entreat, adjure (with word-play on "invoke or effect through magic power")

17. **If I were a woman:** Here the gender-shifts among Rosalind, Ganymede, and Ganymede's playing of Rosalind shift again as the boy actor speaks in his own person.

19. **that liked me:** i.e., that I liked

20. **defied:** despised

22. **bid me farewell:** i.e., applaud

⌐EPILOGUE.¬

ROSALIND It is not the fashion to see the lady the
epilogue, but it is no more unhandsome than to see
the lord the prologue. If it be true that good wine
needs no bush, 'tis true that a good play needs no
epilogue. Yet to good wine they do use good bushes,   5
and good plays prove the better by the help of good
epilogues. What a case am I in then that am neither
a good epilogue nor cannot insinuate with you in
the behalf of a good play! I am not furnished like a
beggar; therefore to beg will not become me. My   10
way is to conjure you, and I'll begin with the
women. I charge you, O women, for the love you
bear to men, to like as much of this play as please
you. And I charge you, O men, for the love you bear
to women—as I perceive by your simpering, none   15
of you hates them—that between you and the
women the play may please. If I were a woman, I
would kiss as many of you as had beards that
pleased me, complexions that liked me, and breaths
that I defied not. And I am sure as many as have   20
good beards, or good faces, or sweet breaths will for
my kind offer, when I make curtsy, bid me farewell.
She exits.

Longer Notes

1.1.45–46. The courtesy of nations: Many editions say that this phrase means "the usage of the civilized world," but neither **courtesy** nor **nations** is recorded as having been used, in Shakespeare's time, in ways that support this meaning. Our sense that this is Shakespeare's way of referring to the custom of primogeniture is supported by a similar usage in *King Lear*. There Edmund is made to refer to the custom of primogeniture as the "curiosity of nations" (1.2.4).

1.1.115. Robin Hood: The story of Robin Hood and his life with his merry men in Sherwood Forest began to appear in ballads in the fourteenth century. Ballads and pageant plays continued to tell his story in subsequent centuries. Robin Hood was also, as "Robert, earl of Huntingdon," the subject of two plays by Anthony Munday and Henry Chettle that were performed on the London public stage in the 1590s. About half the surviving Robin Hood ballads contain some variant of the words that begin Amiens' song in 2.5: "Under the greenwood tree. . . ."

1.1.117–18. golden world: In Greek mythology, the first age was **golden:** laws were not needed, nor was military power; food was abundant without human labor; spring lasted all the year; milk and wine ran in streams, and honey flowed from trees. Hesiod, in his *Works and Days*, 2.106–15, describes "a golden race of mortal men . . . [who] lived like gods without sorrow of heart, remote and free from toil and grief: miserable age rested not on them; . . . they made merry with feasting beyond the reach of all evils." Ovid, in his *Metamorphoses*, 1.90–112, wrote: "Golden was the first age. . . . The earth herself, without compulsion, untouched by hoe or plowshare, of herself gave all things needful. And men, content with food that came with no one's seeking, gathered the . . . fruit. . . . Then spring was everlasting. . . . Anon the earth, untilled, brought forth her stores of grain. . . . Streams of milk and streams of sweet nectar flowed, and yellow honey was distilled from the verdant oak."

1.2.44 SD. **Touchstone:** This character appears most often in the play under the name of "Clown"—which may indicate no more than that his part was played by the theatrical company's comic actor. His function seems to be that of the professional jester or Fool— namely, to entertain his courtly masters through his skillful playing with language. It has been suggested that **Touchstone** is the name he assumes when he accompanies Celia to the Forest of Arden. This suggestion, however intriguing, is based on a misunderstanding of the word *alias* in the stage direction at 2.4.0. While, for us, the word suggests "[under] an assumed name," this meaning had not yet entered the language when the play was written; *alias* then meant only "otherwise called."

1.2.45. **wit:** This word appears frequently in *As You Like It*, with a wide variety of meanings, several of which may be relevant at any given usage. Among these meanings are the following: the mind or the mental faculties, specifically the faculty of reason; intelligence, cleverness, wisdom; and good judgment. While on particular occasions in the commentary we offer specific meanings for **wit**, we do not mean to exclude other possibilities.

1.2.273. **smaller:** Here the Folio reads "taller," thereby making Celia taller than Rosalind. Elsewhere the Folio appears to reverse itself and make Rosalind the taller. In the next scene, Rosalind says she is "more than common tall" (1.3.122), thereby justifying her adoption of a male disguise rather than a female disguise such as is adopted by Celia; the Folio seems here to be representing Rosalind as taller than Celia. Later in the play, Celia's shortness is one of her distinguishing characteristics. Oliver, apparently quoting Orlando's description to him of the disguised Celia, refers to her as "low" or short (4.3.91). All in all, however, the Folio, it seems, cannot agree with itself about who is to be the taller of the two.

Since 1714, editors have felt obliged to resolve the Folio's inconsistency in some fashion, such as the one we have adopted in emending the Folio's "taller" to "smaller," thus making Celia shorter than Rosalind throughout the play. It may be, however, that editorial concerns with consistency are of a different order from concerns evident in early play manuscripts. It therefore may matter little whether editors substitute "lower," "lesser," "shorter," or "smaller" (even if, as some editors suggest, only some of these terms could refer to stature in Shakespeare's time) because editors may not be "restoring" the play's text but rather cleaning it up for readers and directors.

1.3.78. **Juno's swans:** In mythology, as well as in Shakespeare's *The Tempest*, Juno is associated not with **swans** but with peacocks. However, like Shakespeare in this passage, his contemporary the dramatist Thomas Kyd also associated Juno with swans.

1.3.131–32. **Jove's . . . Ganymede:** In classical mythology, Jove, king of the gods, fell in love with the mortal **Ganymede** and carried him off to Mount Olympus, where he served as Jove's cupbearer. *Ganymede* became a term for a catamite.

On the stage of Shakespeare's time, the role of Rosalind would have been played by a boy. Thus, while, in the fiction of the play, Rosalind and Orlando are a woman and a man in love, onstage they were both male actors. In this way the actors, if not the fiction, reproduced the same-sex love of Jove for Ganymede.

2.1.5–6. **feel we not the penalty of Adam, / The seasons' difference:** This passage has proved controversial among editors. While they have offered many different opinions, this present note surveys three of the main ones. (1) Some argue that the **penalty of Adam** and **the seasons' difference** are not connected, as they seem to be in the Folio. They point out that seasonal change is not specifically named in Genesis as a penalty imposed on Adam; instead, Genesis reads "Because thou hast obeyed the voice of thy wife, and hast eaten of the tree . . . cursed is the earth for thy sake: in sorrow shalt thou eat of it all the days of thy life. . . . In the sweat of thy face shalt thou eat bread" (3.17–19, Geneva Bible). They also argue that the Duke and his fellow exiles do not feel the penalty of Adam as it is described in Genesis: they live off the land, shooting deer, rather than sweating to raise crops, as Adam was cursed to do. These editors therefore put a period after Adam. The difficulty with this editorial solution to the problem (or crux) is that, cut off from line 5, lines 6–10 cannot be read as a complete sentence.

Other editors turn to Arthur Golding's translation of Ovid's *Metamorphoses* for evidence that Adam's punishment and seasonal change are linked. They find in Golding an equation of the Golden Age with Adam's time in Paradise; thus Ovid's description of the end of the Golden Age as the beginning of "heate and cold" can be used to defend the equation of **the penalty of Adam** and **the seasons' difference.** This second group of editors then splits over how to explain the Duke's **feel we not the penalty.** (2) Some argue that the Duke clearly indicates that he does suffer the penalty when he says "the winter's wind . . . bites and blows upon my body, / Even till I shrink with cold." These editors therefore change the text to read "Here feel we but the penalty of Adam"; that is, here we experience only the suffering Adam felt, and not other forms of suffering. (3) Other editors, including ourselves, argue that while the Duke speaks of "shrink[ing] with cold," he denies that he experiences the cold as suffering because he says he "smile[s] and say[s] / 'This is no flattery'."

2.3.32–35. **wouldst . . . do:** These lines reflect much sixteenth-century writing about the plight of younger sons and others evicted from their homes. Like Orlando, those thrown off their land in sixteenth-century England had only two options, according to those (like Sir Thomas More) concerned with England's poverty and its crime: to beg or to steal.

2.5.29. **cover the while:** Many editors add a stage direction at this point indicating that food and drink are set out. The difficulty with such a direction is that scene 2.6, represented as taking place in another part of the forest, occurs between Amiens' instructions to "cover the while" and the eating of the food in 2.7. Some editors suggest that the food is left onstage during 2.6, hidden perhaps by a curtain, or visible and thus adding irony to Adam's near-starvation. There is no solution to this problem that takes care of every question. For example, our decision to omit the editorial direction to "set out food and drink" addresses the problem of the intervening scene but leaves hanging Amiens' line "His banquet is prepared" (60–61).

2.5.52. **Ducdame:** The play's dialogue twice indicates that Jaques' word may be nonsense. First, Amiens' "What's that 'ducdame'?" speaks of the word as if it were utterly strange. Then Jaques' identification of the word as "Greek" recalls the proverbial use of "Greek" to mean "unintelligible." Nonetheless, scholars have researched no fewer than seven languages (none of them Greek) in efforts to attach a meaning to "ducdame." Their solutions range from the prosaic "bring him to me" (a loose translation of the Latin *duc ad me*) all the way to the exotic *dukkerdom me* (Romany for "I told fortunes, cast spells").

2.7.46–63, 72–90. **It is . . . man:** In these two substantial speeches, Jaques offers a defense of satire that becomes, in the second speech, an example of satire. Both Jaques' argument and the language in which it is expressed reproduce what is to be found in the satire of Shakespeare's contemporaries, such as John Marston and Joseph Hall. In substance the argument is that the satirist does not libel any particular person, no matter how precisely the satirist's description may seem to apply to that person. Rather, the argument goes, if any person identifies him- or herself as the object of the satiric attack, that particular person bears the entire responsibility for the identification because satire is always general, never personal.

Jaques' second speech (lines 72–90) may be especially challenging to read because the satirists' style was deliberately crabbed, in imitation of the unusually difficult style of the Latin satirist Juvenal, whom they took as their model.

The objects of satire in Jaques' second speech are those people who transgress the sumptuary laws in place in the late sixteenth century. These laws forbade commoners from wearing bright colors and fine cloth, these being reserved for the nobility alone.

2.7.66–71. Most . . . world: In this speech, Duke Senior counters Jaques' speeches in defense of satire by characterizing the satirist as a dissolute person whose own corruption spills out in his attacks on others. Thus, rather than cleansing the world, the satirist corrupts it.

3.2.71–72. God . . . raw: Touchstone's speech may play with two customs, one involving cooking, the other medicine: blood was drawn from raw meat to make it more tender when cooked; blood was drawn from the ill in order to cure them. Touchstone suggests that Corin is inexperienced, untrained (unfinished), or **raw.** To improve or cure him, God must **make** an **incision in** him, and draw off blood.

3.2.120–22. the earliest fruit . . . medlar: This speech plays on a peculiar property (**right virtue**) of the **medlar,** which is not edible until it is rotten. Rosalind says that when she grafts it with Touchstone, the medlar will then be the first fruit to be ready to eat because, like Touchstone, it will be **rotten** before it is **half ripe**—with reference to Touchstone's untimely (that is, unripe) intrusions into Rosalind's reading of her lover's verse.

3.2.147. Helen's cheek, but not her heart: In mythology, the supremely beautiful **Helen** was the daughter of

Zeus and Leda and the wife of Menelaus. Her abduction by Paris caused the Trojan War. Some of Shakespeare's contemporaries, among them Edmund Spenser in Book III of *The Faerie Queene*, represented Helen as complicit in her abduction. She is represented in Shakespeare's *Troilus and Cressida* as beautiful but morally empty.

3.2.149. Atalanta's better part: In mythology, Atalanta was a beautiful, swift-footed maiden hunter who was averse to marriage. She agreed to marry only the man who could defeat her in a footrace. Editors have debated whether her **better part** was her swiftness of foot, her beauty, or her soul.

3.2.150. Lucretia's modesty: Lucretia was a legendary Roman matron who killed herself for shame after being raped by King Tarquin. Her story is told in Shakespeare's *The Rape of Lucrece*.

3.3.6–8. I am here with thee and thy goats, as the most capricious poet, honest Ovid, was among the Goths: In this elaborate and learned joke, Touchstone compares himself to the Roman love poet Ovid (43 B.C.–18 A.D.), exiled by the emperor Augustus to a town on the Danube among a tribe of "barbarians" who could not understand his poetry. Ovid, whose exile was perhaps a punishment for his amoral *The Art of Love*, was forced to live among the Getae, often confused in Shakespeare's day with the **Goths** (pronounced, at that time, "gotes"). Editors have suggested that there is not only a pun on *goats/Goths*, but also that **capricious** may here mean "lascivious, goat-like," from wordplay on the Latin *caper*—i.e., goat.

3.3.13–14. it strikes a man more dead than a great reckoning in a little room: Touchstone is perhaps saying that Audrey's inability to respond to his wit is more deadly than receiving a large bill for food and drink in a small room of a tavern. It has become popular to see this line as a reference to Christopher Marlowe's death in 1593 "in a little room," where he was stabbed in a fight over a "reckoning." The possible echo of Marlowe's line "Infinite riches in a little room," from his play *The Jew of Malta*, has encouraged this association. Many editors, however, remain skeptical.

3.3.42. Sir Oliver Martext: This name, especially the surname "Martext," characterizes Sir Oliver as a priest who mars or ruins the texts that he reads aloud in church. The title "Sir" may also reflect on his lack of learning, since, though this title was given to ordinary priests, it was sometimes used in contrast to the title "Master," given to priests who had graduated from a university. Sir Oliver's appearance in the forest and his willingness to marry Touchstone and Audrey "under a bush" (line 84) may also have connected him in people's minds with the so-called "hedge-priest," a name given to illiterate or uneducated priests.

3.3.49. horn-beasts: Beginning with this line, and through line 62, Touchstone reflects on the commonplace connection between beasts with horns and the fate of the married man, whose wife, Touchstone suggests, will certainly be unfaithful, making the husband a cuckold, or horned man. (See picture, page 184.) The association of cuckolds with horns growing from the man's forehead goes back to ancient times and may originate with the early and prevalent practice of "grafting the spurs of a castrated cock on the root of the excised comb, where they grew and became horns, sometimes of several inches long" (OED, *horn* 7a). In lines 49–62, Touchstone argues that poor men and rich men alike are cuckolded by their wives, but that even so it is better to be married (and, as a horned man, be like a **walled town**) than to be single (and be like an open, undefended **village**).

3.3.83–87. And will you . . . join you together: Jaques' objection to the proposed forest marriage may be, in part, because of Sir Oliver's lack of education (the word **fellow,** line 86, is often a term of contempt), but Jaques seems also to be speaking more generally for the church authorities, who insisted that a marriage be blessed with a sacred ceremony, held in the church before the congregation. Touchstone (lines 48–49) points out that "here we have no temple but the wood, no assembly but horn-beasts"—a setting that goes contrary to the "Form of Solemnization of Matrimony" of the Church of England, which read (in the 1559 Book of Common Prayer): "At the day appointed . . . , the persons to be married shall come into the body of the church, with their friends and neighbors." Jaques' demand that the couple "have a good priest that can tell you what marriage is" (lines 85–86) may also refer to the prescribed marriage ceremony, which has the priest begin with a lengthy description of what "holy matrimony" entails. Jaques' phrase "join you together" may also allude to this ceremony, which begins: "Dearly beloved, we are gathered together here in the sight of God, and in the face of his congregation, to join together this man and this woman in holy matrimony." The marriage that Sir Oliver was asked to perform would have been legal, but would not have been sanctioned by the church. (See Professor Snyder's "Modern Perspective," page 238.)

3.5.109. glean the broken ears: In Leviticus 19:9–10 and 23:22, the Israelites are told by the Lord that, when reaping the harvest, they are to leave some grain unharvested for the poor and the stranger, and they are not to "gather the gleanings," or the ears left behind on the ground by the reapers; in Ruth 2:7, Ruth asks to "glean and gather after the reapers among the sheaves."

4.1.145. commission: While editors do not agree about the precise meaning of Rosalind's statement ("I might ask you for your commission"), or even about the person she is speaking to (some arguing that the words make more sense if addressed to Celia), there is agreement that her words should be seen in the larger context of the mock–marriage which, in fact, follows the prescribed form for legal wedlock in Elizabethan England. Rosalind insists that Orlando put his marriage vow in the present tense (she has him rephrase his "I will" so that it specifies "now"), and she answers him with her own "I take thee," again in the present tense. The presence of a third party adds an additional legal sanction. For an Elizabethan audience, then, this scene would have had resonances of an actual exchange of marriage vows, resonances that are not immediately available today because of changes in customs.

4.2.4. like a Roman conqueror: Sir Thomas Elyot, in *The Governor* (1531), writes: "To them which, in this hunting [of the deer] do show most prowess and activity, a garland or some other like token to be given in sign of victory and with a joyful manner to be brought in the presence of him that is chief in the company. . . ." A hunter celebrated in this manner would be **like a Roman conqueror** who had been awarded wreaths of laurel bows to celebrate his military victory. See illustration, page 158.

4.2.13SD. The rest shall bear this burden: In the Folio, these words are printed continuously with our line 13, so that the line reads "Then sing him home, the rest shall beare this burthen." Since the early 18th century, editors have tended to print "The rest shall bear this burden" as a stage direction, with the suggestion that "burden" carries its meaning of "refrain." Although some editors today print the line as part of the song, we agree with those who feel that it reads much more like a direction than as part of the lyrics, though we acknowledge the uncertainty here.

Whether part of the lyrics or a stage direction, the word *burden* is puzzling. Musically, it could mean either a refrain (that is, lines sung at the end of each stanza) or an accompaniment or "undersong"—the bass part sung along with the melody. Neither quite works here: there are no lines repeated at the ends of stanzas, and "this burden" is an awkward way to refer to an undersong. It has been suggested that "this burden" may refer instead to the deer's horns, and some editors have worked out elaborate stagings that involve sets of horns being attached to "the rest"—i.e., all the other lords singing.

One can only acknowledge the uncertainties surrounding this line.

5.2.34–39. no sooner met . . . marriage: Rosalind's speech exhibits elaborately patterned language, which calls attention to itself: "no sooner met . . . looked, no sooner looked . . . loved, no sooner loved . . . sighed," and so on. This rhetorical scheme is called *gradatio* (gradation) by Roman rhetoricians and "the staircase" by the Greeks. So Rosalind's use of "degrees" (steps) and "a pair [i.e., flight] of stairs" are both puns, referring not only to the progress of Oliver and Celia's love but also to the way in which she has described it.

5.2.65. not damnable: The practice of magic carried with it many dangers, including the danger, to the magician, of being executed by the state. It was also dangerous for the magician's soul, since magic practice was thought to involve spirits that were often evil (and connected to Satan). "Ganymede" argues that this magician does not call on evil spirits or otherwise endanger his soul. "Ganymede" makes the point again (lines 70–72) that, though "he" will set Rosalind before Orlando's eyes through a kind of magic, it will be the living Rosalind (not a phantom or a supernatural image of her), and that the producing of Rosalind will not carry with it the danger that goes with the summoning of spirits—including the danger of being put to death.

5.3.16–39. It was a lover and his lass: The words and music to this song were published in Thomas Morley's *The First Booke of Ayres* in 1600. (The only copy of this book still in existence today is in the Folger Shakespeare Library. We include, on pages xxxvi–xxxvii, a photograph of the song as printed in Morley.) There is no agreement among scholars about who wrote the words or the music. It is possible that Shakespeare wrote the words and Morley the music, or that Morley wrote both words and music and Shakespeare used them for his play, or that this was a popular song used by both Shakespeare and Morley.

The final stanza of Morley's *First Booke of Ayres* appears as the second stanza in the Folio text of *As You Like It*. Editors of the play (including the editors of this edition) have, since the eighteenth century, followed the arrangement as it appears in Morley, since the narrative structure of the song argues for this arrangement rather than for the Folio's.

5.4.49. I have had four quarrels: According to Vincentio Saviolo, a leading London rapier instructor in the

sixteenth century, a gentleman or nobleman who is
mocked or who is accused of dishonor, slander, or libel
must respond in quite specific ways in order to protect
his honor. In Saviolo's "Of Honor and Honorable **Quarrels**" (the second part of his *Saviolo his practice*, 1594), a
quarrel is, variously, "the action that determines the
truth of an accusation," "the cause of the hostility," "the
charge leveled against the defendant," and "the state
resulting from a person's feeling injured, either by word
or deed, or from one man charging another with
dishonorable conduct." In the context of the "code
duello" described by Saviolo, we might translate Touchstone's "I have had four quarrels, and like to have fought
one," as "I have been involved in four formal contentions that, had they not been resolved in a court of law
or otherwise settled, would have been resolved with
swords; one of the four contentions came close to such a
violent resolution."

Many of the words used by Touchstone in lines 49–55
and 71–107 are precise terms from the code duello:
taken up, cause, the lie, and *to give the lie* are some of
these terms.

**5.4.74–75. if I said his beard was not cut well, he
was in the mind it was:** This is a comic example of an
insult and of the mildest form of response to that insult.
The most extreme form of response would be for the
insulted courtier to say: "You said my beard was not
well cut. You are a liar." This is "the lie direct," which a
gentleman, to protect his honor, must answer in one of
three ways: (1) He can say "I never said your beard was
not well cut." (2) He can prove that, in fact, the beard
was "not well cut," and thus that he was not lying. (3)
He can challenge the courtier to single combat. Touchstone's parody provides several intermediate responses
between **the retort courteous** and **the lie direct.**

5.4.135. If truth holds true contents: The critic Malcolm Evans has shown that when one takes into account the possible meanings of **truth** (that which is true, that which is faithful), **holds** (supports, restrains, sustains, interrupts), **true** (true, faithful), and **contents** (substance, pleasures), then multiplies these permutations by the differing implications of **If** (as a conditional implying an invitation to consent and as indication of a fiction), and, finally, adds these readings of the line as they apply to the stage fiction to the readings as they apply to the audience, one comes up with 168 ways this line can be read; many of the readings throw interesting and helpful light on the play as a whole. (See Evans's "Truth's True Contents," *Signifying Nothing: Truth's True Contents in Shakespeare's Text* [Athens, Georgia: The University of Georgia Press, 1986], pp. 143–91.

5.4.194–98. You . . . bed: Since Nicholas Rowe's edition of 1709, these three verse lines have been marked as directed to the three different men in order of their current status or rank, first Orlando, then Oliver, and then Silvius. While rank counted for a great deal in Shakespeare's time, it needs to be noted that the selection of addressees for the individual lines is merely an editorial choice. The same considerations apply to the selection of addressees for lines 136 and 137 above. In this latter case, no editor specified the addressees before Deighton in 1891.

Textual Notes

The reading of the present text appears to the left of the square bracket. Unless otherwise noted, the reading to the left of the bracket is from **F**, the First Folio text (upon which this edition is based). The earliest sources of readings not in **F** are indicated as follows: **Morley** is Thomas Morley's *The First Booke of Ayres, Or Little Songs, to Sing and Play to the Lute* of 1600; **F2** is the Second Folio of 1632; **F3** is the Third Folio of 1663–64; **F4** is the Fourth Folio of 1685; **Ed.** is an earlier editor of Shakespeare, beginning with Rowe in 1709. No sources are given for emendations of punctuation or for corrections of obvious typographical errors, like turned letters that produce no known word. **SD** means stage direction; **SP** means speech prefix; **uncorr.** means the first or uncorrected state of the First Folio; **corr.** means the second or corrected state of the First Folio; ~ stands in place of a word already quoted before the square bracket; ∧ indicates the omission of a punctuation mark.

1.1	12. manage] F (mannage)
	61. so.] ~, F
	83. SD *Ex. Orl. Ad.* F
	108. she] F3; hee F
	160. SP OLIVER] F2; *omit* F
	160. SD *Exit.* F *1 line earlier.*
	168. misprized] F (misprised)
1.2	3. I] Ed.; *omit* F
	43. No?] ~; F
	44 SD *and hereafter in SDD.* Touchstone] Ed.; *Clowne* F, *where SD is 2 lines earlier.*
	53. and] Ed.; *omit* F

57 *and hereafter.* SP TOUCHSTONE] Ed.;
     Clow. F
58. father] farher F
82. SP CELIA] Ed.; *Ros.* F
82. him.] ~ ∧ F
90. Le] F2; the F
96. *Bonjour*] F (*Boon-iour*)
104. rank—] ~. F
114. sons—] ~. F
143 SP *and hereafter.* DUKE FREDERICK]
     Ed.; *Duke* F
152. you,] ~ ∧ F
174. misprized] F (misprised)
239–40. deserved. . . . love ∧]~, . . . ~; F
241. justly,] ~ ∧ F
244. fortune,] ~ ∧ F
251. quintain] F (quintine)
257. SD *Rosalind . . . exit*] Ed.; *Exit* F
261. SD *2 lines earlier in* F
263. To] Te F
273. smaller] Ed.; taller F
1.3   37. SD *2 lines earlier in* F
60. likelihood] F2; likelihoods F
80. smoothness,] ~; F
81. her] per F
86. lips.] ~ ∧ F
87. doom] F (doombe)
93. SD *Exit Duke, &c.* F
127. martial] F (marshall)
133. be] F2; by F
138. travel] F (trauaile)
144. go we in] F2; goe in we F
2.1   51. much] F2; must F
53. friends] Ed.; friend F
2.2   10. gentlewoman] Centlewoman F
21. SD *They exit*] *Exunt* F

2.3   8. prizer] F (priser)
      10. some] F2; seeme F
      16. SP ORLANDO] F2; *omit* F
      19. lives.] ~ ∧ F
      30. SP ORLANDO] F2; *Ad.* F
      72. seventeen] Ed.; seauentie F
2.4   1. weary] Ed.; merry F
      18. SD *1 line earlier in* F
      32. heartily.] ~, F
      43. thy wound] Ed.; they would F
      71. you] F2; your F
      76. travel] F (trauaile)
      84. recks] F (wreakes)
      86 *and hereafter.* cote] F (Coate)
      100. me.] ~, F
2.5   1. SP AMIENS] Ed.; *omit* F
      3. *turn*] tnrne F
      28. not,] ~ ∧ F
      36. SP ALL *together here*] this ed; *Altogether heere* F
  42–43. *No . . . weather*] Ed.; &c. F
      47. SP JAQUES] F2; *Amy.* F
2.7   0. SD *Senior*] F (*Sen.*)
      0. SD *Lords*] Ed.; *Lord* F
      39. brain] braiue F
      50. Withal] Wiithall F
      57. Not to] Ed.; *omit* F
      66. chiding sin] F2; chiding fin F
      91. comes] F2; come F
      102. say.] ~, F
      119. been] bcene F
      120. sat] F (sate)
      139. find] sinde F
      158. sudden ∧] ~, F
      167. wide ∧] ~, F
      169. treble,] ~ ∧ F

	173.	SD *carrying*] Ed.; *with* F
	182.	SP AMIENS *sings*] Ed.; *omit* F
	190.	*Then*] Ed.; *The* F
	193.	*bite*] F (*bight*)
198–201.	heigh-ho . . . jolly] &c. F
	209.	master] F2; masters F
3.1	15.	Well,] ~ ∧ F
3.2	11, 86.	Master] F (Mr)
	21.	Hast] F (Has't)
	27.	good] pood F
	32, 40.	Wast] F (Was't)
	49.	court ∧] ~, F
	75.	good,] ~ ∧ F
	85.	SD *2 lines later in* F
	127.	a] Ed.; *omit* F
	130.	*show*] F (*shoe*)
	137.	*boughs*] F (*bowes*)
	145.	*enlarged.*] ~, F
	147.	*her*] Ed.; *his* F
	161.	now?—Back,] ~ ∧ ~ ∧ F
	165.	SD *Exit.* F
	197.	whooping] F (hooping)
	241.	such] F2; *omit* F
	248.	thy] Ed.; the F
	250.	heart] F (*Hart*)
	255.	SD *1 line earlier in* F
	262.	God be wi'] F (God buy)
	277.	conned] F (cond)
	303.	is 't] i'st F
	353.	lectures] F (Lectors)
	369.	deifying] F2; defying F
	377.	are] F2; art F
3.3	0.	SD *followed by*] Ed.; *and* F
	55.	Horns? Even so. . . . alone?] Ed.; ~, ~~ ∧ . . . ~ : F

	66.	*and hereafter*. SP OLIVER MARTEXT] F
		(*Ol.*)
	73.	Monsieur] F (Mr)
	96.	SP TOUCHSTONE] F2 (*Clo.*); *Ol.* F
	98.	Master] F (Mr)
	107.	SD *Exeunt.* F
3.4	13.	the] thc F
	29.	a] F2; *omit* F
	41.	puny] F (puisny)
3.5	1.	Phoebe.] ~ ʌ F
	12.	pretty,] ~ ʌ F
	32.	wounds] wouuds F
	70.	hear] F (here)
	138.	I] F2; *omit* F
	147.	straight] F (strait)
4.1	1.	be] F2; *not in* F
	21.	my] F2; by F
	31.	travel] F (trauaile)
	32.	SD *4 lines earlier in* F
	34.	be wi'] F (buy)
	41.	gondola] F (Gundello)
	52.	whole] F (hole)
	73.	holiday] F (holy-day)
	163.	hyena] F (Hyen)
	176.	wilt] F (wil't)
	178.	wife's] F (wiues)
	192.	o'clock] F (a clock)
	197.	hour?] ~. F
	223.	in, it] F2; in, in F
4.2	13.	SD *printed as part of the song in* F
4.3	1.	o'clock] F (a clock)
	5.	SD *2 lines earlier in* F
	12.	tenor] F (tenure)
	30.	huswife's] F (huswiues)
	78.	SD *Silvius*] F (*Sil.*)
	82.	bottom;] ~ ʌ F
	109.	boughs] F (bows)

115. threats,] ~ ∧ F
116. suddenly,] ~ ∧ F
150. place—] ~. F
151. In] F2; I F
164. his] F2; this F

5.1   9. SD *1 line later in* F
11. clown.] ~, F
15. gi'] F (ye)
18. covered] eouer'd F
21. SP TOUCHSTONE] F *corr. (Clo.); Orl.* F
        uncorr.
22. SP WILLIAM] F *corr. (Will.); Clo.* F
        uncorr.
23. Wast] F (Was't)
27. SP TOUCHSTONE] Ed.; *Cle.* F
37. sir] F2; sit F
56. policy] F2; police F

5.2   7. her] Ed.; *omit* F
27. swoon] F (sound)
33. overcame] F2; overcome F
59. are] F2; arc F
68. straits] F (straights)
71. human] F (humane)
120. will] wlll F
121. satisfy] Ed.; satisfi'd F

5.3   5. SD *1 line later in* F
19. *springtime*] Ed.; *the spring time* F
19. *ring*] Morley; *rang* F
24. *lie* ∧] ~. F
25–27. *the only . . . the spring*] Ed.; *&c.* F
31–33. *the only . . . the spring*] Ed.; *&c.* F
34–37. *And . . . springtime*] Morley; *printed in* F
        after line 21
36. *prime,*] ~. F
37–39. *the only . . . the spring*] Ed.; *&c.* F
46. be wi'] F (buy)

5.4   26. SD *Rosalind*] F (*Ros.*)
                 30. daughter] daughrer F
                 35. SD *1 line earlier in* F
                 84. to] ro F
                 84. the] F2; *omit* F
                 117. hither,] ~. F
                 118. her] his F
                 153. daughter,] ~ ∧ F
                 169. them] Ed.; him F
                 177. here were] here vvete F
                 180. share] sharc F
                 189. SP SECOND BROTHER] F *corr.* (*2. Bro.*);
                          2. Bri. F *uncorr.*
                 192. bequeath;] ~ ∧ F
                 205. see] F *corr.*; sce F *uncorr.*
                 207. rites] F (rights)
                 208. trust ∧] ~, F
                 208. SD *Exit.* F
Epilogue 9. play!] F *corr.* (~?); ~. F *uncorr.*

As You Like It:
A Modern Perspective

Susan Snyder

In some ways, *As You Like It* is as difficult to pin down as its permissive name suggests. Plot provides the usual framework for investigating a play, but here the plot is all huddled into the beginning and the end. For the middle three acts, the normal impetus of dramatic action is more or less left on hold. In the opening act, things happen quickly. Oliver plots against his hated younger brother, Orlando, who wins the wrestling match anyway; Rosalind and Orlando fall in love; Rosalind is banished; Orlando comes to blows with Oliver and runs off to escape his brother's hostility. At the other end of the play, in the very last scene, the usurper Duke Frederick is converted, repents, and gives up the throne to the rightful duke, Rosalind's father; and all the young people get married. In between, very little happens, in a plot sense. Oliver, a bad brother like Duke Frederick, has a change of heart and falls in love with Celia. (This "action," like the repentance and abdication of Duke Frederick himself, is not shown onstage but only related to us.) And in a subplot Rosalind straightens out the cross-wooings of Phoebe and Silvius so that they can be one of the happy couples at the end.

That's not much for three acts. Compared with most of Shakespeare's comparable plays, *As You Like It* noticeably lacks a strong forward thrust. The other comedies have pressing questions: Can Antonio be saved from Shylock (*The Merchant of Venice*)? Will the mixups created by Oberon's magic love-juice in *A Midsummer Night's Dream* be sorted out? How will the shrew be tamed in the play of that name? Instead of forces like these pressing us onward, what we have in the Forest of Arden is something like "time out" in a basketball game. While the clock is on, the action rushes forward. Then the clock is stopped, and there is a period of time that doesn't "count." Urgencies are suspended. Time is out: out of its customary course, displaced from the usual relentless sequence, not pressing on with problems to be solved and deadlines to be met, liberated from its own rules. In Arden, we are told, people "fleet the time carelessly, as they did in the golden world" (1.1.117–18): in Arden, freed from the court imperative to "sweat . . . for promotion" (2.3.61), one can enjoy moments as they happen without any sense of waste. Time in *As You Like It* is, as Helen Gardner says, "unmeasured": rather than events pushing us forward, we get more a sense of space, "a space in which to work things out."[1]

Space in the more literal sense, geography, plays its part in this suspension of urgency. The Forest of Arden is somewhere other, a "world elsewhere": part of the dukedom, presumably, but beyond the courtly sphere of influence. It is rural rather than urban or courtly, though its pastoral nature has more to do with literary tradition than with real country life.[2] Silvius and Phoebe are pure pastoral artifice, invoking a long-established literary convention of lovelorn swains and disdainful shepherdesses by their names as well as their situation: The forest itself is not an ordinary woodland, harboring as it does not only deer and gilded snakes but palm trees and a lioness. Even the sheep are peculiar, when you come to think of it. Sheep eat grass, which is not plentiful in forests. But what is a pastoral without sheep, however improbable they may be in practical terms?

The landscape created by the play's dialogue is a kind

of composite literary wilderness, it seems, a construction of the mind. It is appropriate, then, that Arden is a place to test out poses and hypotheses: to take on a different role or position in a playful, temporary way to see how it feels or find out what can be learned from a perspective that is not your habitual one. Time-out in a game means, as in Arden, discussion rather than action. It is also an opportunity for substitutions: A, who has been central before, comes back to sit on the sidelines for a while, and B, who has been an onlooker, takes on a new role in the action. The analogy breaks down at this point because, in a game, stepping into the new role means abandoning the former one. You can't be both participating in the game-action and watching from the sidelines. In *As You Like It*, though, new roles expand characters as they add the roles onto their usual selves. Duke Senior is still the ruler while he plays Robin Hood in the forest. Touchstone the Fool struts around among the yokels as a courtier while still being the witty commentator—that is, the Fool. Jaques the complainer aspires to Touchstone's role himself ("O, that I were a fool! / I am ambitious for a motley coat": 2. 7.43–44)—but he keeps on complaining. Most of all, Rosalind remains the woman in love while also entering into her acquired persona of the scoffing boy Ganymede, who jeers at love and lovers.

Role-playing and debating stand in for dramatic complications in the central section of *As You Like It*. The typical "action" is a discussion—an unresolved discussion with no winner or loser. This part of the play is made up of conversational encounters as one pair after another meets, talks, separates: Rosalind-Orlando, Orlando-Jaques, Jaques-Touchstone, Touchstone-Corin, Rosalind-Touchstone, Phoebe-Silvius, Corin-Silvius, and so on. Talking about love, talking about time, talking about country life. To every proposition, there is a counterview. Amiens sings of the joys of life in the forest, and then Jaques sings his

own contrary verse of the same song to show what fools he
and his friends are for leaving the civilized comforts of the
court. Rosalind reads Orlando's courtly love poem:

> From the east to western Ind
> No jewel is like Rosalind.
> Her worth being mounted on the wind,
> Through all the world bears Rosalind.
> (3.2.88–91)

But, after more such couplets, Touchstone, bored with
this idealizing love, carries on in the same rhythm and
rhyme scheme to stress the more earthy side of wooing
and mating:

> If the cat will after kind,
> So be sure will Rosalind.
> Wintered garments must be lined;
> So must slender Rosalind.
> (3.2.103–6)

In these debates, there is no victor. We may sometimes
think that one speaker has the better of it—Orlando in
this same scene, for example, seems to best Jaques both
in his witty putdown and in the values he espouses (lines
258–98)—but such advantages have no consequences
for the action. As in the more even exchanges, each
speaker has his say, and they pass on to other things:
"Farewell, good Signior Love. . . . Adieu, good Monsieur
Melancholy" (lines 295–98). In a pinch, a single character can carry on a debate with himself. When Touchstone
is asked how he likes the shepherd's life, he manages to
be pro and con simultaneously:

> Truly, shepherd, in respect of itself, it is a good life;
> but in respect that it is a shepherd's life, it is naught.

In respect that it is solitary, I like it very well; but in respect that it is private, it is a very vile life. Now in respect it is in the fields, it pleaseth me well; but in respect it is not in the court, it is tedious. As it is a spare life, look you, it fits my humor well; but as there is no more plenty in it, it goes much against my stomach. (3.2.13–21)

The debate may not be posed as a debate at all, but emerge from simple juxtaposition. In the first Arden scene, Duke Senior paints an idyllic picture of life in the forest: away from the pomp and envy of the court, nature supplies all they need.

> And this our life, exempt from public haunt,
> Finds tongues in trees, books in the running
>   brooks,
> Sermons in stones, and good in everything.
> (2.1.15–17)

How pleasant, how benign. But almost in the next breath the Duke has to acknowledge that their living off nature is hard on the deer they kill for food. And one of his fellow hunters then tells very graphically of seeing a wounded deer die in anguish, cut off from the herd. Life in harmony with nature looks more Darwinian from the perspective of the suffering deer. And how natural is it, anyway? Duke Senior cannot describe what is good about their existence in the wild without referring to civilized products and practices like sermons and books. As soon as we enter it, the forest is represented as an imaginative construction—imagined by civilized people who hear sermons and read books.

In all these exchanges—between Amiens and Jaques, Orlando and Touchstone, Touchstone the courtier and Touchstone the pastoralist, even Duke Senior and the deer—the point seems to be not which is right and which is wrong, but the dual view itself: the rhythm in which a single, limiting perspective is qualified/expanded/countered by another based on a different "truth."[3] Even the most celebrated speech in the play, Jaques' summing up of human life that begins "All the world's a stage" (2. 7.146–73), is not left unqualified. In his bravura performance Jaques demonstrates to his audience how all men enact one standard role after another through their lives, from the infant mewling and puking, to the decrepit old man in his second childhood. Summarized in this reductive way, the entire human journey is pointless and arbitrary, especially since no stage brings with it any joy or satisfaction. The schoolboy isn't seen as empowered by learning new things, but only resisting instruction. The lover's sighs and woeful ballads don't win him his lady. Any fame the soldier wins for facing danger is discounted as "the bubble reputation." In Jaques' gloomy vision, we move through a series of stances imposed on us by the passage of time, with no say in the matter and no rewards along the way. But much later in the play, Jaques' sour view of things is forcefully countered by the pages' song "It was a lover and his lass" (5. 3.16–39). This cheerful, energetic lyric does not seek to deny that "life is but a flower": time passes quickly, the blooming season is short. But the song's answering exhortation is to make the most of each season, especially spring—the mating time. There is fulfillment for those who seize the day.

> And therefore take the present time,
>   With a hey, and a ho, and a hey-nonny-no,
> For love is crownèd with the prime,
>   In springtime, the only pretty ring time.
> (5.3.34–37)

Versions of love also play off one another—romantic and cynical, equal and hierarchical, spiritual and animal.

Rosalind as Ganymede, like Touchstone, encloses opposites in her double self and displays them, almost simultaneously, to the bemused Orlando. But there is some danger in all this. Multiplying perspectives without any clear priority or strong direction can be liberating. Yet it can also destabilize, erasing fixed meaning and denying any resolution that allows us to conclude one phase in order to move on to the next. Intellectual sparring can become a substitute for getting on with life, in that it holds real action, including sexual consummation, at a remove. When Oliver and Celia fall in love and immediately move toward marriage, Orlando becomes impatient with the game he is playing with Ganymede-pretending-to-be-Rosalind. Perhaps this realization that he "can live no longer by thinking" (5.2.53) is exactly the effect intended by the disguised Rosalind when she describes so forcefully to Orlando the sudden mutual desire of Oliver and Celia, their close relatives and peers.[4] In any case, each hears the signal to rejoin real time.

As we would expect, it is Rosalind who achieves this resolution; more surprisingly, she announces she will do it by magic. "I can do strange things," she says. "I have, since I was three year old, conversed with a magician, most profound in his art. . . . I am a magician" (5.2.62–65, 75). Why this elaborate appeal to supernatural powers, we wonder, since to bring this devious courtship to conclusion on the level of plot, she need only reveal her true identity? Perhaps the insistent gesture toward magic is a way of reaching to another level, quite beyond the endlessly repeated exchanges and qualifications—a transcendence felt to be necessary to resolve the "action" of Arden, because there is really no logical end to deconstructive games. Without some deus-ex-machina intervention, they could go on forever. So, by "magic" of some undefined sort, Rosalind undoes the spell of Arden and pairs up the couples, including herself in one of them. Since this disentangling and settling is so clearly her work, we are made to feel that the sudden appearance at the play's close of Hymen, the Roman god of marriage who "bar[s] confusion" and "make[s] conclusion" (5.4.130–31), is somehow her doing as well. This supernatural visitation also signals the end of suspended time and the return of the forest visitors to the court, and not merely because these final ceremonies are interrupted by news that the usurper has abdicated and left the way open for the exiles' return. In the forest we have seen a couple of "dry runs" toward marriage: Celia pretends to be a priest marrying Orlando with Rosalind-Ganymede-Rosalind (4.1.129–48), and Touchstone enlists Sir Oliver Martext to join him to Audrey with only the trees for a temple and only the beasts for witnesses (3.3.40–107). But the play-wedding breaks down in laughter—Celia "cannot say the words," and Rosalind wants to say more than her assigned ones. Touchstone's woodland nuptials are interrupted by Jaques, who points out their irregularity: Sir Oliver may know the words somewhat better than Celia, but he omits the counseling of bride and groom on "what marriage is" that begins the traditional ceremony, as well as the calling of the banns that should precede it—in short, the all-important social dimension of marriage. Hymen, however, is "god of every town" (5.4.151). The settled marital commitment that he represents has to do not with the unstructured casual engagements of the forest but with civilized society, which is founded on the ordered relation of wedlock. Of all the forest expatriates, only Jaques goes on standing aside, withholding commitment. He joins the converted Duke Frederick in order to take up yet another pose, that of intellectual hermit, and presumably go on posturing and deflating the posturings of others.

The Arden interlude is "time out," not only from exigencies of plot-action, but also from the power relations inherent in the usual social structure (usual in the court of the early scenes and in the world of Shakespeare's audience as well). This normative society is hierarchical, vesting power in the senior male: the father, and then the eldest brother, who under the law of primogeniture inherited all the father's power and wealth. Women and younger brothers were subordinate. But not in the Forest of Arden.

For instance, paternal control of marriage, which was a given in the everyday social order and is a powerful normative force that most Shakespearean comic plots have to reckon with, is simply a non-issue here. Rosalind and Celia choose their husbands on their own, and neither one gives much thought to her father's wishes when she agrees to marry. Rosalind's father is nearby, but she does not seek sanction from him for her choice, a choice that is itself a violation of social hierarchies in that she is a princess and Orlando merely a gentleman. While she does set up Duke Senior to give her to her husband, the ritual is quite opposite to the usual arranged marriage. The daughter has done the arranging, and the father simply ratifies her choice. When Rosalind finally reveals herself in woman's clothes to Duke Senior, she sounds a note of daughterly duty: "To you I give myself, for I am yours." But then she turns to Orlando and repeats the same words: "To you I give myself, for I am yours." We get the impression that she is choosing her father as well as her husband. "I'll have no father, if you be not he. / I'll have no husband, if you be not he" (5.4.120–21,126–27). In this world of upended hierarchies, the only candidate for marriage who does ask for permission is Oliver, who asks his brother—his younger brother.

Which brings us to that other prominent feature of social hierarchy, primogeniture. In economic terms, this system of inheritance settling everything on the eldest son functioned to keep an estate intact by denying any

share in it to younger children. But what then happened
to those younger sons, caught between their good birth
and their lack of the income needed to sustain a gentleman's life? Primogeniture could create enormous in-
equalities between siblings, turning the brother-brother
relationship into one like that of father-child, or even of
master-servant. It was the heir's moral responsibility to
settle his brothers in appropriate positions, but if he
didn't do so, they had no recourse.[5] Oliver in *As You Like
It*, eldest of the three sons of the late Sir Rowland de
Boys, does right by the middle brother, sending him to be
educated, but he keeps the youngest one untrained, in a
servile condition. Why? Oliver wonders that himself.
After sending Orlando into a potentially fatal fight with
the Duke's wrestler, he says in soliloquy,

> I hope I shall see an end of him, for my soul—yet I
> know not why—hates nothing more than he. Yet
> he's gentle, never schooled and yet learned, full of
> noble device, of all sorts enchantingly beloved, and
> indeed so much in the heart of the world, and
> especially of my own people, . . . that I am altogeth-
> er misprized.

>   (1.1.161–68)

What to Oliver is a contradiction—I hate him, yet he is
full of good qualities and admired by everyone—sounds
to the audience more like psychological cause and effect:
I hate him because he puts me in the shade. Not for
nothing is this society called "the envious court" (2.1.4);
the same resentment of another's good also shapes the
play's other fraternal relationship. In the ducal family it
was the younger son who usurped the dukedom held by
his elder brother. While Frederick has seized power some
time before the play opens and there is no direct discussion of his motives for it, we can see traces of an abiding

envy of his brother when he banishes his niece Rosalind, not for anything she has done but for what she is: her father's daughter. Frederick defends his arbitrary cruelty by assuring Celia that Rosalind's popularity diminishes Celia: "She robs thee of thy name, / And thou wilt show more bright and seem more virtuous / When she is gone" (1.3.83–86). Since his daughter has no such feelings, we suspect that Duke Frederick is projecting onto Celia his own envy of his elder brother, as he repeats his act against Duke Senior by banishing Rosalind.

With primogeniture as with marital choice and class divisions, the play seems to resist the status quo on various fronts, enacting the wish to choose one's marriage partner freely and to measure the worth of men independent of any conferred superiority. But the dramatic outcome is carefully balanced. An across-the-board challenge to primogeniture, especially on the state level, would strike at the foundations of social order. To be sure, younger brother Orlando does come out on top of elder brother Oliver. But Duke Senior (emphasize the word *senior*) is restored to rightful rule. And in approving his daughter's choice of a non-noble younger son as husband, he also makes Orlando heir to the dukedom. The father-duke thus accepts Rosalind's independent selection of her own husband but at the same time makes sure that the ruler who succeeds him will be male and erases the class difference by elevating Orlando's rank. Anarchic wishes are acted out and satisfied, but contained.

"Time out" does not mean that a whole social system can be cast permanently into anarchy. At the very end of the play, the actor who plays Rosalind stands alone onstage to deliver the epilogue. It is a position of power, and the speaker accentuates how unusual it is by starting out, "It is not the fashion to see the lady the epilogue." It was not the fashion, either, in Shakespeare's time to see a

lady as autonomous and powerful as Rosalind has been
in this play. But we should bear in mind that Shakespeare's Rosalind was played by a male actor. This
epilogue functions, like any of Shakespeare's epilogues,
to effect a transition from the fictional world of the play
to the real world in which the spectators live. Proceeding
with this transition, the Rosalind-actor continues, "If I
were a woman. . . ." But he is no longer a woman, and
the woman has lost her special power. "Time out" is over,
and the game goes on.

---

1. *"As You Like It," Twentieth-Century Interpretations of
"As You Like It"* (Englewood Cliffs, NJ: Prentice-Hall,
1968), p. 60.

2. The pastoral convention in literature, which *As You
Like It* both incorporates and interrogates, pictures shepherds in an idealized version of country life, sometimes
tending sheep but mainly engaged in amorous courtship
and creating songs.

3. My discussion of pluralism and qualification in *As
You Like It* is to some extent a development of Harold
Jenkins' observation: "One must not say that Shakespeare never judges, but one judgment is always being
modified by another. Opposite views may contradict one
another, but of course they do not cancel out. Instead
they add up to an all-embracing view far larger and more
satisfying than any one of them in itself" (*"As You Like
It," Shakespeare Survey* 8 [1955], 45).

4. Mario DiGangi, "Queering the Shakespearean Family," *Shakespeare Quarterly* 47 (1996), 284.

5. Primogeniture and fraternal relations are examined
in depth by Louis Adrian Montrose in "'The place of a
brother' in *As You Like It*: Social Process and Comic
Form," *Shakespeare Quarterly* 32 (1981): 28–54.

Further Reading

As You Like It

Adelman, Janet. "Male Bonding in Shakespeare's Comedies." In *Shakespeare's "Rough Magic": Renaissance Essays in Honor of C. L. Barber*, edited by Peter Erickson and Coppélia Kahn, pp. 73–103, esp. pp. 81–87. Newark: University of Delaware Press; Toronto and London: Associated University Presses, 1985.

Adelman examines fantasies of male bonds and the threat posed to them by women. Through strategies of isolation (male and heterosexual relations operate in total separation from one another in the plot) and camouflage (Rosalind's disguise as Ganymede permits Orlando's wooing to be experienced as "simultaneously homosexual and heterosexual"), *As You Like It* provides "a suggestive model" for managing the conflict between male friendship and heterosexual love, thereby avoiding the magical solution to the problem favored in the early comedies and the disastrous consequences explored in the tragedies and romances. Because marriage functions as "the means by which Orlando is restored to his rightful place in the male order of things," the married state is ultimately experienced not as "problematically related to male identity" but as "joyous resolution."

Barton, Anne. "*As You Like It* and *Twelfth Night*: Shakespeare's Sense of an Ending." In *Shakespearian Comedy*, edited by Malcolm Bradbury and D. J. Palmer, pp. 160–80. Stratford-upon-Avon Studies 14. London: Edward Arnold; New York: Crane, Russak, 1972.

As You Like It, which unfolds through a network of

parallels and contrasts that constantly test a variety of love relationships and attitudes toward life, represents for Barton the culmination of Shakespearean form. Shakespeare "mitigate[s]" the violence in the original story (Thomas Lodge's *Rosalynde*) to create a play distinguished by poise, balance, and classical stability. The "fullest and most stable realization" of this harmony emerges in the final moments, where Shakespeare achieves a masterful balance of romance and realism.

Belsey, Catherine. "Disrupting Sexual Difference: Meaning and Gender in the Comedies." In *Alternative Shakespeares*, edited by John Drakakis, pp. 166–90, esp. pp. 180–85. New York: Methuen, 1985.
    Belsey includes *As You Like It* in her discussion of how Shakespeare's comedies radically challenge patriarchal values by disrupting the stereotypical differences between masculine and feminine. In its use of the transvestite boy heroine who speaks from a position that "is not that of a full, unified gendered subject," *As You Like It* can be read as raising at certain moments the basic question, "Who is speaking?"—Rosalind or Ganymede? With the added dimension of a male actor playing the part of a female, as was the case in Shakespeare's theater, it becomes possible "to attribute a certain autonomy" to the voice of Ganymede, especially where the voice is not "so palpably feminine" (e.g., the passages where Rosalind as Ganymede mocks women). The comedy of the Epilogue owes its "resonance" to the fact that "a male actor *and* a female character is speaking." Heroines like Rosalind may "dwindle" into wives but "only after they have been shown to be something altogether more singular—because more plural."

Berry, Edward I. "Rosalynde and Rosalind." *Shakespeare Quarterly* 31 (1980): 42–52.

Berry focuses his comparative study of *As You Like It* and its narrative source, Thomas Lodge's *Rosalynde,* on the alterations Shakespeare introduced into his heroine: greater scope of activity, magical power, a "strong dose" of antifeminism, an obsession with time, and a link between parental and romantic love. The invention of "diverse sounding boards" in Touchstone and Jaques, foils to Rosalind, creates further "resonances" not found in Lodge. With her pervasive consciousness and control, Shakespeare's Rosalind emerges as "a figure of the playwright himself." A close examination of 1.2 reveals her capacity for compressing thought and feeling, thus making "her every exchange a rich psychological event."

DiGangi, Mario. "Queering the Shakespearean Family." *Shakespeare Quarterly* 47 (1996): 269–90.
In the choice of the name Ganymede for Rosalind's male disguise, DiGangi finds the key to a homoerotic interpretation of *As You Like It.* Focusing on the Jupiter-Juno-Hebe-Ganymede myth (in which the boy Ganymede supplants the daughter Hebe as Jupiter's cup-bearer), the author contends that "anxieties about homoeroticism [in *AYL*] are manifested and managed through the asymmetrical, shifting erotic roles taken by or imposed on characters." In Arden, Rosalind will play *both* Ganymede *and* Jupiter: Ganymede to Orlando's Jupiter, and Jupiter to Celia's Hebe/Juno. What Rosalind hopes to ensure through her male disguise is that, by playing Ganymede in the wooing process, she will not assume the role of Juno (the rejected wife) when she marries. The female homoeroticism of Celia in relation to Rosalind is eventually transferred onto Phoebe. The marriages that conclude the play "succeed to the extent that premarital female homoerotic desire and postmari-

tal male homoerotic desire have been successfully banished." The Epilogue reveals "the homoeroticism of the theater [and] establishes the theatricality of homoeroticism."

Erickson, Peter. "Sexual Politics and Social Structure in *As You Like It.*" In *Patriarchal Structures in Shakespeare's Drama*, pp. 15–38. Berkeley, Los Angeles, and London: University of California Press, 1985.

Erickson claims that, contrary to celebrating female liberty, *As You Like It* is "primarily a defensive action against female power." It is the men—the banished courtiers who depict an "idealized male enclave" in 2.7 and Orlando in his rescue of Oliver from the lioness— who are the real beneficiaries of androgyny, manifesting maternal nurturing, gentleness, and compassion. Rosalind's disguise does not provide "sex-role fluidity" because she remains essentially female throughout. The happy ending is made possible only by her abandonment of the male masquerade and her reinscription within the patriarchal structure as daughter and wife. The revelation in the epilogue that she is really male marks the complete "phasing out" of Rosalind, the message being that "not only are women to be subordinate; they can, if necessary, be imagined as nonexistent."

Garber, Marjorie. "The Education of Orlando." In *Comedy from Shakespeare to Sheridan: Change and Continuity in the English and European Dramatic Tradition: Essays in Honor of Eugene M. Waith*, edited by A. R. Braunmuller and James C. Bulman, pp. 102–12. Newark: University of Delaware Press; London and Toronto: Associated University Presses, 1986.

Observing that disguise is not central to the plot of *As*

You Like It, Garber asks why Rosalind holds onto her male masquerade for so long, especially since no compelling reason remains once she has safely arrived in Arden. The answer lies not in the liberation that the male disguise affords the heroine but in Orlando's need to be educated about himself, his beloved, and the substance of love. Depicting the three stages he goes through—tongue-tied youth; self-absorbed, Petrarchan wooer; and "articulate and (relatively) self-knowledgeable husband"—the play could be subtitled "The Education of Orlando."

Gardner, (Dame) Helen. *"As You Like It."* In *More Talking of Shakespeare,* edited by John Garrett (London: Longmans, Green & Co., Ltd.; and New York: Theatre Arts Books, 1959), pp. 17–32. [Reprinted in *Twentieth Century Interpretations of As You Like It: A Collection of Critical Essays,* edited by Jay L. Halio, pp. 55–69. Englewood Cliffs, N.J.: Prentice-Hall, Inc., 1968.]

In its elegance and refinement, *As You Like It* is Shakespeare's "most Mozartian comedy." Gardner attributes the play's universal appeal (as indicated by the title) to its eclectic mix of romance, débat, pastoral, burlesque, song, and spectacle. What plot there is consists in the juxtaposition of various perceptions so as to provide a balance of "sweet against sour, of the cynical against the idealistic." While Arden is juxtaposed to the corruption of the Court, it is not Elysium, but a place of self-discovery where both positive and bitter lessons can be learned.

Hodges, Devon L. "Anatomy as Comedy." In *Renaissance Fictions of Anatomy,* pp. 50–67. Amherst: University of Massachusetts Press, 1985.

Hodges examines literary, theological, and scientific

"anatomies," a generic "fad" in sixteenth-century England. Maintaining that "the mechanism of release [as articulated by C. L. Barber], of breaking through forms," is the method of the anatomist, Hodges discusses *As You Like It* under the heading "the anatomy as comedy." Love, language, and social order are all anatomized in Arden, "a kind of antiworld . . . where all that is repressed in the 'working day world' can be figured forth." The play's chief anatomists are Rosalind, Touchstone, and Jaques: the first strips away the conventions of Petrarchanism; the second cuts through the artifice of the pastoral ideal; and the third dissects the body of human life, gradually reducing it to nothing in the "seven ages of man" speech. At the end it is Jaques who "expose[s] the inadequacies of the 'clarified' order of comic resolution": a voluntary exile, he shows that what appears to be a permanant order is really just the beginning of a new journey—the paradox at the heart of all anatomies.

Jackson, Russell, and Robert L. Smallwood, eds. *Players of Shakespeare 2: Further Essays in Shakespearean Performance by Players with the Royal Shakespeare Company.* Cambridge: Cambridge University Press, 1988.

The volume includes essays by Alan Rickman on his performance of Jaques (pp. 73–80) and Fiona Shaw and Juliet Stevenson on their portrayals of Celia and Rosalind (pp. 55–71) in Adrian Noble's RSC 1985–86 production. In addition to discussing their respective characters, the actors make passing reference to the decision to use modern dress and to the efforts of the stage designers to reject the traditional depiction of Arden "as a kind of theatrical arcadia reminiscent of Suffolk," since the play "is so clearly *not* a rural romp."

Jenkins, Harold. *"As You Like It."* *Shakespeare Survey* 8 (1955): 40–51. [Reprinted in *Twentieth Century Interpretations of As You Like It: A Collection of Critical Essays*, edited by Jay L. Halio, pp. 28–43. Englewood Cliffs, N.J.: Prentice-Hall, Inc., 1968.]

In this seminal study of the play's structure, Jenkins describes the technique of reconciliation through the juxtaposition of opposites as central to *As You Like It*'s compositional rhythm. The dialectical pattern in which each judgment/attitude/position is modified by another yields "an all-embracing view" that is far more satisfying than any one perspective. Jenkins insists that the play is more than "some mere May-morning frolic prolonged into a lotos-eating afternoon"; its idyllic quality is only one of many—a point made clear by Corin in his function as the "touchstone with which to test the pastoral." For Jenkins, *As You Like It* is the clearest example of Shakespeare's excellence as a writer of comedy.

Leinwand, Theodore B. "Conservative Fools in James's Court and Shakespeare's Plays." *Shakespeare Studies* 19 (1987): 219–37, esp. pp. 225–29.

A review of prominent fools associated with the Court and great houses of the English Renaissance reveals that marginality was not the fool's defining characteristic. Leinwand singles out Touchstone and Lear's Fool to demonstrate that, like their counterparts outside the theater, Shakespeare's fools "are less naturals than artificials, less wise than clever, and less spokesmen for topsyturvydom than for conservatism." As "inbred" as the rest of the courtly visitors to Arden (none of whom recreates himself/herself as a genuine shepherd or shepherdess) and as the only visitor to interact directly with the country folk (see especially his encounter with

Corin in 3.2), Touchstone is the one who establishes the "antipastoral gesture of Shakespeare's pastoral comedy."

Montrose, Louis Adrian. "'The Place of a Brother' in *As You Like It*: Social Process and Comic Form." *Shakespeare Quarterly* 32 (1981): 28–54.

Where Gardner (see above) reads *As You Like It* as "untouched" by time, Montrose firmly situates it in early modern family politics, specifically in the fraternal rivalries at the root of primogeniture. The sibling conflicts between Orlando and Oliver and between Duke Senior and Duke Frederick are central to the play. Before he is worthy of marrying Rosalind, Orlando must repair a fractured relationship with his brother and seek a "social" father in Duke Senior. Arden works its miraculous power in restoring the male bonds at the core of the play's patriarchal order, thus enabling events to unfold and relationships to be transformed "in accordance with a precise comic teleology." By containing and discharging the tensions that are released through different social relations (brother/brother, father/son, master/servant, male/female), *As You Like It* is both "a theatrical *reflection* of social conflict and a theatrical *source* of social conciliation."

Rackin, Phyllis. "Androgyny, Mimesis, and the Marriage of the Boy Heroine on the English Renaissance Stage. *PMLA* 102 (1987): 29–41.

Rackin examines the theatrical convention of the transvestite boy heroine in five plays (Lyly's *Gallathea;* Shakespeare's *The Merchant of Venice, As You Like It,* and *Twelfth Night;* and Jonson's *Epicoene*) to focus her discussion of changing conceptions of gender and theatrical mimesis in the Renaissance, a moment of cultural transition when gender definitions were still fluid. *Gal-*

lathea (1587) and *Epicoene* (1609) represent two poles in the depiction of the transvestite heroine—the former idealizing the androgyne as an image of transcendence over human limitations; the latter seeing only an object of ridicule, an image of monstrous deformity. Shakespeare's comedies occupy a "middle position" between the celebration of androgyny and homophobic satire, his plays being more "ambivalent" in both celebrating and satirizing romantic love. In *As You Like It*, the multiple implications of the heroine's sexual ambiguity—for relations between actor and role, dramatic representation and the reality imitated, play and audience—are most pronounced in the Epilogue.

Wilson, Richard. "'Like the Old Robin Hood': *As You Like It* and the Enclosure Riots." *Shakespeare Quarterly* 43 (1992): 1–19.

Wilson reads *As You Like It* in the context of the subsistence riots of the 1590s, arguing that the play's "violent plot and implausibly romantic ending have their material meaning" in that socio-economic crisis. "No Shakespearean text transmits more urgently the imminence of the social breakdown threatened by the conjuncture of famine and enclosure." As one of a group of texts in the late 1590s to adapt the legend of Robin Hood to the contemporary agrarian crisis— elevating the outlaw to the rank of gentleman—*As You Like It* dramatizes "the divided loyalty of the propertied class." Presenting the entire band of Sherwood outlaws and "parad[ing] all the felonies associated with forest rioters," the play reveals "how discourses work through social change and are never indeterminate."

Wofford, Suzanne. "'To You I Give Myself, for I Am Yours': Erotic Performance and Theatrical Performatives in *As You Like It*." In *Shakespeare Reread: The*

Texts in New Contexts, edited by Russ McDonald, pp. 147–69. Ithaca: Cornell University Press, 1994.

Wofford uses speech act theory (specifically extending the views of J. L. Austin on performative utterances) to demonstrate how *As You Like It* confirms the patriarchal order. The invocation of the wedding performative in "I take thee Rosalind for wife" and the "potentially subversive representation of a wedding onstage" (which by its nature is fictive) allow *As You Like It* to participate "in a complex way in a cultural debate about the power of fathers and of the state to control the language that gives such actions a social reality." Observing the play to be one of proxies—i.e., "of actions enacted in or undertaken by an alternative persona"—Wofford explores the effects of using a proxy "on the performative language necessary to accomplish such deeds as marriage." The Rosalind/Ganymede erotic performance receives special attention since it carries implications for questions of gender and enjoys an "apotropaic" function in warding off threats to a comic resolution.

Young, David. "Earthly Things Made Even: *As You Like It.*" In *The Heart's Forest: A Study of Shakespeare's Pastoral Plays,* pp. 38–72. New Haven: Yale University Press, 1972.

By creating a forest that is both subjective and relative—"constant in its imaginary character and changeable in each contact with a separate imagination"—and by favoring the iteration of the hypothetical "if," Shakespeare creates in *As You Like It* a play that is self-consciously pastoral, one firmly within the tradition while at the same time providing commentary on the stylistic features, themes, and attitudes associated with it. Instead of isolating the two polarities of pastoral—idealism and satire—Shakespeare engages in a constant interchange of judgment, adjustment, qualification, and reversal of position that allows for the testing of one pole against the other in a journey toward the comic reconciliation of both. According to Young, *As You Like It* yields not wish-fulfillment or escape but a "prospect on life."

Shakespeare's Language

Abbott, E. A. *A Shakespearian Grammar*. New York: Haskell House, 1972.

This compact reference book, first published in 1870, helps with many difficulties in Shakespeare's language. It systematically accounts for a host of differences between Shakespeare's usage and sentence structure and our own.

Blake, Norman. *Shakespeare's Language: An Introduction*. New York: St. Martin's Press, 1983.

This general introduction to Elizabethan English discusses various aspects of the language of Shakespeare and his contemporaries, offering possible meanings for hundreds of ambiguous constructions.

Dobson, E. J. *English Pronunciation, 1500–1700*. 2 vols. Oxford: Clarendon Press, 1968.

This long and technical work includes chapters on spelling (and its reformation), phonetics, stressed vowels, and consonants in early modern English.

Houston, John. *Shakespearean Sentences: A Study in Style and Syntax*. Baton Rouge: Louisiana State University Press, 1988.

Houston studies Shakespeare's stylistic choices, considering matters such as sentence length and the relative positions of subject, verb, and direct object. Examining plays throughout the canon in a roughly chronological, developmental order, he analyzes how sentence structure is used in setting tone, in characterization, and for other dramatic purposes.

Onions, C.T. *A Shakespeare Glossary*. Oxford: Clarendon Press, 1986.
This revised edition updates Onions's standard, selective glossary of words and phrases in Shakespeare's plays that are now obsolete, archaic, or obscure.

Robinson, Randal. *Unlocking Shakespeare's Language: Help for the Teacher and Student*. Urbana, Ill.: National Council of Teachers of English and the ERIC Clearinghouse on Reading and Communication Skills, 1989.
Specifically designed for the high-school and undergraduate college teacher and student, Robinson's book addresses the problems that most often hinder present-day readers of Shakespeare. Through work with his own students, Robinson found that many readers today are particularly puzzled by such stylistic devices as subject-verb inversion, interrupted structures, and compression. He shows how our own colloquial language contains comparable structures, and thus helps students recognize such structures when they find them in Shakespeare's plays. This book supplies worksheets—with examples from major plays—to illuminate and remedy such problems as unusual sequences of words and the separation of related parts of sentences.

Williams, Gordon. *A Dictionary of Sexual Language and Imagery in Shakespearean and Stuart Literature*. 3 vols. London: Athlone Press, 1994.
Williams provides a comprehensive list of the words

to which Shakespeare, his contemporaries, and later Stuart writers gave sexual meanings. He supports his identification of these meanings by extensive quotations.

Shakespeare's Life

Baldwin, T. W. *William Shakspere's Petty School.* Urbana: University of Illinois Press, 1943.

Baldwin here investigates the theory and practice of the petty school, the first level of education in Elizabethan England. He focuses on that educational system primarily as it is reflected in Shakespeare's art.

Baldwin, T. W. *William Shakspere's Small Latine and Lesse Greeke.* 2 vols. Urbana: University of Illinois Press, 1944.

Baldwin attacks the view that Shakespeare was an uneducated genius—a view that had been dominant among Shakespeareans since the eighteenth century. Instead, Baldwin shows, the educational system of Shakespeare's time would have given the playwright a strong background in the classics, and there is much in the plays that shows how Shakespeare benefited from such an education.

Beier, A. L., and Roger Finlay, eds. *London 1500–1700: The Making of the Metropolis.* New York: Longman, 1986.

Focusing on the economic and social history of early modern London, these collected essays probe aspects of metropolitan life, including "Population and Disease," "Commerce and Manufacture," and "Society and Change."

Bentley, G. E. *Shakespeare's Life: A Biographical Handbook.* New Haven: Yale University Press, 1961.

This "just-the-facts" account presents the surviving

documents of Shakespeare's life against an Elizabethan background.

Chambers, E. K. *William Shakespeare: A Study of Facts and Problems*. 2 vols. Oxford: Clarendon Press, 1930.
   Analyzing in great detail the scant historical data, Chambers's complex, scholarly study considers the nature of the texts in which Shakespeare's work is preserved.

Cressy, David. *Education in Tudor and Stuart England*. London: Edward Arnold, 1975.
   This volume collects sixteenth-, seventeenth-, and early-eighteenth-century documents detailing aspects of formal education in England, such as the curriculum, the control and organization of education, and the education of women.

Dutton, Richard. *William Shakespeare: A Literary Life*. New York: St. Martin's Press, 1989.
   Not a biography in the traditional sense, Dutton's very readable work nevertheless "follows the contours of Shakespeare's life" as he examines Shakespeare's career as playwright and poet, with consideration of his patrons, theatrical associations, and audience.

Fraser, Russell. *Young Shakespeare*. New York: Columbia University Press, 1988.
   Fraser focuses on Shakespeare's first thirty years, paying attention simultaneously to his life and art.

De Grazia, Margreta. *Shakespeare Verbatim: The Reproduction of Authenticity and the Apparatus of 1790*. Oxford: Clarendon Press, 1991.
   De Grazia traces and discusses the development of such editorial criteria as authenticity, historical periodization, factual biography, chronological development,

and close reading, locating as the point of origin Edmond Malone's 1790 edition of Shakespeare's works. There are interesting chapters on the First Folio and on the "legendary" versus the "documented" Shakespeare.

Schoenbaum, S. *William Shakespeare: A Compact Documentary Life*. New York: Oxford University Press, 1977.
  This standard biography economically presents the essential documents from Shakespeare's time in an accessible narrative account of the playwright's life.

Shakespeare's Theater

Bentley, G. E. *The Profession of Player in Shakespeare's Time, 1590–1642*. Princeton: Princeton University Press, 1984.
  Bentley readably sets forth a wealth of evidence about performance in Shakespeare's time, with special attention to the relations between player and company, and the business of casting, managing, and touring.

Berry, Herbert. *Shakespeare's Playhouses*. New York: AMS Press, 1987.
  Berry's six essays collected here discuss (with illustrations) varying aspects of the four playhouses in which Shakespeare had a financial stake: the Theatre in Shoreditch, the Blackfriars, and the first and second Globe.

Cook, Ann Jennalie. *The Privileged Playgoers of Shakespeare's London*. Princeton: Princeton University Press, 1981.
  Cook's work argues, on the basis of sociological, economic, and documentary evidence, that Shakespeare's audience—and the audience for English Renaissance drama generally—consisted mainly of the "privileged."

Greg, W. W. *Dramatic Documents from the Elizabethan Playhouses.* 2 vols. Oxford: Clarendon Press, 1931.

Greg itemizes and briefly describes many of the play manuscripts that survive from the period 1590 to around 1660, including, among other things, players' parts. His second volume offers facsimiles of selected manuscripts.

Gurr, Andrew. *Playgoing in Shakespeare's London.* Cambridge: Cambridge University Press, 1987.

Gurr charts how the theatrical enterprise developed from its modest beginnings in the late 1560s to become a thriving institution in the 1600s. He argues that there were important changes over the period 1567–1644 in the playhouses, the audience, and the plays.

Harbage, Alfred. *Shakespeare's Audience.* New York: Columbia University Press, 1941.

Harbage investigates the fragmentary surviving evidence to interpret the size, composition, and behavior of Shakespeare's audience.

Hattaway, Michael. *Elizabethan Popular Theatre: Plays in Performance.* London: Routledge & Kegan Paul, 1982.

Beginning with a study of the popular drama of the late Elizabethan age—a description of the stages, performance conditions, and acting of the period—this volume concludes with an analysis of five well-known plays of the 1590s, one of them (*Titus Andronicus*) by Shakespeare.

Shapiro, Michael. *Children of the Revels: The Boy Companies of Shakespeare's Time and Their Plays.* New York: Columbia University Press, 1977.

Shapiro chronicles the history of the amateur and quasi-professional child companies that flourished in London at the end of Elizabeth's reign and the beginning of James's.

The Publication of Shakespeare's Plays

Blayney, Peter. *The First Folio of Shakespeare*. Hanover, Md.: Folger, 1991.

Blayney's accessible account of the printing and later life of the First Folio—an amply illustrated catalog to a 1991 Folger Shakespeare Library exhibition—analyzes the mechanical production of the First Folio, describing how the Folio was made, by whom and for whom, how much it cost, and its ups and downs (or, rather, downs and ups) since its printing in 1623.

Hinman, Charlton. *The Printing and Proof-Reading of the First Folio of Shakespeare*. 2 vols. Oxford: Clarendon Press, 1963.

In the most arduous study of a single book ever undertaken, Hinman attempts to reconstruct how the Shakespeare First Folio of 1623 was set into type and run off the press, sheet by sheet. He also provides almost all the known variations in readings from copy to copy.

Hinman, Charlton. *The Norton Facsimile: The First Folio of Shakespeare*. Second Edition. New York: W. W. Norton, 1996.

This facsimile presents a photographic reproduction of an "ideal" copy of the First Folio of Shakespeare; Hinman attempts to represent each page in its most fully corrected state. The second edition includes an important new introduction by Peter Blayney.

Key to
Famous Lines and Phrases

. . . fleet the time carelessly, as they did in the golden
world. [*Charles*—1.1.117–18]

. . . I show more mirth than I am mistress of . . .
[*Rosalind*—1.2.2–3]

. . . the little foolery that wise men have makes a great
show. [*Celia*—1.2.88–89]

Well said. That was laid on with a trowel.
[*Celia*—1.2.103]

. . . one out of suits with fortune . . .
[*Rosalind*—1.2.244]

Hereafter, in a better world than this,
I shall desire more love and knowledge of you.
[*Le Beau*—1.2.285–86]

Not one [word] to throw at a dog. [*Rosalind*—1.3.3]

O, how full of briers is this working-day world!
[*Rosalind*—1.3.11–12]

Beauty provoketh thieves sooner than gold.
[*Rosalind*—1.3.116]

Sweet are the uses of adversity . . .
[*Duke Senior*—2.1.12]

And this our life, exempt from public haunt,
Finds tongues in trees, books in the running brooks,
Sermons in stones, and good in everything.
[*Duke Senior*—2.1.15–17]

. . . He that doth the ravens feed,
Yea, providently caters for the sparrow,
Be comfort to my age.   [*Adam*—2.3.44–46]

Though I look old, yet I am strong and lusty,
For in my youth I never did apply
Hot and rebellious liquors in my blood . . .
                                 [*Adam*—2.3.48–50]

. . . now am I in Arden, the more fool I. When I was at
   home I was in a better place, but travelers must be
   content.   [*Touchstone*—2.4.15–17]

If thou rememb'rest not the slightest folly
That ever love did make thee run into,
Thou hast not loved.   [*Silvius*—2.4.33–35]

[Song]
Under the greenwood tree
Who loves to lie with me . . .   [*Amiens*—2.5.1–8]

I can suck melancholy out of a song as a weasel sucks
   eggs.   [*Jaques*—2.5.12–13]

[Song]   Who doth ambition shun . . . [*All*—2.5.36–43]

[Song]
If it do come to pass
That any man turn ass . . .   [*Jaques*—2.5.48–55]

A fool, a fool, I met a fool i' th' forest . . .
                                 [*Jaques*—2.7.12–35]

If ever you have looked on better days . . .
                                 [*Orlando*—2.7.118]

All the world's a stage . . .   [*Jaques*—2.7.146–73]

[Song]   Blow, blow, thou winter wind. . . .
                                 [*Amiens*—2.7.182–201]

. . . let us make an honorable retreat, though not with bag and baggage, yet with scrip and scrippage.
[*Touchstone*—3.2.163–65]

O wonderful, wonderful, and most wonderful wonderful, and yet again wonderful, and after that out of all whooping!   [*Celia*—3.2.195–97]

Dead shepherd, now I find thy saw of might:
"Who ever loved that loved not at first sight?"
[*Phoebe*—3.5.86–87]

Men have died from time to time, and worms have eaten them, but not for love.   [*Rosalind*—4.1.112–13]

Forever and a day.   [*Orlando*—4.1.152]

. . . "Wit, whither wilt?"   [*Orlando*—4.1.176]

[Song]   It was a lover and his lass . . .
[*Pages*—5.3.16–39]

A poor virgin, sir, an ill-favored thing, sir, but mine own.*   [*Touchstone*—5.4.60–61]

. . . good wine needs no bush . . .
[*Rosalind*—Epilogue.3–4]

---

*Usually misquoted as "A poor thing but mine own."